Exploration into
Contemplative Prayer

Exploration into Contemplative Prayer

HERBERT SLADE 'S.S.J.E.

PAULIST PRESS
New York, N.Y./Paramus, N.J.

First published in Great Britain in 1975
by Darton, Longman and Todd Ltd
85 Gloucester Road, London SW7 4SU

©1975 Herbert Slade S.S.J.E.

ISBN 0-8091-1904-8

Published by Paulist Press
Editorial Office: 1865 Broadway, N.Y., N.Y. 10023
Business Office: Paramus, New Jersey 07652

Printed and bound in the
United States of America

Contents

Preface

This book is an account of an exploration leading to a discovery. The subject of the exploration is prayer, the main concern of the profession of the religious. The discovery is about many things of interest to many people who have their own explorations in prayer still to complete or even to begin. It is as various and unexpected as the discoveries made during Scott's last expedition. Primarily an expedition to the South Pole it led to discoveries about many other things: the courage of men, life under limitless strain and uncertainty, the conditions under which men are transformed into heroes. Our journey has led to similar discoveries.

The prayer of the exploration with which this book is concerned is deliberately called contemplative though undertaken by many who were not professionally religious but very amateur and inexperienced. It has been called contemplative prayer because this prayer is the prayer of all who are seeking the vision of God as the end of man. One of our discoveries is the number of people who are being led to desire this end and are still essentially human. This is to be expected for the contemplation of God is leading them not away from the world but into a relationship with One who is engaged in an adventure of cosmic renewal in which human beings of every nation and kind are being inspired and prepared to take a part. As fragments of this one humanity we find ourselves caught up in a process of earthly and heavenly reconstruction and are convinced that it is as important to everyone else as it is to ourselves.

Some forms of prayer are for the professional and expert: liturgical prayer is of this kind and much of that technical meditation on God and His creatures which Karl Barth defines as theology. But contemplative prayer, loving and seeing God, is for all men because as the psalmist so rightly and repeatedly says they can all open the mouth and draw in the breath and delight in Him.

Contemplation is what we are made for and our goal, whatever our form of religion. That is why in our exploration we have drawn on the ways of others outside of our own tradition as well as of many within. The same Word speaks in all and the same Spirit inspires.

7

This we have found especially true of Patanjali and the Yoga Sutras. It has not led us to belittle our own tradition or attempt the impossibility of an unnatural synthesis between our Christian and the Eastern scriptures. We have, in a phrase of a great Indian teacher, 'kept our own seat firm'. Many have done this before us, notably St. Thomas Aquinas in his use of Aristotle and the result has been not confusion but an increased precision, a widened sympathy and the forging of a theological instrument capable of communicating to many outside the boundaries of the Christian tradition. This has been our intention in our use of Indian contemplative traditions. The exercise has deepened our understanding and evoked an admiration for the great Indian spiritual culture which the author shared for eleven years in that country by daily personal contact with some of its living exponents.

The exploration has led to many discoveries, some capable of verbal sharing, most going beyond verbal forms into that apophatic silence to which the peaks of the Himalayas and much spiritual experience must always belong. The most important discovery has been that contemplation is a relationship given by God in which we receptively share and that our response is to co-operate with—His work of cleansing the doors of our perception. Some of the ways of doing this form the heart of this book. They are described in graded form, milk first as St. Paul would say and then meat. This is done in outline and by no means exhaustively and without any compulsion. It is a shared experience of a small group of explorers who have formed a family and have been the experimental raw material of this book. Others will find other ways and use other methods.

The book is in many ways a map drawn during our journey. It is incomplete and will require endless amendment. All we can hope is that it will help and stimulate others in their own journey. We look forward to sharing their experiences and receiving their corrections.

Herbert Slade, S.S.J.E.

The Anchorhold, 1974

Chapter 1

Beginnings

It was the Lambeth Conference of 1968 which gave authority and respectability to the Anchorhold venture. In the report of this conference it was stated that one of the most important ways of renewing the Church in faith was through a growth in prayer and contemplation. It emphasised the need for Christians to play their part in this by learning to keep still and listen to God, and it pointed out that this involved 'fostering each man's capacity for contemplation'. A further direction was given in the reminder that there was much to learn from the approach of oriental religions to silence. Special reference was made to religious communities and the part they could play in this work. They were asked to take the lead and advised to make 'a reappraisal of traditional methods of prayer and to develop new and modern methods'. All this came as a challenge to religious communities at a time when many of them had just finished looking back thankfully over their first hundred years and with the celebrations over, were stepping out rather bewildered and uncertain into their second century.

The Society of St. John the Evangelist, true to the vision of its founder that its members should be men of the present moment, responded to this call and sent one of its members on 31 January 1969 to begin an exploration into contemplative prayer at the Anchorhold, Haywards Heath.

1

THE ANCHORHOLD

The Anchorhold, a small property in Paddockhall Road, Haywards Heath, was given to the Society of St. John the Evangelist at the death of its owner, Dorothy Ivatt, in 1967. It has proved an admirable place for the exploration into contemplative prayer. Neither too large nor too small, situated on the outskirts of Haywards Heath, within easy distance of London and sufficiently removed from the

Mother House of the Society, it had all the advantages needed at the beginning of this venture. A brief description of the house and garden will show how suitable it was for the exploration.

The house was built in 1931 and the inscriptions over the front door leave no doubt with what intentions. A.M.D.G. is a reminder that it was for the glory of God. And the welcoming words: 'Lodge here that thine heart may be merry' sums up its attitude towards its guests. We have tried to develop these two intentions and have found them an adequate summary of the two aspects of contemplation. The property is in two parts: the main house and a gardener's cottage. The main house has been slightly modified to supply a training room for movement in contemplative prayer, a chapel for the daily office, a library, a refectory and kitchen and six cells. These are all of modest and unpretentious proportions. They could not be described as quite 'a goodly heritage' but they are a suitable place to live in and put us all in the same situation as our neighbours. This is not one of the least advantages of the house. The gardener's cottage has gradually grown into a guest house.

The garden is as important as the house. It is a place to work in and has recently been enlarged by the kindness of the Mother of the Holy Cross convent who has shared her kitchen garden, giving enough land to grow our own vegetables and make manual work the hard reality it ought to be. The garden is also a place of beauty and in so many ways symbolises the essentials of contemplative prayer. This is especially true of the oak tree and the pond.

The oak tree at the entrance of the garden is very much older than the house. It is of massive proportions, spreading out in a wide arc over much of the house and garden. It stands guard over the Anchorhold and is a home for many small creatures who are almost full members of the Anchorhold family, at least the birds treat the house as their home and one squirrel comes in as an honoured guest. This tree symbolises our purpose and speaks to us continually of the need to stand firm in the tradition we have received and yet to be open and receptive as it grows. It has weathered many storms and been a faithful support during the trials of our journey.

The pond is the other significant feature of the garden. Heart-shaped and set in a delightful water-garden, it symbolises the heart, that deep centre of contemplative prayer. It teems with life. Each year during March it is visited by an army of frogs who use it for procreation and then leave us in the company of their children who teach us so much about dangerous and patient transformations and then disperse about the garden to take their part in its life. This pond is a place of unfailing peace, a constant reminder of our purpose and the kind of prayer we are called to explore.

T. S. Eliot writes in *Little Gidding* of 'the timeless moment' and the particular place where it is experienced as 'the intersection'. He does not limit this to any one place but he does insist that these places are valid and of special importance to prayer. Such a physical place of intersection the Anchorhold has become to those who have lived in it for the past six years. It has grown into a place where prayer is valid. It has become a sign to us and to others of some of the necessary physical conditions which either hinder or stimulate contemplation.

Negatively it has taught us that large numbers and vast buildings create places where the 'intersection of the timeless moment' is impossible. Once a contemplative family grows beyond a certain size it becomes a congregation where certain stable forms of structure are essential and prayer takes on a liturgical form. This does not imply a condemnation of buildings and numbers but it makes the point that they change the form of prayer. In these days of reappraisal in religious communities it becomes urgent that those who lead should decide what kind of spiritual life they intend. If it is the active life of good works then the programme should be concerned with enlarged and modernised buildings and every care should be taken to imitate the Taizé example of a liturgy which will move large numbers. But if prayer, and especially contemplative prayer is intended, then there will have to be a ruthless reduction of buildings and a dividing up of communities into small, family houses where this prayer may become valid. One of the lessons which the Anchorhold has taught us is that our exploration into contemplative prayer has been possible simply because our buildings have been small enough to limit our numbers and to compel the few to live as a closely compact family.

The positive lesson of the Anchorhold is that physical conditions matter a great deal in making possible contemplative prayer. Beauty, peace and order, simplicity and conditions for a balanced life of action and prayer are essential if this life is to be lived without undue strain and mental breakdown. All these things have been given to us by the Anchorhold house and garden. The shape of the building is conducive to peace. The old garden sheds were converted into simple workshops which made manual work possible. The size and beauty of the garden enable us to work with pleasure and without strain. There is enough withdrawal to guard silence and at the same time to keep us in living touch with our neighbours. The eastern prayer called hesychasm required that the monk should find a place of withdrawal (anachoresis) where he could train the heart for contemplation. In theory it should be possible to do this training under the ordinary conditions of the world but our experience teaches us that this may be possible for a time but not for all the time

11

and that especially in the early stages of contemplation the physical help of a house like the Anchorhold is of the greatest importance. When stillness of heart has been reached one may then go out to share ordinary life in the world but again the special conditions of an Anchorhold are still necessary to provide places and times of retirement when hearts may be healed and re-charged from the injuries they have sustained in the present-day world. This again is a lesson which has special significance to religious communities. One of their functions is to provide places of retreat for people whose lives must be lived in the world. Such places need to be more than convalescent homes or places of physical silence. The Anchorhold model suggests that they need to consider the provision of forms of healing and contemplative activity, to counteract the complication of life in the world, with simplicity both of life and food, to train people not merely to relax but to deepen their ways of contemplation so that their time in such conditions may be something more than mere consolation. Anchorholds were places for training in contemplative prayer. It would not be impossible to multiply such conditions in the many religious houses of this country.

2

SOME PREDECESSORS

Looking back over the last six years it is easy to imagine that the intentions for the development of our life at the Anchorhold were clearer in their beginnings than in fact they were. At the Chapter which decided to authorise the venture we deliberately refrained from forming any detailed plan and limited ourselves to that general objective which is the title of this book. It was to be an exploration into contemplative prayer. Yet in our minds there were certain ideas and already some of the leaders for the work had been chosen. Two stand out with special clarity: Father Richard Meux Benson and Father Thomas Merton.

Richard Meux Benson. Father Benson is chiefly known as the founder of the Society of St. John the Evangelist but he has many other claims to greatness. He was himself a great explorer. He did his own exploration into contemplative prayer and in using the word 'mental' for this prayer gave precise instructions for the daily hour he set aside in the rule for the practice of this art. He also did much to revive the use of retreats in the Church of England and planned and conducted many parish missions.

12

Canon A. M. Allchin has recently emphasised a feature in the life and teaching of Father Benson which has mostly been overlooked. Quoting from a sermon preached at his funeral by Bishop Gore who there described him as 'a very orthodox and great theologian' he maintains that this orthodoxy was 'related at its heart to the orthodoxy of the Eastern tradition' (*The Nature of Theology*, A Study of R. M. Benson by A. M. Allchin, Sobornost, Series 6, No. 2, Winter 1971, p. 89). Canon Allchin does not overstate his case. He points out that Father Benson could not have had much close personal contact with Eastern Orthodox Christians. There were considerable linguistic and cultural barriers at the time. Yet he admits that the theological teaching of Father Benson could be 'paralleled by that of Orthodox writers, either of the Byzantine Middle Ages, or of the nineteenth or twentieth centuries'.

To prove this, it is fortunately not necessary to plunge into the profuse and often disordered theological writings of Father Benson. It is sufficient to go to that summary of his teaching and practice which is contained in the Rule of Life he gave his Society. There we find many of the principles that marked the forms of Eastern contemplative prayer, particularly the hesychastic discipline as manifested in the life of the Staretz Silouan. He insists on the importance of the house and cell as places of prayer. He lays down detailed instructions for the observance of silence as a contemplative training. He provides for the daily recitation of the Office in choir and prefers to have it sung. He insists under all conditions on the practice of a long period of mental prayer each day in addition to further retreat days each month and two long retreats a year.

It has already been mentioned that Father Benson described meditative prayer as 'mental' prayer. One can remember older Fathers of the Community reminding the brethren that this description referred to the concept of St. Augustine that this prayer should be done with the *mens* or heart and not be a merely discursive act of the reason. Such prayer resembles the prayer of the heart in the Eastern tradition.

In another way Father Benson was within the Eastern tradition. He stressed the relationship between the natural and spiritual body and their relationship to prayer. He followed the scriptural tradition that this body was destined to become a 'transparent temple' of the divine presence. To prepare it for this future he laid down disciplines for fasting and moderation in food and sleep. He provided for manual work which was an essential part of the novices' training. He accustomed them to the practice of stillness and movement in preparation for mental prayer. Haste and noise were always to be avoided, the habit of sitting and standing straight was to be cultivated; lounging

13

on chairs and tables and sitting cross-legged were forbidden. This physical discipline went beyond externals to the inner practices of maintaining recollectedness of demeanour when walking and cultivating an attitude of joy under all conditions. Devotional composure rather than any external excitement was to be aimed at in chapel and obtrusive exaggeration of voice and gesture were to be avoided. To this was added the physical discipline of kneeling upright and not leaning back when seated at Office. Above all, Father Benson taught the value of walking in the country as a training of the body for prayer. The novices were to go for a walk in the country at least once a week and the professed members used this exercise as their main recreation.

All this could be called contemplative training with considerable Eastern overtones and was intended through long practice to become deeply rooted habit, inspired by a strong inner life from the heart. Not only was it in harmony with the discipline of hesychastic prayer: it was also in harmony with the oriental disciplines of Yoga which the author of this book experienced during some eleven years in India and by further reading. There was no intention when we first came to the Anchorhold of rejecting this wise teaching in favour of the contemporary demand for a more complete freedom. What we found needed was a translation of its principles in terms of the present day and in harmony with the Patanjali teaching about contemplative Yoga.

Thomas Merton died suddenly in Bangkok on 10 December 1968. He died a long way from his Abbey, Gethsemani, where he had lived since 1941, and during those years had made a long journey. This was more than a physical pilgrimage to the Far East. He had also made a long pilgrimage of mind and spirit which was vividly described in his many writings during the whole of that period. It was a journey from the narrow, defensive positions of his conversion to the wide, attacking position in which he died. At the time of his death he was engaged in a mission of encouragement and exploration among the abbots of catholic religious orders in the Far East and representatives of many Asian religions. He was also steadfastly pursuing his own inner pilgrimage which involved him in the task of what he called 'monastic renewal'; and he was convinced of an urgent need to get into contact with Buddhist monasticism.

During the months before his death Merton revealed the working of his inner mind through an address which he gave at the Spiritual Summit Conference held between 22 and 26 October 1968 and a series of intimate letters written to his community and since shared with the world. These described some of his spiritual discoveries and the

14

growth of his thought on the future of monasticism and prayer. They give glimpses of a man catching sight of visions beyond the horizon of most of his contemporaries and provide inspiration for those who would embark on the same kind of exploration into the monastic life as Bonhoeffer and his contemporaries did for the Church.

In spite of his long journey from his trappist home Thomas Merton never lost sight of his religious vocation. This he summed up in a letter written from his abbey at the beginning of his last journey. He wrote: 'Our real journey in life is interior; it is a matter of growth, deepening, and of an ever greater surrender to the creative action of love and grace in our hearts. Never was it more necessary for us to respond to that action. I pray that we may all do so.'

In Merton's own life this prayer was answered in a faithfulness unto death through which he discovered certain truths about the monastic life and contemplation and in part handed on. These truths have played an important part in the Anchorhold venture.

Monica Furlong has used a striking phrase to describe Thomas Merton in the later stages of his spiritual growth. She calls him 'the trappist untrapped' and speaks of him as a man returning with a great simplicity to a world he had once furiously renounced, with a holiness which reproduced the Buddhist ideal of being 'just ordinary and nothing special' (see *New Fire*, No. 5, p. 20). Of course he was much more than that but this simplicity was the foundation of the new Thomas Merton. Like St. Anthony he returned renewed to the world he had left. We must carefully examine the changes in his attitudes and thinking which he brought with him on this return.

The root of these changes lies in his mature conviction of a deep relationship between Eastern and Western spirituality, both in contemplation and community life. He envisaged sanskrit as a lingua franca for those engaged in the exploration of this relationship. In reaching this position he was not alone. John Macquarrie in his *Principles of Theology* has said the same thing in more general terms. There he has written of the need for theology always to keep in close touch with biblical sources but described as absurd any attempt to exclude non-biblical categories. He insisted that theology must use the language of the culture within which it is done. He insists that there is no final theology.

On 9 November 1968 Merton wrote in the same attitude of open expectancy: 'I hope you will pray for me and all those I will be meeting. I am sure the blessing of God will be upon these meetings and I hope much mutual benefit will come from them. I also hope I can bring back to my monastery some of the Asian Wisdom with which I am fortunate to be in contact—but it is something very hard to put into words.'

Here was one of his main discoveries: Western and Eastern forms of the spiritual life were related; each had much to contribute to the other. He realised that he was now living in a climate of openness following Vatican II and was convinced of the urgency of making full use of 'free and productive communication' which the council had encouraged.

During his last journey there were many opportunities for practising this openness and free communication. He met the Dalai Lama at Dharamsala and made preliminary contacts with Tibetan mysticism. He met representatives of Theravāda Buddhism and was deeply impressed by an English buddhist monk in Bangkok. Then there was the conference sponsored by the Temple of Understanding attended by representatives of a wide variety of religious traditions where he played a leading part just before his death. It was at this conference that he summarised his position in these words: 'Without asserting that there is complete unity of all religions at the top, the transcendent or mystical level ... it is certainly true to say that even where there are irreconcilable differences in doctrine and in formulated belief there may still be great similarities and analogies in the realm of religious experience. There is nothing new in the observation that holy men like St. Francis or Shri Ramakrishna (to mention only two) have attained to a level of spiritual fulfilment which is at once universally recognisable and relevant to anyone interested in the religious dimension of existence. Cultural and doctrinal differences must remain but they do not invalidate a very real quality of existential likeness' (Notes for a paper delivered at Calcutta. October 1968).

This is a very great confession of a very great man. He has left the working out of the details to those who follow him.

Another legacy of Thomas Merton to the future was a clear appraisal of the present-day monasticism and some outlines for its future growth. This he did in a paper read at Calcutta in October 1968. In this he shared some of his ideas about the monastic life and its future.

For him the monastic life was essentially concerned with 'a special contemplative dedication' expressed in 'a certain distance or detachment from the ordinary and secular concerns of worldly life', largely concerned with 'the radical inner depth of one's religious and philosophical beliefs' and with 'inner transformation'. He saw these activities as essentially communal though without any smothering of the personal and individual contribution. Because these concerns are shared by Western and Eastern forms of monasticism, Merton judged the time ripe for a deeper communion between them in terms of one contemplative vocation. This led him to look into the future where he saw both opportunities and dangers in the growth of a closer communication.

The dangers were primarily the repudiation of the contemplative vocation through 'an obsession with relevance to the new generation' and the pursuit of that goal by wrong means, such as an over-concern with verbal forms of communication, 'interminable empty talk' and 'the inexhaustible chatter with which modern man tries to convince himself that he is in touch with his fellow man and with reality'. Against the background of such dangers Merton saw great opportunities.

Among them was the Sanskrit language. He saw this language as 'a workable inter-religious lexicon of key words' providing a kind of spiritual lingua franca and making possible a deep understanding between many traditions. For him the monastic life provided an ideal environment for this exchange, 'conditions of quiet tranquillity, sobriety, leisureliness, reverence, meditation and cloistered peace'. With these he was convinced there could be 'non-hurrying and patient waiting' and a safeguard against the Western passion 'for immediate and visible results'.

The end of Thomas Merton's life has been movingly described in a letter to his Superior from the six trappist delegates at the conference during which he died. It was both an end and a beginning: an end of one part of his pilgrimage in terms of exodus and the beginning of an entrance into the eternal country of truth and beauty which he so genuinely sought. Had he lived longer he would have shared with us deeper discoveries than any made during the first part of his religious life. Like Sādhu Sundar Singh he disappeared into a world of silence when many were most eager to hear him. But he left outlines of his plans and approach which have been most helpful in our own Anchorhold exploration: the need to penetrate fearlessly and in much greater depth into forms of contemplative prayer outside our own traditions, the urgent need to re-formulate and intensify our monastic vocation, the search for a wider communion with all who share this life, not in terms of facile compromise and shallow imitation but with 'a scrupulous respect for important differences' and patience 'to wait until a moment of greater understanding dawns'.

Thomas Merton was one of a great band of explorers in Eastern and Western contemplative prayer who have played a part in inspiring and guiding the Anchorhold venture. They include on the Eastern side such men as Shri Ramāna Mahārshi, Ramakrishna and his great disciple Vivekananda, Shri Swami Brahmabandhab Upadyaya and Sādhu Sundar Singh, R. S. Rādakrishnan and a teacher of Marathi in Pune, Shri Kanetkar, who introduced the author of this book to the Yoga Sutras. On the Western side is an even greater number which includes that great pioneer, Jack Winslow and his fellow worker, Verrier Elwin, Bishop Lash, Dom. Le Saux and those exploring Roman Catholic religious: Dom. Bede Griffiths, Dom. Aelred Graham and Dom. J. M. Déchanet. On the more purely theological side there has been the inspiration of Karl Barth and Dietrich Bonhoeffer who have opened doors and windows in the mind and sounded the call to go forward fearlessly in faith, doubting nothing.

3

THE FIRST SHAPE

We came to the Anchorhold with many unsolved problems, some personal, some communal and some general. In ourselves we were conscious of having reached the middle of the wood, one of the many crisis situations of life. The old ways had worn thin. New roads had to be made. We needed to find a new direction. The same was even more true of the religious life in which we had lived so long. Vatican II and its sequel had burst the banks of the old ways and traditions, making possible for the first time the widest forms of experiment without disloyalty to our inherited positions. There was also the urgent need to reconcile many of the insights gained during eleven years in India with other experiences of contemplative prayer. Here were problems and opportunities enough but they were dangerous and mistakes which would wreck the venture in its beginnings could easily be made. To guard against them we decided to move slowly and to write a very general outline of principles and objectives at the Anchorhold, as a means of both checking our own tendency to jump to conclusions and to answer the questions of those who were interested in our welfare. This first shape which has stood up remarkably well to five years of living is given in much the same form as it was first produced.

THE OBJECT of the Anchorhold was described as a home of growing prayer in which the three faculties of body, heart and mind would be fully used. The prayer was to be contemplative according to the pattern defined by St. John of the Cross as 'a permitted infusion of God which enkindles love'. The motive of the prayer was not mere personal experience but the renewal of the world. We used a rather high-sounding word to describe this which we have since dropped. We called it cosmic contemplation. In order to stimulate

18

this kind of prayer four conditions were provided: a planned environment, a rule of life, a training pattern and certain forms of prayer.

THE PLANNED ENVIRONMENT was in the Anchorhold house and garden. Both were seen as symbols manifesting God and showing some of the ways to Him. In the garden we were reminded of the teaching of St. Paul in the epistle to the Romans that the everlasting power and deity of God are revealed through the things He has made. We found this especially true in the Anchorhold garden where His power and deity were shewn in the great variety of beauty it contained: the flower garden, the vegetable garden and above all the water garden around the pond. Each part of the garden we found was speaking particular truths about God and ourselves. Part of the prayer of the Anchorhold we found was expressed through work in this garden and enjoyment of its beauty. Here we saw God through His works and heard His voice when we became quiet and listened. The house we came to love as a kind of House of Interpreter and a Palace Beautiful. It immediately welcomed us and all who came and introduced some of the mysteries of life hidden with Christ in God. This life was particularly revealed in the training room, the prayer room, the community room and the cells. The training room outlined the way to contemplation and was a place where some of its actions could be demonstrated and practised. The prayer room was the place where the Divine Office was said and corporate meditations shared. The community room, divided into refectory and library, was a centre for eating and recreation. The cell was a place for solitude and sleep. We quickly realised that if the house were to be able to speak clearly in all its parts silence and tranquillity would have to be cultivated.

The house and the garden spoke most clearly through symbols. We defined a symbol as a sign with many meanings. Christian symbols are signs of Christ and our life in Him. In the Anchorhold we made much of the symbols and centred them in the training room as teaching aids and a focus for concentration, in the prayer room as an expression of meditation, in the community room in the form of bread and the bible and in the cell we had a cross. We were sure that symbols must be allowed to have many individual interpretations and so, unlike the symbols of Interpreter's House we left them undescribed and free to speak for themselves. This was a cause of much speculation and misunderstanding, but so were the symbols of the early Church. We were content to wait for meanings to grow. Through symbols God reveals Himself and He must be allowed to make His own meanings plain.

THE ANCHORHOLD LIFE was a development from principles of both Western and Eastern origins and experiences learnt from living together. They had to do with life in its personal and family forms.

The personal life of each member of the Anchorhold family was based on the baptism conditions of self-denial, faith in Christ and obedience to His Spirit. We found that these demands increased with growth in prayer and so we made no attempt to formulate them in any further detail. They could only be completely fulfilled through a holy death and the processes of glorification which follow. They must always make further demands on each person while he is living *in via* on earth.

Family life is essential for contemplative prayer which requires the support of a closely knit family if it is to grow in a balanced and healthy form. Such a family need not be more than two or three. It should never be more than twelve. The centre of this family must be Christ as He now is. We marked this presence by the use of certain symbols and by recognising each member of the family as a living vessel of His presence. Anything like a legal rule of life for the family we avoided from the start and we are resolved not to have one. Instead we recognised certain regulations for our life which we left to be interpreted by the Spirit whenever difficulties arose. These regulations were summarised for us in the principles of poverty, chastity and obedience. We saw poverty as the family form of self-denial, chastity as the love of each other in Christ, obedience as the family response to the indwelling Spirit. We have no written rule of life and we go on getting along very well without one.

TRAINING FOR CONTEMPLATION we found essential. We accepted St. Paul's description of Christians called to be like men stripped for action, perfectly self-controlled. The asceticism of the Anchorhold was from the first designed to meet these demands. It was not repressive but liberating, planned to prepare every member to act fully under the power of the Spirit. It was concerned with both the body and the heart and endeavoured to bring each faculty under the power of the Spirit, correcting inadequacies and stimulating the growth needed for an adult form of contemplative prayer. We aimed at bringing the body to full health, stillness and obedience to the Spirit and the heart to the full contemplative use of its powers of listening to God, seeing Him and loving Him, as He reveals Himself in Christ and creation. In drawing up a form of training we used some of the teachings and practice of the Eastern spiritual technique of Yoga.

Yoga goes back beyond 2000 B.C. The word yoga is related to the word yoke. It appears in our Lord's invitation: 'Take my yoke upon you and learn of me.' It may be translated as union. It is a spiritual technique, a method, a way, a path. It is not a religion but a spiritual exercise or meditative technique. Forms of technique resembling yoga are to be found in hesychastic forms of prayer and the Ignatian Exercises. Yoga provides a detailed form of bodily and mental training which when wisely selected and used under proper direction prepares the body and the heart for contemplation. The most helpful teaching of yoga has to do with posture, breathing, detachment, concentration, meditation and contemplative silence.

The body is the temple of the Spirit. It is an instrument of prayer. Each bodily act, when purposefully carried out under the control of the Spirit, is prayer. Such bodily acts include eating, sleeping, working, recreation and posture.

There are some 84 postures in the teaching of hatha yoga. Of these no more than a few are needed to train the body for the stillness and relaxation required for prolonged meditation. We have found the following most helpful: the deep obeisance, the shoulder stand, the plough, the backstretch, the cobra, the headstand, the folded leaf. When these postures cannot be carried out it is sufficient to aim at sitting still, straight and relaxed.

The heart is the centre of man, the point where he meets God and creation. The heart is disordered and its faculties for love and contemplation are immature. Some of the training which corrects these disorders and co-operates with the work of the Spirit in bringing full growth is: breathing, detachment and concentration.

Rhythmical breathing is done with the Spirit to expel evil from the heart and inspire it with good. Such breathing develops the energy of love in all its forms, physical (eros), personal (philia), family (sterge) and divine (agape). The evil expelled is desire, pride, lust, anger, sloth, gluttony and envy. The good inspired is hope, faith, love, prudence, fortitude, moderation and justice. This breathing is especially helpful at the beginning and the end of meditation.

Detachment and concentration with the Spirit develop the heart's capacity to hear and understand God. The main instrument of detachment is silence. The main instrument of understanding is a focus of concentration.

The focus of concentration is always used as a symbol of Christ or His Spirit. It may be a sound or an image or both. It is used physically, mentally and spiritually. The most valuable sources for these focuses of concentration are the bible, the divine office and the eucharist. These focuses of concentration are described by St. John of the Cross as 'deeply imprinted images' and he recommends that they be recalled 'for the purpose of enkindling love'. They are used in this way during the time of meditation and at other times as well.

THE ANCHORHOLD PRAYER FORMS are the divine office, the eucharist, meditation and work.

The divine office is an instrument for regular and corporate concentration on God in union with the Spirit. The form of this office is that in use at the Mother House. The normal times for the office are: 6.30 a.m. Morning office. 9.00 a.m. Terce. 12.30 p.m. Sext. 2.30 p.m. None. 5.00 p.m. Evensong. 8.30 p.m. Compline. All members of the family try to share terce, sext, evensong and compline. After these offices some form of meditation is used.

The eucharist is the instrument which unites the family of the Anchorhold with the whole Church and gives an outline and materials for meditation. Normally there is a eucharist once a week in the house and on Sundays the parish eucharist is shared in the parish church. To emphasise the contemplative nature of the eucharist silence is used after the gospel and the communion.

In meditation the heart comes under the control of the Spirit and thinks with love on God and His creation. All the faculties of the heart are used for this purpose, the emotions, the reason and the understanding. Through the regular practice of meditation in union with the Spirit the powers of the heart are developed; the ear is sharpened to hear the Word of God, the eye of the understanding is opened to contemplate Christ in glory and the will is kindled in love. There are four periods of meditation each day and in at least one of them the use of the postures. The main actions in a meditation are physical relaxation through the use of the postures, concentration on a symbol, interior thinking around the symbol leading on to silence. These meditations are corporate and the leader gives what guidance he feels is necessary.

Since we are commanded to pray continually we find that this is only possible when we include work as a form of prayer. We find that work shared with the family and done in obedience to the Spirit is a form of contemplation. The work within the Anchorhold is divided into sections with one member responsible for each. To develop the contemplative spirit in work we make use of short ejaculatory prayers and often make the work a subject of meditation.

This preliminary outline concluded with the statement that the Anchorhold prayer was for the whole kingdom of Christ and that this kingdom was to be seen in embryo in every part of creation. This was intended to widen the scope of our concern beyond Church and community and to find all men in some way related to this kingdom and all events part of its continuous growth.

4

GROWTH

All life is growth. This is especially true of the spiritual life. It continually grows. To stand still, to look back is death. This is a law of life on both sides of death. Before His death there was an uninterrupted growth in our Lord's life which came to completion on the cross. After His resurrection this growth continued. He revealed to Mary Magdalene that He was ascending to His Father. Later St. Paul applied this same principle of growth to the Body of Christ and in the epistle to the Ephesians taught that His body was still growing through the incorporation of new members and their growth in the Spirit.

We came to the Anchorhold at the end of a long period of growth. This was both personal and communal. The personal growth had gone on through a lifetime, beginning with adolescent and Wordsworthian experiences of the divine presence, moving on to the more theological experiences given through ordination and the ministry, growing into the life of prayer as it was taught in the novitiate of the Society of St. John the Evangelist and as it grew through the many experiences of professed life and reading. Then came the years in India with the privilege of meeting other traditions and other ways of prayer. And finally there was the need to re-think much of the past when Vatican II opened the closed doors of the Roman Catholic Church and forced us all to go out into the ways of faith again leaving many of the accepted traditions behind us.

And there was community growth as well. The Society founded by Father Benson travelled fast and quickly during its first hundred years. It held in tension two forms of the religious life which were very roughly joined together under the ambiguous description of the mixed life. There was a vigorous strain of action expressed in the energetic missionary work of the Society, particularly in South Africa and India, and there was the more hidden contemplative vocation which had certainly shone through the teaching of Father Benson and been absorbed and practised by such people as Father O'Neill at Indore, Father Hollings in Oxford and Father Congreve in his life and writings. All this growth came to a state of particular tension at the time of the centenary celebrations. The numbers of the Society had dropped to the point when it became essential to close down the missions in India and South Africa. Many of the Society were sharing with thoughtful people in the missionary Societies a questioning attitude towards the methods of the earlier forms of missionary work and some were beginning to listen to the

23

Archbishop of Canterbury as he went round presiding at various centenary celebrations, always asking religious communities to remember their contemplative vocation. When the time for opening the Anchorhold came it was a very different Society from the one founded by Father Benson which faced the opportunity.

The growth of the Society has continued. In the last six years the Society has re-written its rule of life and considerably modified its work and prayer. Altars have been moved in response to present-day fashions, new forms of the office and the eucharist have been accepted, many of the more rigid parts of the community life have been changed. For this we are deeply thankful, not only to the leadership but also to the trusting response of the members of the Society who have not been afraid to strike camp and go on pilgrimage again. No one can predict the future changes. All one can hope is that we shall continue to realise that we are strangers and sojourners and were never intended to be anything else. Provided this detachment from the past and flexibility to the present and the future are maintained there will always be work for the Society to do and men available to do it.

The growth at the Anchorhold from the days when we tentatively drew up our first plans has been even swifter and more profound. This was inevitable. The early years of any venture are always the years of more rapid change and we have learnt to live with the changes and recognise the hand of God in them. There have been changes in the outer conditions of our life and still more fundamental inner ones.

The outer changes have been made to meet the needs of the growing family. This has meant making not only more room to live but more room to work. The early members of the family re-built the workshops. The greenhouse was made into a pottery, the garden shed became a woodwork shop and the garage gradually took the form of a weavery and shop. This necessarily brought changes to our way of life. Some became more involved in what we called the Anchorhold industries and found themselves learning for the first time the way to throw pots, to master a loom and to work the lathe. We were sensitive to the danger of going into trade and going out of prayer and so limited our times of work and carefully guarded the times for prayer. The growth in this part of our life has been considerable but not, we believe to the detriment of our first duty to explore ways of contemplative prayer.

The inner changes have been concerned with our family life and prayer.

Father Benson used to warn the first members of the Society that they must be ready for the most acute form of poverty in poverty of numbers. So far, except for the first few weeks of our life at the Anchorhold we have been given a generous supply of recruits for the family, some staying no more than a few days and others long enough to become integrated and helpful members. They have been of all kinds which has demanded skill in learning to respond to their needs and recognise, often by instinct, why they had come. This demand has forced the family to be in a state of continuous and receptive movement. Sometimes the response has had to be to a guest in sickness, often to one in doubt and when they recovered balance then it has been necessary to provide creative work as well as the opportunity for prayer. We have still much to learn. Of one thing we are certain: the contemplative family must be a healing family of both the body and the heart and this demands constant meditation as well as compassionate service.

As the family constantly grows and changes so our prayer grows, too. This has taken the form of many changes in our vocal prayer. We have adopted the new forms of the morning and evening office and we allow the eucharist to form around the pattern given in series III. A deeper study of Patanjali has helped us to see many more implications of yoga with contemplative prayer than at first we recognised and there is still a long way to go. We begin to glimpse the situation in which there is no fixed method of prayer beyond an increasing response to the movement of the Spirit in the heart. Whatever methods there are relate to the preparation for prayer and not to the prayer itself. There is still much to learn about this preparation and we see it including every part of our life together. Much of this book will describe our discoveries in this region and the situation we have so far reached. But there is no final position, no final rule. We move into new territory all the time and there is no finality. Love is infinite and it is ultimately with love that we have to do.

We can look forward in hope and backwards with thanksgiving. So much has been given and so much shown. The Anchorhold stands as a sign of the inexhaustible generosity of God and as an encouragement to go unafraid into the future.

Chapter 2

Contemplation

There is always a danger in over-definition. It tends to freeze what should be moving and often kills what has meaning only when it is alive. But this does not excuse us from the work of trying to think as clearly as possible and to construct some pattern of thought which can be easily understood by others. While we are very conscious that contemplation has often been so over-defined that many of the ordinary Christians with a capacity for it have been seriously discouraged yet in the work of exploring this theme some outlines are necessary. We have tried to keep them simple, drawing from all traditions and leaving as much freedom as possible to move between them.

The word contemplation contains in its many forms clues as to its meaning. It comes from the Latin word *contemplāri* which describes the acts of the Roman augurs when they looked for God's will within a sacred enclosure called the templum. It is related to the Greek word *theoría* which means to look towards God and to the Sanskrit word samādhi which describes an act of concentrated thought. Contemplation may therefore be partly defined as looking towards God and thinking deeply about Him.

This activity in some form or other is found in many traditions, both Eastern and Western. It is common to both Christian and non-Christian experience. There is a mature contemplative tradition in the Yoga Sutras of Patanjali which teaches us much about the Eastern approach and in many ways parallels and illuminates our own Christian tradition. We shall extract certain parts of this teaching before examining the essence of the Christian view.

Patanjali describes contemplation (samādhi) as part of a three-action centring of the mind which he calls mind-poise (samyama). In this process the mind is centred on an image in the heart. Then the mind is trained to think discursively towards that image and finally it is led to a mental balance or stillness of insight (samādhi). This insight is of varying degrees of intensity. It begins as an insight into the real significance of the image (samprājnāta samādhi) and eventually develops through various stages into an imageless state of identification with the Lord (asamprājnāta samādhi). This comes to

26

fruition in the act of loving union with the Lord and the state of freedom (kaivalya). This detailed analysis of contemplation given by Patanjali in various parts of the Yoga Sutras may seem over-complicated but it is reflected in the Christian tradition and contributes many insights into its present forms.

The present descriptions of Christian contemplation are almost as many as there are people to make them and most are of varying degrees of complexity. This has not always been so. Early descriptions of contemplation in the Bible and in writers like St. Thomas Aquinas are simple and avoid over-definition. In the Bible contemplative prayer is vividly described in the Song of Songs in the form of a delightful love poem. The Johannine writings veil it in discourses attributed to the Lord and to the working models called signs. This freedom from precise definition marks the teaching of the Church until the Reformation. In the writings of St. Thomas there is an almost light-hearted approach when he compares contemplation with playing because, he says, play is delightful and sports are not means to ends but are sought for their own sake. For him contemplation was an affair of images. The Counter-Reformation altered all this and brought precise and controversial definitions Contemplatives argued about their art and in doing so got confused and often lost its living meaning. One has only to read such descriptions of contemplative prayer as were given by Père Poulain in his *Graces of Contemplative Prayer* to realise how far the idea of contemplation had moved from the earlier, spontaneous approach to God. He defines contemplation in many ways. It is a simple regard of God accompanied by love, a simplification of the understanding, a prayer of simplicity, an obscure night, a mystic state. He goes on to distinguish between acquired and infused contemplation. All this not only complicated prayer but raised doubts and scruples in the minds of contemplatives as they tried to discover which of the many categories reflected their own condition.

This description of contemplation from Dr. Cross's *Dictionary of the Christian Church* fairly summarises the present state of contemplation-definition in the Church today. He writes: 'As used by modern religious writers contemplation describes non-discursive mental prayer as distinguished from meditation. In so far as this stage of prayer is held to be reached by the normal development of the natural faculties it is termed "acquired contemplation" (as also "the prayer of simplicity"); but when considered as the fruit of supernatural grace, directly acting on the soul, it is known as "infused contemplation". Mystical writers such as St. Theresa of Avila distinguished between several forms of mystic contemplation.' All this is very true but contemplation in these terms could not be, as the

27

Archbishop of Canterbury has said, the prayer of ordinary Christians. Something simple and more spontaneous in technique and description is required.

This can be supplied when definitions are put aside and another mode of description used—the Bible and early Church method of images and models. Then contemplation comes alive as the prayer of living people inspired by God and it is in following their example that others can find their way. For our purpose we have chosen the model of the mystery of the Transfiguration as a living exposition of the meaning of contemplation and as a model of the ways in which its experiences can be shared by those ordinary Christians who are prepared to take a way of faith in and imitation of its principles. To it we have added the account St. Augustine gives of his contemplative experience at Ostia as a kind of subsidiary model of the way in which the experiences of the Transfiguration can be applied and shared.

1

THE TRANSFIGURATION

There are many interpretations of St. Mark's account of the Transfiguration (8.27–9.29). In using it as a contemplation model we shall use the method recommended by William Temple who wrote: 'As we read the story, though it all happened long ago, we apprehend present fact. It is not only the record of a historical episode that we read; it is the self-expression of that God in whom we live and move and have our being; so that whatever finds expression there is true now, and the living Jesus who is the same yesterday and today and for ever still deals with our souls as He dealt with those who had fellowship with Him when He tabernacled among us. Our reading of the Gospel story can and should be an act of personal communion with the living God.' (*Readings in St. John's Gospel* Vol. 1, p. 15).

This is a combination of the literal, allegorical and mystical interpretations of scripture with a strong emphasis on the anamnesis method of the eucharist. It enables us to use the Transfiguration mystery as the main guide for our exploration into contemplative prayer.

The Transfiguration divides into three parts: the preparation, the transfiguring experience and the consequences.

THE PREPARATION is in stages and experienced by all the disciples. Our Lord had taken them away from their ordinary environment. They were going through the alien villages of Caesarea Philippi, away from their usual Jewish surroundings. They were in close touch with the larger world of Greek thought and custom. Under these conditions our Lord asked them to give their witness to the reputation He had won among others and among themselves. He asked them what men thought of him and received the answer that to some he was John the Baptist, to others Elijah and to others one of the prophets. He then asked for their opinion and this was given by Peter, the leader of the rest: 'You are the Messiah.' This title of Messiah was full of deep implications and involved the disciples in the acceptance of our Lord both as their own leader and as the one who was going to lead the revolution which would rescue the Jewish people from their Roman overlords and inaugurate the kingdom of God on earth. It was the most dangerous and significant conclusion they could have reached and no wonder our Lord gave them strict orders not to reveal this to anyone.

This was the first part of the preparation, the commitment to Jesus as the divine leader. From this point our Lord continued the preparation, first by describing what kind of Messiah he intended to be and then by making his demands as this Messiah upon them.

He was going to be an unexpected type of Messiah. Instead of bringing victory he was going to suffer great sufferings, rejection, death and resurrection. When Peter dared to dispute this prediction he is given the most crushing rebuke of his life: 'Away with you, Satan, you think as men think, not as God thinks.'

Our Lord's demands upon his disciples have been described by St. John of the Cross as the most central part of the whole gospel. He makes them not only upon the disciples but upon the people as well whom He calls to hear them. They must be accepted by all who would follow Him, from the highest ecclesiastic to the humblest novice. They are needed to fulfil the Christian discipleship of those who would follow Him in the villages and of those who would share in transfiguration. No one is exempt from them. They sum up what is required from the followers of the Messiah. 'Anyone who wishes to be a follower of mine must leave self behind; he must take up his cross, and come with me. Whoever cares for his own safety is lost; but if a man will let himself be lost for my sake and for the Gospel, that man is safe. What does a man gain by winning the whole world at the cost of his true self? What can he give to buy that self back? If anyone is ashamed of me and mine in this wicked and godless age, the Son of Man will be ashamed of him, when he comes in the glory of his Father and of the holy angels' (St. Mark 8 : 34–8).

These preparatory events to the Transfiguration are an integral prelude to all who would lead the Christian life and share in the Christian form of contemplative prayer. We find them in the great initiation rites of all genuine Christian communities and they are embedded in the classical non-Christian forms of contemplation as well. Self-denial, self-affirmation and an unswerving perseverance are the essential conditions which must be fulfilled by those who would arrive at a contemplative experience of God.

THE TRANSFIGURING PRAYER begins with the selection of a nucleus of people. Not all the disciples, still less any of the people, are chosen. Peter, James and John, the disciples who shared the Lord's most intimate experiences and were later to be with Him in Gethsemane were selected. Later on this nucleus was to be enlarged by the inclusion of Moses and Elijah. Meanwhile the preliminary nucleus was trained by the physical discipline of being taken into a high mountain and by a period of seclusion. Under these conditions the disciples saw the Lord transfigured with his clothes a dazzling white. They penetrated to that spiritual world where Moses and Elijah were seen conversing with Jesus. We need to let the mind flow around this description a long time in order to penetrate its full significance. Blake would say that under the conditions of climbing the mountain and the seclusion with Jesus the doors of sense perception were cleansed and the disciples saw the world as it really is—infinite. That is certainly part of the truth. The disciples were given a moment of supreme insight. But the experience went much further. They saw the reconciliation in Jesus between the law of religion as symbolised by Moses and the law of spiritual freedom as symbolised by Elijah. Into this unity they were themselves taken and when Peter wanted to capture this moment of perfect insight and make it into an unchanging tradition he was ignored and the living form of the mystery was revealed as the cloud covered not only the Lord but themselves as well as the divine voice proclaimed the total mystery: 'This is my Son, my Beloved; listen to Him' (Mark 9 : 8). It was then that the three disciples have their moment of perfect awareness, when they glimpse for a moment the cosmic Christ as the centre and heart of the whole creation. 'Suddenly, when they looked around, there was nobody to be seen but Jesus alone with themselves.' Again this insight finds a parallel in other non-Christian experience for when Gautama received his enlightenment he went out and saw the Buddha in all things.

THE CONSEQUENCES. The contemplative experience revealed in the Transfiguration was something more than an intense insight into

God and His kingdom. It led on to certain essential consequences. Although the disciples wanted to crystallise the experience by making tents to contain the glory they were forced to share in its movement. They had to come away from the place of vision, they had to absorb some practical teaching, they had to witness the dazzling power of our Lord once more working under the hidden conditions of a ministry to fallen man. It was all an anti-climax and yet true to the full contemplative experience. The mountain must be left behind. Those who share such insight must accept a period of incoherence when they are ordered not to tell anyone what they have seen and insight into the spiritual world must always lead to a greater awareness of the spiritual disorder of this world and the need to take a part, according to one's strength, in healing those who suffer like the spirit-possessed boy. Contemplation and action go together. As our Lord reminded all the disciples: capacity for transfiguration does not mean incapacity for meeting the needs of this world. On the contrary, the prayer of transfiguration is the necessary condition for being able to deal effectively with the needs of this untransfigured world.

This is the essence of what St. Mark describes in his account of the Transfiguration. This is the working model out of which we must construct our own analysis of the ingredients of contemplative prayer. Before doing so we shall compare the Transfiguration prayer of contemplation with the contemplative experience of St. Augustine and his mother at Ostia.

2

ST. AUGUSTINE AT OSTIA

St. Augustine describes this experience in the ninth book of his *Confessions*. He writes of a state in which bodily pleasure had been transcended and of a growth in love which he shared with his mother one evening after a long journey at Ostia. As they stood together looking out to sea he experienced an ascent through all the stages of creation until he reached the presence of the Divine Wisdom. There he reached out for a moment and touched the mystery. Then followed a reluctant descent 'to the sound of our own speech in which each word has a beginning and ending', so different from the immediacy of the eternal Word.

Compared with St. Mark's description of the Transfiguration this account of St. Augustine is wordy and imprecise but yet it follows the same pattern of contemplation. It is a corporate experience, shared with his mother. It is centred around our Lord under the symbol of the Divine Wisdom. It leads first of all through a series of physical experiences as his thought ranges through the whole compass of material things. It culminates in that mental insight in which he penetrated to the presence of the Divine Wisdom. And the experience was more than intellectual. His other senses were involved: he touched and loved. All this was for a moment but in that moment there was a transforming experience which made him identify with the object of contemplation so that his independent ego was transcended.

Compared with the Transfiguration St. Augustine's contemplative experience may be inadequate but it supplies a subsidiary model which confirms the principles of the main model and helps us in formulating the essential principles of contemplation.

3

PRINCIPLES OF CONTEMPLATION

By concentrating on the mystery of the Transfiguration and allowing the mind to flow around the inner image we make of St. Mark's account certain principles evolve. And because the mystery of the Transfiguration is a transcendent and universal experience these principles are general and unlimited. They can apply to all forms of contemplation, whether Christian or not. We can test them, as we have done in the case of St. Augustine with other accounts of contemplative experience and we shall find that they apply to all. These principles may be summarised as follows.

1. CONTEMPLATION IS AN INSIGHT EXPERIENCE of both mental and emotional proportions. The disciples see the divine–human glory. Their insight is both into the glorious depths of the humanity of Christ and also into the depths of His divinity. They pass through the experience of creation and reach the uncreated glory of God. But it is more than an intellectual penetration. It is an emotional experience as well. They pass through the whole emotional range. There are fear and love and indignation and hope. They fear to enter the cloud, they share in the love of the Father for the Son, there is a period of indignation when Peter tries to oppose the Lord and is crushingly rebuked: 'Away with you Satan.' And the mystery ends on the note of hope in a future resurrection. Contemplation is not just insight. It is loving insight into God.

The many words used to describe the act of contemplation convey these various meanings.

32

Contemplation derived from the Latin contemplari emphasises the act of looking intently as the Roman augurs looked within the sacred enclosure of the templum. The Greek word theoria takes the meaning a stage further and stresses that the mind looks intently on God. And the sanskrit word samādhi describes the mental concentration as filled with understanding of the object so that there is an identity between the instrument of seeing and the thing seen.

Wordsworth's exposition goes even further for he combines the mental and emotional act in this extract from Tintern Abbey:

'That blessed mood,
In which the burthen of the mystery,
In which the heavy and the weary weight
Of all this unintelligible world
Is lightened:—that serene and blessed mood,
In which the affections gently lead us on,—
Until, the breath of this corporeal frame,
And even the motion of our human blood
Almost suspended; we are laid asleep
In body, and become a living soul:
While with an eye made quiet with the power
Of harmony and the deep power of joy,
We see into the life of things.'

2. CONTEMPLATION IS A GIVEN EXPERIENCE. Christ selects and takes three disciples to the experience of transfiguration. It is true that these disciples are not compelled but neither could they achieve it by themselves. They are led and they willingly follow. Certain Western descriptions of contemplation divide it into acts of acquired and infused contemplation. This is confirmed by the Transfiguration model. This contemplation is given and received. God takes the initiative and the disciples respond. They are asked to receive what is freely given. This balanced principle in full contemplation, the given and the received, denies two great errors of the contemplative forms of prayer: Pelagianism which denies the need for God's initiative and co-operating grace; Quietism which denies the reality of the act of reception. The Body of Christ is given as a free gift, but it is given with the command to receive, take and eat and only when both actions are done can there be that contemplative feeding on Christ in the heart.

3. CONTEMPLATION IS A CORPORATE EXPERIENCE in its developed forms. The Transfiguration is shared by Christ and his disciples, by Moses and Elijah, by Christ and the Father and the

33

Spirit. Christ is the centre of this fellowship; his disciples form the outer nucleus and the Father is its goal. The corporate nature of contemplation has often been overlooked. In the West this has been done by the over-emphasis on enclosure and the insistence on some forms of the solitary life. In India the Ashram form of life and the relationship between guru and disciple have done much to correct the balance. Not only was the contemplative experience of the Transfiguration a corporate experience: the same conditions held good in Gethsemane and the insights into the resurrection life of glory stress the corporate form of this heavenly prayer. Under those conditions it is shared by a great multitude which no man can number.

4. THE TRANSFIGURATION PRESENTS CONTEMPLATION AS A GROWING EXPERIENCE. For the disciples it was a process of selection, training and ascent and the manifestation of the glory was in stages. This element in contemplative prayer is stressed in the Western tradition by the symbol of the ladder and by the division of the way into discursive meditation, affective and then contemplative prayer. In the East there are even more detailed divisions which emphasise the same point. There is no rocket propulsion to any of the states of contemplation. They are all reached by climbing mountains on foot.

5. THE CONTEMPLATIVE STATE IS EXPRESSED PARTLY IN WORSHIP but in other ways as well. There is intercourse between our Lord and his predecessors. This takes the form of dialogue. There is the silence in the cloud. There is the moment of verbal insight. There is the obedience to the Lord's commands about the use of the experience. The contemplation described in the Transfiguration model also makes a deliberate connection between the insight and the service which followed in the healing of the young man. Contemplation and action are brought so closely together that they form parts of a single act and our Lord deliberately links the power to serve with the prayer of contemplation. In the Western tradition there has often been an unnatural separation between service and contemplation. This is not the principle given in the Transfiguration. Action and prayer are one insight.

6. THE TRANSFIGURATION TRANSFORMED ALL WHO SHARED IT. Our Lord was changed into glory: the disciples were illuminated by the divine presence and voice. The whole universe was transformed by the cloud of glory. In India the sign of the contemplative is partly in his physical appearance. Like Moses the experience makes his face shine and so it is sufficient for the contemplative to display this glory in a darshana. The over-emphasis on the mortifying preparation which has often distorted Western views of contemplation has tended to play down this sign. There are other signs, too. The most impressive is the one insisted on in the New Testament. It is growth in charity. It is in this virtue that the contemplative is changed from glory to glory through the work of the Spirit.

7. *ALTHOUGH THERE WAS SELECTION IN THE TRANS-FIGURATION PRAYER*, and no more than three of the disciples were chosen, yet they were types of everyman. Not intellectually brilliant, not of outstanding holiness, not of importance by any worldly standards: they were typical men whose normal abilities when touched by the Spirit flamed into contemplative insight. In other words: contemplation is open to all who are ready to believe and follow the leading of the Lord. This was the early teaching of the Church as recalled in this quotation from Abbot Butler: 'It was the standard teaching of the Catholic ages of modern times that contemplation is the natural term of a spiritual life seriously lived and it is a thing to be desired, aspired to, aimed at and not infrequently achieved by devout souls. We shall see that it is explicitly taught by St. Augustine and St. Gregory that contemplation is open to all, and that this was the great Catholic tradition is shewn by Abbé Sandreau in the book *La Vie d'Union à Dieu*. The old view is being reasserted increasingly by Catholic writers on the subject in these days. It is the hope that the teaching of these great western doctors may promote the return to the old Catholic tradition' (*Western Mysticism*, p. 192). This open-to-all approach to contemplation is one of the repeated teachings of Archbishop Ramsey and it is assumed by non-Christian traditions. Those who have been to India will have their experiences of simple and untrained people practising a deep form of contemplative prayer and doing so without any idea that they were doing something unusual. The teaching that contemplation is for a few specialists, living under almost hothouse conditions, is not the conclusions we can draw from the Transfiguration model nor is it part of the earlier traditions of Christian and non-Christian spirituality.

Many of the conclusions we have drawn from this study of the Transfiguration about contemplation are common to all its forms, Christian and non-Christian, for contemplation is not an exclusively Christian experience. It is found in all religions and in none. What makes contemplation specifically Christian is the object contemplated. Where this is Christ contemplation assumes Christian forms. But even so there are still many things in common between the

Christian and other forms. That is why Thomas Merton is right when he insists that Christian contemplatives should be in touch with their brothers of other faiths and should seek ways of light and renewal by studying the teaching of the best non-Christian contemplatives and by incorporating some of its best techniques to improve their own prayer. This happened naturally in the past. There was much common ground between the hesychasts and the practisers of meditative yoga. Today this way has been opened up again by such men as Déchanet, Abhishiktananda and a group of Roman Catholic writers who are leading us back to the rock of contemplation which is a common posession of us all.

4

CONTEMPLATIVE MATERIALS

Before an artist can create he must have certain raw materials: his paints, his canvas and a model. These materials are both within and outside himself. Within there must be an inspiring vision; outside, the instruments for its expression. He must grow to know his materials, their limitations and possibilities, and then through long and persevering practice so master them that they become responsive to his creative will and able to express his inner vision. So it is with the contemplative. He is an artist and his art is prayer. His inspiring vision is God, his instruments are himself, his friends and a controlling tradition. He must also be aware of the obstacles to his prayer and be ready to learn the way of mastering them.

All this we find in the prayer of Transfiguration. There we see our Lord acting as the great master of contemplation. He has the inner vision and he expresses it through the materials at hand: the disciples, creation and the tradition into which He was born. He also overcomes obstacles: the inadequacy of the disciples, the demands of the crowd, those spiritual forces which through this prayer became particularly active. Against the background of His achievement we shall study our own materials for contemplative prayer and the obstacles which hinder our use of them.

1. GOD is the environment in which we all live and in whom we pray. St. Paul reminds the Athenians of this and makes the point that God is the environment of prayer for everyone by quoting from a non-Christian poet to prove it: 'As some of your own poets have said, "We are also his offspring" ' (Acts 17 : 28). God is the centre of contemplation whether we think of that centre as immanent or

36

transcendent or both. At some periods of man's history this centre has been more clearly sited and described than it is today, although we still live and move in God. But it is realistic to recognise that we live in a time of special theological crisis which has been described under the heading of 'The Debate About God' in the Lambeth Conference Report of 1968 in this way: 'In the West the theological scene is characterised above all by the Debate about God. This debate is a lively discussion regarding the assertions that can be made with confidence about God, man and the world. Its context is one of theological bewilderment set against the background of the challenge, the successes and despairs of secular civilisation. Among its many causes are certain trends in current biblical and theological schools of thought, which are themselves related to the swing from traditional metaphysics to existentialism. Other causes are man's confidence in his ability to be master of his environment, and a widespread conclusion that belief in God on the part of Christians does not make any distinctive difference to the way in which they behave.' This is an accurate if somewhat committee description of the present-day attitude towards God but it certainly does not describe the God who is the object of transfiguration contemplation. The God who emerges from this debate is a hypothesis for discussion but certainly not a God for contemplation.

Baron von Hügel described the God of prayer as 'a tremendously rich reality' and this is the God revealed in the Transfiguration. He is the being who shines through all creation and makes a dazzle of glory. He is the Lord of the mountain and the overshadowing cloud. Creation is not a superfluous structure but a symbol of His being and presence. Again, He is not the empty name of the philosphers, or the nirvāna of the Buddhists but the threefold God of the Christian revelation. He is Father, Son and Holy Spirit and He offers, not something merely to look at, but someone to love. He is appropriated not by debate and argument but by faith.

The God of the Transfiguration is a God who reveals Himself continuously 'in fragmentary and varied fashion'. He reveals Himself in creation, especially through the human body transfigured. He reveals Himself both individually and corporately through the body of Christ, through the written tradition and in the heart of all who turn to Him. This God crams Himelf into all things and all things are aflame with Him. He is not the God of the theologians but the God of the living faith of those who have been taken and shown His glory. He is God in His tremendous richness, not only of being but of personality, Father, Son and Holy Spirit.

The God of the Transfiguration, not the God of debate is the God of the contemplative. He is not a God to discuss, to systematise, to doubt. He is the God of the symbols, an overwhelming presence with whom the contemplative must strive as he finds himself taken into the glory and sees God in all things, not only in the Christ transfigured but in the possessed young man, the inadequate disciples, those who ventured no further than the foot of the mountain and those who having ventured further so misunderstood as to attempt to contain the divine presence in structures of their own making. He is a centre never to be defined, never to be totally experienced, never to be described. Growth in His love is infinite. This centre is inexhaustible and always new.

All this does not belittle the work of the theologians or the precision of dogma. The Chalcedonian definition is a magnificent attempt to formulate the great facts about God and admirably guards against the danger of trying to reduce Him to the measure of our understanding. The constant struggle to express our worship in liturgical form must always go on and the God revealed in scriptures must be continually sought in order to grow into the truth. But it makes the point that the God known in these ways is a God imperfectly described and described from the experience of others. The God of the contemplative is the Lord to whom he commits himself in faith and with whom he ascends into the centre of his being. This God is the Supreme Self who fills the surrendered ego with increasing measures of His being. He is the God revealed and experienced on the mount of Transfiguration.

2. THE CONTEMPLATIVE. The nature of man is as much in debate as the nature of God. 'Lord, what is man?' is a question which has always received many and conflicting answers. We live in a time which is well described as 'a crisis of identity'. This is true of everyman but especially of the contemplative who has a special vocation and a particular sensitivity and is called to make a creative response to the mystery of himself. The model of contemplative man is contained for us in the total manifestation of man in the Transfiguration.

Herman Hesse in his book *Steppenwolf* makes the point that no individual character can fully express the mystery of man. A theatre of characters is required. So when Shakespeare gives his answer to the question 'Lord, what is man?' he uses not the one character of Hamlet, but a stageful of other characters as well. So it is in the Transfiguration. The total mystery of contemplative man is not revealed in the transfigured Christ alone but in the disciples, in Moses and Elijah, in the cloud of glory and the voice as well. What kind of answer does this complicated stage give us?

That contemplative man is an individual, centred in Christ. This comes out in the character of Peter. His individuality is not lost in

38

the group. He goes on being Peter, making his mistakes, but he is Peter locked into Christ. He is entirely dependent on Christ who takes him and leads him often to places he would naturally have avoided. So dependent is he on Christ that he can best be described as 'a member of Christ' with Christ as his true self, his head.

But Peter the individual is a divided person. At one time he penetrates the mystery of the Messiahship of Christ; at another, he is opposed to Christ and identified with Satan. This state of division and alternation from glory to abject failure is an essential of the mystery of Peter the individual. But it is not permanent. Contact with Christ leads to a transformation. Even during the Transfiguration we can watch his growth as he emerges from the blindness which made him want to build tents to contain the divine glory to the obedience which led him down the mountain and on to the eventual fulfilment of his ministry.

Peter is a combination of both physical and spiritual forces. His body is an important part of his total being. That body carries him up the mountain to his own partial transfiguration where in the cloud his body picks up the light of glory. But there is also a spiritual element which makes him sensitive to the divine manifestation and after a lifetime's meditation on it led him to write this remarkably deep description of the experience: 'It was not on tales artfully spun that we relied when we told you of the power of our Lord Jesus Christ and his coming; we saw him with our own eyes in majesty when at the hands of God the Father he was invested with honour and glory, and there came to him from the sublime Presence a voice which said: "This is my Son, my Beloved, on whom my favour rests." This voice from heaven we ourselves heard; when it came we were with him on the sacred mountain' (1 Peter 1 : 16–18). The Transfiguration model of contemplative man also insists that he is a member of a family, energised by the Spirit and centred in Christ. On this occasion the family is made up of four and to them is added the extra membership of Moses and Elijah. The family of contemplative man is not merely a selection of earthly people; it has a relationship with those on the other side of death. His family is also the company of heaven. Life in the family is not optional for the contemplative individual. It is essential for the fulfilment of his vocation. In this family he is taken into Christ and shares the richest corporate life, a harmony of past, present and future. He sees the Lord more clearly through the varied characters of the family and he is also trained and deepened by the impact of many human relationships and tensions. This family is something more than the natural family. It is formed for the purpose of contemplation, specially selected and trained for this work. It is small, flexible, responsive to change and without those rules and legal obligations which so often make the natural family a prison rather than a home. Its purpose is not primarily to do good but to become good in terms of transfiguration. Peter, James and John made an excellent contemplative family because they were ready to share the Transfiguration of their Lord. Any attempt to make this family permanent was too dangerous to consider. Peter's suggestion that shelters should be made was absurd. The family forms and disperses as its contemplative purpose requires.

The history of the Church and of religious communities is a warning to all who would enlarge the structure of the contemplative family beyond its effective size. This is the warning of the ruins of Cluny and of many another ecclesiastical structure. When man tries to universalise the contemplative family it fragments into its original components. The Transfiguration family in its intense nucleus was made up of three with the Lord as its centre. Its outer circumference included the other nine disciples at the foot of the mountain. This made a total family of twelve with Christ the centre. This seems the maximum size for a such a family. It can be shown that a model made up of thirteen balls, all of the same diameter is the maximum number in which each ball touches the other and the centre. This is a warning of what must happen when the contemplative family exceeds that number: its mutual contact is destroyed and communication with the centre is broken.

This contemplative family which is so essential for the individual contemplative exists not merely for its members nor for the world but for the Lord. Its function is to share in His Transfiguration, in His Gethsemane prayer and to be His instrument for communicating with the world. It cannot work on its own, achieving its own degree of insight, being itself an instrument of healing. It is completely dependent on the Lord and His Spirit. It lives by being completely receptive to the Spirit of the Lord and in growing sensitivity to the presence of the Lord who is the source of its identity.

All contemplatives share in these features revealed in the Transfiguration model. They are individuals primarily concerned with an inner centre of being; they have been called to an awareness of the divine presence, often against their will; they agonise in a state of divided and obscured identity. They are also members of a family called into being for a contemplative purpose. This family is truly ecumenical by the fact that it can be made up of members of many religious groups, united in the Christ centre, the Spirit energy and the Father of the Lord Jesus Christ as its goal.

3. SOME WESTERN CONTEMPLATIVE TRADITIONS. Both Elijah and Moses shared in the Transfiguration. 'They saw Elijah

40

appear, and Moses with him, and there they were conversing with Jesus' (Mark 9 : 4). These two figures have been interpreted in the liturgy of the Church as symbols of two great contemplative traditions, the Law and the prophets. The antiphon for Lauds says this explicitly: 'The law was signified by Moses, and the prophets by Elias: who were shining in glory with the Lord and speaking with him in the mount.' Elijah achieved the highest degree of contemplative awareness: 'He went up by a whirlwind into heaven' (2 Kings 1 : 11). Moses turned away from the invitation to contemplate God in the burning bush and instead substituted a law and ways of serving Him. 'And Moses hid his face, for he was afraid to look at God' (Exodus 3 : 6). Both of these men were contemplative geniuses and both taught ways leading to deep awareness of God. As they talked with Jesus during the Transfiguration they were speaking to the greatest contemplative of all, one in perfect union with the Father and the Spirit who not only taught the way to God but claimed himself to be the way and the truth and the life. He is the primary source of the Christian contemplative tradition and the main secret of Christian contemplation is to turn to Him.

Jesus initiates the conversation but others talk to Him and communicate through Him to others. This communication is of two kinds: the tradition of religion as symbolised by Moses and the tradition of inspired, prophetic leadership as symbolised by Elijah. To reach the Transfiguration state of contemplation the influence of both these traditions, controlled and rooted in the incarnate Lord, is needed.

Religion is given harsh treatment by Karl Barth in his commentary on St. Paul's Epistle to Romans. He writes: 'Neither obedience, nor resurrection, nor God can be embraced within the possibility of religion' (p. 231). Religion is obviously an inadequate substitute for God. But on the other hand Barth is equally clear that religion provides a training ground for union with Him. The so-called 'religionless Christianity' is a small part of the truth. Barth puts the other side when he writes: 'For in religion the spirit veritably enters in on our behalf with groanings which cannot be uttered' (p. 240). In other words, religion is a discipline which prepares for the presence of God. There is a place for Moses, for religious tradition in contemplation, even though religion can lead no further than to a Pisgah glimpse of the Promised Land.

There are many religious traditions to choose from, both Christian and non-Christian. In the past it has been the fashion to deplore the multiplicity of Christian traditions and disastrous attempts have been made to harmonise them into a meaningless compromise. Equally there are innumerable non-Christian traditions and

41

again there are disastrous attempts to synthesise them into a con-fused harmony. The right attitude to this rich variety seems to be selection from the many of a few traditions which most meet the needs of the group and individual, using this small selection as a structure of experience from which to develop one's own path of contemplation. Often the traditions most useful are those which form part of one's inherited environment or which have been met with in life's pilgrimage. Our own choice has been made on these principles and this has resulted in the religious tradition of the Church of England forming one part of the tradition and the teaching of Patanjali in the Yoga Sutras the other.

The religious tradition of the Church of England is something to be lived rather than to have explained. To those who have not done this it seems a contradictory system which compared with the strict consistency of other traditions can hardly be taken seriously. Many would dismiss it as an unworkable compromise, but those who have lived in it long enough find that it is a *via media* which holds in balance the two extremes and finds truth in between them. This is particularly suitable for contemplative prayer which is much more about insight than clear-cut solutions and definitions, and it leaves the mind free to come to its own awareness of truth without having its freedom of exploration curtailed by premature and unsuitable answers. In the East the end of contemplation is described as a state of freedom: for this freedom the Anglican tradition is a wonderful preparation.

The materials of this tradition are primarily contained in the Bible but the Bible without too detailed an interpretation. It is the word of God but we are left to hear that Word in our own way. All that is laid down is that there should be no contradiction between parts of the Word in one part of the Bible and another. We have to learn to hold in balance contradiction and we have to work patiently towards a resolution. Any other teaching from any other source must be com-pared with the Bible teaching and nothing which is against that teaching is to be accepted. So, although the Bible is a primary source this does not preclude the use of other writings as helps to growth in awareness of God. The Bible remains a standard of comparison but not an exclusive authority.

The Anglican tradition is formulated in many ways. There is the Catechism, to which all divinity may be reduced, according to George Herbert. This has recently been revised and is a valuable summary of the Anglican tradition in a shorthand form, in some ways like the brief summary of Yoga in the Yoga Sutras. There is the liturgy which has become a much more living expression of the tradition since the Church has claimed the right to revise this

42

liturgy as and when she thinks necessary. Until this freedom was won liturgy was much nearer what Archbishop Ramsey has called 'archaeological religion' than the expression of a living tradition. Now in its recently revised forms it is a contemporary expression of the tradition, put into prayer forms which give considerable help in the construction of personal and corporate prayer patterns. It combines regular use of the psalms, planned readings from the Bible and above all the structure of a yearly cycle of festivals through which the main parts of the tradition are expressed. This use of the mysteries of the Christian gospel in the cycle of festivals is one of the most effective ways of expressing the tradition and it is shared in method at least by many other religious traditions. Hinduism has a similar method with a combination of agricultural festivals; and birth, death, marriage and puberty observances parallel this in simpler religions.

The most immediately contemplative part of the liturgical expression of the Anglican tradition is the eucharist. In this service, which is even more an action than a verbal statement, are brought together all those contemplative principles we have already observed in the Transfiguration. There is the insistence on preparation. This is expressed in the preliminary rites of baptism and confirmation and in the pattern of Christian life they imply. In this service are all the materials needed for contemplative prayer: the presentation of the mystery of God and man through the scripture readings, the sermon and the creed; the use of symbols of bread and wine to stimulate the mind to contemplative acts; the command to identify with the Lord in the most intimate of all ways, 'Feed on him in your heart by faith with thanksgiving.' This pattern-form of all acts of communion with God provides the materials we need for contemplation. What is lacking in the Anglican tradition is any serious method of responding to the material in an adequately contemplative way. We have little teaching about 'The Mass in the heart'. True, Teilhard de Chardin dropped hints in his description of 'Mass on the World' but the Church has a lot of practice to do with the eucharist in terms of silence, posture, concentration and contemplative prayer before it comes to an adult response to what is given. Perhaps the restoration of contemplation in the West will eventually come about most effectively, not by borrowing from Eastern traditions but by taking seriously our own tradition in the eucharist and then learning how to use it with mature contemplative action. To do this we shall certainly have to reduce the size of the eucharistic congregation and be quite uninhibited about the explorations into the way of using it for contemplation. This is the great ministry for which the clergy should be prepared during their theological training.

43

We have already seen that contemplative prayer requires a contemplative family and this is provided for in the Anglican tradition. The structure of the ministry, bishops, clergy and laity is designed to develop a most closely knit relationship, even though it does not always work. The Anglican communion is now made up of a glorious variety of people of all countries and languages and gradually there is a growing interpenetration of custom and ways of living. There is even provision for a close relationship between the Church and those who do not share her membership and this is something to develop rather than deplore. The more varied the family the richer it becomes.

The Anglican tradition has recently passed through an unfortunate phase in which it attempted to reform itself by means of a revision of its canon law. This was an enormous expenditure of time and energy and from it emerged one valuable discovery. It was that the canons were irrelevant and unworkable. Families are not made by rules. They are the result of a free play of Spirit on groups of people who are learning to love one another. This potential freedom lies at the heart of the Anglican tradition and waits courageous development by those who are prepared to run the risk of growing into a family of contemplation.

Discipleship is the other way of growing in contemplation. As there was an essential place for Moses in the Transfiguration even more so was there a place for Elijah. There is an Indian saying that when the disciple is ready the spiritual leader (guru) will appear. In his book *Guru and Disciple* Abhishiktananda described the relationship between disciple and spiritual leader in this way: 'Beyond the experience of things and places, of watching or participating in rites, of reading or meditating on the scriptures, or of attending lectures, there is the experience of meeting with men in whose heart the Invisible has revealed himself and through whom his light shines in perfect purity—the mystery of the guru' (Abhishiktananda, *Guru and Disciple*, p. 28, S.P.C.K., 1974). He went on to show how the guru and disciple in the Indian tradition formed a couple, mutually attractive and complementary. The guru must be much more than an intellectual guide. He must himself have attained the Real. The disciple must be prepared to trust him and to see through him his real self and vocation.

This is a precise description of the relationship between Elijah and his disciple Elisha, between the Christian contemplative and those he guides along the path he has already taken.

In the course of a contemplative life several spiritual guides may be needed. In retrospect I am conscious of a number of different men who performed this service for me. The first was a congregational lay

44

preacher whose knowledge of Western prayer was so much deeper than my own. Then there was the novice master with his practical handling of the delicate problems of community life. Then in India a Brahmin language teacher who was in touch both with Western and Eastern traditions and could see where they enriched each other. And now the guru appears in the stranger who stays no more than a day and in that short time reveals so much and in that great host of leaders who have written their teaching for those who come after them.

The Anglican tradition is particularly rich in what might be called its writing prophets. There is an outstanding collection of spiritual writers in the school of the Early English Mystics which includes Mother Julian of Norwich, Walter Hilton, the author of *The Cloud of Unknowing*, and Richard Rolle. In the post reformation period there were men of the stature of George Herbert, John Donne and Jeremy Taylor. The later writers maintained this great tradition through the writings of William Law and Bunyan in his spiritual classic, *Pilgrim's Progress*. In the nineteenth century there was the recall to contemplation sounded by Wordsworth and the romantic poets and this was taken up in the Church by the catholic movement and by such spiritual leaders and writers as Father Benson and John Keble, Father Longridge who re-introduced the Ignatian Exercises to the Anglican Church and a host of others. We still live in a period when the number of spiritual leaders increases and are now reinforced by the retailers of various forms of oriental mysticism who with the support of Western methods of advertisement persuade many to forsake the leaders of their own traditions for others much more difficult to understand.

In the course of his spiritual life a contemplative may use several guides both within and outside his tradition. This was the experience of Thomas Merton. He began with the great masters of his own tradition: St. Benedict, St. Bernard of Clairvaux, St. Ignatius of Loyola, St. Theresa and St. John of the Cross. Later he came more under the influence of the Desert Fathers and made use of an almost hesychastic form of prayer. In his final period he moved towards the Buddhist masters of contemplation. This did not mean that he abandoned his own tradition. His final letters make it quite clear that there was no question of this. But he turned to the Buddhist contemplation methods as a source of experience to enrich his own. In doing this he was acting true to his own Christian traditions. The early Church learnt much about contemplative prayer from the masters of the Greek traditions. Through the Desert Fathers she took into herself some of the oriental techniques. And now encouraged by the highest authority we are being asked to examine some of these oriental guides more closely.

4. PATANJALI AND THE ORIENTAL CONTEMPLATIVE TRADITION.

Thomas Merton was certainly not alone in his search for guidance among Eastern teachers. He was one of a great company of explorers. Some of them concentrated on Buddhist forms of prayer, some were more interested in the Indian techniques of Yoga.

Dom. J.-M. Déchanet was one of the first pioneers of yoga and in his book *Christian Yoga* (Search Press), he attempted to combine the use of certain parts of hatha yoga with Christian meditation. It was a courageous beginning and won the approval of his superiors and was welcomed by many Christians. The book was first published in 1960 and has passed through many reprints. Déchanet does not seem to have drawn on the specifically meditative form of yoga called raja yoga nor does he seem to have used the classic source of that teaching in Patanjali's Yoga Sutras. But it was an important beginning which was to inspire many others to explore this Indian technique of prayer.

Some years before Déchanet published his book Father Jack Winslow was leading a pioneer movement in India at the Christa Prema Seva Sangha community in Pune where an attempt was made to found a religious community which would combine the ashram type of structure with some of the Western disciplines. In 1931 he published a book called *The Art of Contemplation* in which he brilliantly introduced the 'Eight Limbs' of Patanjali's teaching in the Yoga Sutras to an Indian audience. It was more than an introduction. It was an attempt to show how much of Patanjali's teaching could be paralleled in the Christian contemplative tradition. One of his disciples, Verrier Elwin at about the same time in his book *Christian Dhyāna* showed how much of the teaching in *The Cloud of Unknowing* could be found in Indian forms of meditation. These two leaders were a little too early to receive the recognition given to Déchanet but in many ways they had a more profound knowledge of the methods of Yoga contemplation and presented a more complete picture for others to use. The great work of Jack Winslow and Verrier Elwin was to point to Patanjali as the chief source of the Indian form of Raja Yoga and to indicate some of the ways in which his teaching could be used to develop and renew our Western tradition.

Meanwhile in our own day Yoga continues to be given to the West in a variety of forms by a host of teachers. Some present it in the form of karma yoga, a way of life with the *Bhagavad Gita* as the source of teaching. Others stress yoga as a form of worship and prayer, using the many forms of bhakti Yoga for their teaching. Most popular of all is hatha yoga which treats yoga as a way of health to be practised by regular performance of a number of postures and complicated breathing exercises. Yoga as a way of training for contemplation as taught in the Yoga Sutras of Patanjali still awaits adequate exposition and application and it is one of the purposes of this book to make a small contribution towards this end.

Patanjali wrote the Yoga Sutras according to many Indian authorities about 300 B.C. They are a collection of less than 200 verses, divided into four books which describe the application of certain techniques to contemplative prayer. The subject-title of each book roughly describes its contents: Book 1. *Contemplation* (Samādhi Pāda); Book 2. *Training for contemplation* (Sādhana pāda); Book 3. *Contemplation exercises* (Vibhūti pāda); Book 4. *Freedom* (Kaivalya).

This small book has been fairly described by Radakrishnan in his great work on Indian Philosophy in these words: 'The Yoga Sutras are the crystallisation of ideas on asceticism and contemplation extant at his time in a more or less hazy and undefined way. He codified the nebulous tradition evolved under the pressure of life and experience. His system bears the marks of the age in which it was produced. While we have in it the most refined mysticism, we have also mixed up with it many beliefs derived from the prevailing religions of the time. Yoga, according to Patanjali, is a methodical effort to attain perfection through the control of the different elements of human nature, physical and psychical.... The main interest of Patanjali is not metaphysical theorising but the practical motive of indicating how salvation can be attained by disciplined activity' (S. Radakrishnan, *Indian Philosophy*, Vol. 2, p. 338, Allen & Unwin, 1929).

This is a fair description of Patanjali's great work by an outstanding Indian scholar. It does not make higher claims than a study of the work justifies. It is no more than a summary, a codification rather than a work of great originality and in its over-compressed form it presents serious difficulties to the present-day student.

Radakrishnan makes the important point that Patanjali was rather concerned with describing techniques than with enunciating a philosophy. His philosophy had already been done for him by the Sankhya exposition of Yoga. Patanjali was concerned with applying its principles to contemplative prayer. For this reason he is a particularly suitable guide for Christians and reduces to a minimum any tension between his teaching and the Christian faith. Those who follow him are not required to go into a kind of synthetic wilderness of compromise: they can leave their Christian theology unchanged and without tension incorporate many of the profound insights of Patanjali's methods into their prayer. This is an important reassurance for those Christians who are uneasy about going outside

47

of their own tradition, who are at ease with Moses and the law but embarrassed by Elijah and the individual explorers. As we try to respond to the Church's invitation to explore oriental techniques of silence we can be certain that in using Patanjali as our main guide we are following one who most completely expounds his own tradition and at the same time makes no conflicting demands on our loyalty to our Christian faith.

Geraldine Coster in her book *Yoga and Western Psychology* points out that Patanjali has been badly served by his translators. This is one of the problems of sharing his teaching with Western readers. The translations are either inaccurate in an attempt to be coherent or else they are translations of the sanskrit in a form which leaves them incomprehensible. The standard literal translation is still *The Yoga System of Patanjali* by James Haughton Woods (1966), but his English is often obscure, as obscure as his sanskrit original. Geraldine Coster tried to solve her problem of translation by attempting a paraphrase of the sutras she needed for her study and by some re-arrangement. We have partly followed her example in the version of the Sutras which is in the appendix to this book.

Patanjali's account of yoga includes all the forms of yoga in outline and in harmonious balance. He also directs them towards their true end in some form of contemplation. His study of yoga gives an acute analysis of the principles of contemplation in its various stages and although his arrangement is often haphazard there are in his book all those acts leading to contemplation which we have found so clearly demonstrated in the model of the Transfiguration. We have found much help in applying these acts to our own contemplative prayer by comparing Patanjali's work with the teaching and practice of our own traditions. This is what the Lambeth Conference hoped would result from a communication between different traditions and it is an exploration which needs still further development.

Patanjali describes two forms of contemplation: one using an image (samprājnāta samādhi) and the other without an image (asam-prājnāta samādhi). These correspond to the two experiences of the disciples at the Transfiguration. First, they contemplated with the image of Jesus in various forms: as the Master leading them up the mountain, as the transfigured Lord on the mountain. Then this image was absorbed by the cloud of glory and they contemplated without an image the glory of the Lord and became identified with Him.

Contemplation with an image Patanjali divides into several stages. There is contemplation with the use of the imagination (savitarka samādhi), contemplation with the use of the discursive reason (savichāra samādhi), contemplation with the emotions (sānanda

48

samādhi), contemplation on the self (sasmita samādhi). This is followed by an experience of what is called the rain cloud of knowledge (dharma-megha-samādhi) in which the ordinary rational processes are transcended into some form of insight.

Again, all these stages are present in the Transfiguration model. There was the physical ascent of the mountain during which many images were presented and pondered. There was a discursive form of prayer when Jesus conversed with Moses and Elijah. Even Peter joined in this stage with his inadequate contribution about building tents for the divine glory. There was an emotional sequence when the emotions of fear and joy were present. Then came the obliterating cloud and within that cloud the transforming experience out of which they came to see Jesus only.

The rain cloud or the cloud of unknowing is the dividing experience between contemplation with and without an image. Patanjali teaches that passing through the cloud to the imageless experience beyond requires great faith, energy, recollection and a deep understanding. It comes as the climax of single-minded devotion to the Lord.

We see the disciples at the Transfiguration and St. Augustine at Ostia share a momentary touch of this state. They become simply aware of God. They become unconsciously united with him. For that moment all life is summed up in one experience of Jesus only. But it is Jesus in His relationship with the Father, Son and Spirit. Patanjali does not take us as far as this. He never attempts a detailed analysis of the God to whom contemplation leads. He is content to describe him as 'a unique Self' but his very reticence adds value to his description of the way to Him and makes it possible to harmonise this way with the path revealed to us in the Transfiguration.

For Patanjali contemplation is not the end. Contemplative clarity leads on to freedom (kaivalya). This is an identification between the object of consciousness and the enlightened consciousness. This was the final goal of the Transfiguration. It was fully attained by the Lord who was proclaimed as the well-beloved Son, united to the Father's will and empowered to perform it as he heals the sick and passes through death to resurrection. For the disciples this freedom was a momentary touch. They had to stumble and fall and rise many times before they reached that stable freedom of glory.

There is much in the Yoga Sutras about the spiritual life which is for the specialist and not suitable for our present needs. This is true of Book 3 where various experiences arising from different acts of contemplation are described. They should be no means be dismissed as irrelevant exaggerations even though they bring their own temptations which have been recognised by Radakrishnan. Of them he wisely writes: 'The acquisition of these powers (siddhis) is subordinated to the chief end of samādhi in the Yoga system. ... In Bunyan's allegory the pilgrims to the celestial city find, even at the very gateway of heaven, a little wicket gate that admits to a path leading down to hell. He who falls a victim to the magical powers rapidly goes downward' (ibid., pp. 366–7). Our Lord gives a similar warning after the Transfiguration when he 'enjoins them not to tell anyone what they had seen until the Son of Man had risen from the dead' (Mark 9 : 9).

This descriptive part of the Yoga Sutras is of lesser value compared with the training for contemplative prayer which is the subject of the second book. Here a preliminary and advance course of training is given, not in order to achieve contemplation by self-effort but in order to reduce the hindrances to that state. This is an important distinction and avoids the error of a pelagian self-sufficiency. Patanjali's training adds detailed guidance to the bare outline of the three stages to contemplation which are given in the Transfiguration model. There we have a summary of the preparation of the disciples, a brief description of the transfiguration experience and an outline of the consequences. In Patanjali all this is done in careful detail. As a result his teaching provides the expert guidance needed for mapping a course of preliminary and advanced training and helps us to construct a plan of contemplation exercises which is both balanced and has been tested over a long period. In these days when so many are casting about for a reformed asceticism which shall include the best principles of the old ways and be open and responsive to the ways of other traditions this work of Patanjali can be of immense value. We have used it as a way of by-passing many old theological differences by going behind the conditions of their origin to a wider and more general foundation in our common human nature to which the work of Patanjali bears witness. We have also used his work to complement our own tradition and to map a path up the mount of Transfiguration to meet our present needs. Just as St. Thomas Aquinas renewed Christian doctrine in the Middle Ages by building his *Summa* around the intellectual structure of Aristotle so it may well be that in our century, with its pressing need for a contemporary asceticism and contemplative form of prayer, Patanjali could supply a similar model on which to work. There are at present many Eastern leaders competing for this responsible position. We must each make a contribution to this search and then wait for the most suitable leader to survive.

OBSTACLES TO CONTEMPLATION

The model of the Transfiguration does not suggest that the way to contemplation is easy and unobstructed. On the contrary, it describes many obstacles and the ways they were overcome. These obstacles were of two kinds: general and particular.

Some of the general obstacles to contemplation at the Transfiguration were: the inadequacy of the disciples as a contemplative family; the disorders of creation; and the distraction of the crowd, symbolised by the devil-possessed son, the perplexed father and the turbulent spectators. These obstacles are always with us. Ideally the Church is the great contemplative family, but the Church is always inadequate to its task. Like the disciples there are many of its members who want to remain at the foot of the mountain, absorbed in good works. The energy of the family is dissipated in innumerable concerns which distract from the main vocation. The whole creation still groans and travails in pain, giving us no more than 'puzzling reflections in a mirror' when we look for a transparency of God. And the world of men is still a chaos in which the divine presence is almost totally concealed.

The particular and individual obstacles are equally serious. We see them summarised for us in the character of Peter. He had contemplative genius but how much the process was hindered by his blindness and over-confidence and misinterpretation. St. Paul sums up what we see in Peter for everyman: 'Unspiritual, the purchased slave of sin . . . for what I do is not what I want to to do, but what I detest. . . . The good that I want to do, I fail to do; but what I do is the wrong which is against my will' (Romans 7 : 15).

While being realistic about our own obstacles to contemplation we must avoid being too pessimistic. We are not totally disordered nor with the faculties completely incapable of contemplative prayer. Our Lord's view at the Transfiguration was that there were varying degrees of disorder. He selected for the experience those of His family most able to respond at that time. He took and led them. Then the transforming luminosity of the uncreated light was increased to illuminate both Himself and his creation. Through this He cleansed the senses of perception of the disciples to make them capable of seeing and hearing events beyond their normal range. In this way He led them to a brief contemplative experience of God and the removal of all obstacles to the awareness of the divine vision and the hearing of the divine voice. The divine intervention can overcome all obstacles and transform men of quite ordinary ability into contemplatives of the highest order. This needs to be remembered as we analyse the obstacles and guard against the danger of being depressed by their number through forgetting the power and adequacy of divine grace.

The obstacles to contemplation revealed through the Transfiguration have been analysed and described in many contemplative traditions. We shall consider two of them: the Christian and the Eastern as reported by Patanjali in the Yoga Sutras.

1. THE OBSTACLES TO CONTEMPLATION IN CHRISTIAN TRADITIONS. Starting from the Bible picture of man the Christian tradition has included all obstacles to contemplation under the general heading of sin. Sin has then been divided into two categories: original and actual. These have been variously described, often with the unfortunate emphasis on the penal aspect of sin with God as the avenging judge. This approach is less acceptable today and there is a danger of minimising the gravity of sin. In the types of instant meditation often purveyed to Western customers, eager for an easy and rapid way to spiritual experience, by astute Eastern teachers, sin is often ignored altogether with the result that sooner or later the disciple finds his progress blocked. Sin is much more than punishment and God's treatment of it is much more sophisticated than that of an angry judge. Sin is the obstacle to contemplation and with the co-operation of the sinner God is engaged in the complicated ministry of a forgiveness which both removes the obstacle and restores the harm it has done to the sinner. It is sin as an obstacle to contemplation that we shall accept as our interpretation in examining the distinction between its two main forms.

Original sin is an inherited obstacle to the vision of God which is shared in varying degrees by the whole creation. John Macquarrie emphasises this in his definition of original sin as 'a massive disorientation and perversion of human society as a whole' (*Principles of Christian Theology*, p. 61, SCM Press, London, 1966). It affects all creation which as St. Paul says 'groans in all its parts as if in the pangs of childbirth' (Romans 8 : 22). The result is that creation and our own faculties included can only provide us with 'puzzling reflections of God'. This is far from saying however that creation is totally opaque to his presence. The Transfiguration takes place, not in heaven but on earth, and God is still able to use his creation to reveal Himself. Neither creation nor man is completely depraved. In both there are signs of the divine presence and when these are magnified and made luminous, as in the Transfiguration event, then God shines through a distorted universe and is recognised through the damaged faculties of man. There is, in spite of inherited sin, an embryonic capacity for God in creation and in man; and with man's co-operation God can and does develop this into 'a wakening up after his likeness' leading on to a face-to-face vision as man makes his journey through the planned and remedial experiences of this world. Original sin is therefore a partial obstacle to the revelation of God in creation and man which is inherent in their essential structures. It is removable and the discipline of contemplative prayer is the way man co-operates with God in this healing.

Actual or individual sin has been described in greater detail. It is the obstacle man puts between himself and contemplating God by his own choice. St. Gregory analysed the root forms of this sin in what are called the seven capital sins, and provided we remember that these seven sins are attempts to probe the roots of all forms of sin they still have much value in helping us to diagnose our condition. The root of them all, pride, concerns our relationship with God. Lust, sloth, gluttony relate to our use of the body and its faculties. Anger, envy, covetousness are disorders in our family life. These sins appear in many forms from the obvious physical forms of such a work as Boccaccio's *Decameron* to the more subtle spiritual forms analysed by St. John of the Cross in *The Dark Night of the Soul*. In whatever form they are found they hinder the heart in its work of contemplation. This is the experience of all, whether Christian or not, who have set out on this path and for all the prayer of the psalmist rings true: 'Make me a clean heart, O God: and renew a right spirit within me' (Psalm 51 : 10).

There is at the present time a healthy reaction against a former over-emphasis on sin with mostly negative overtones. Modern psychology rightly warns us of the danger in terms of an unhealthy self-consciousness, an over-concern with our failed selves; and Christians need to take this warning seriously. But there is also a need, especially for the Christian engaged in growing contemplative prayer, to diagnose the obstacles to this growth clearly so that he may play an intelligent part in the removal of those which hinder the fulfilment of his vocation. There is no need to elaborate the traditional sevenfold division of actual sin but there is a need to be aware of the sins in that division which are the special obstacles to contemplative prayer at the present moment. We see this specific awareness being given to the disciples at the Transfiguration by the careful guidance of our Lord. His presence reveals their blindness, their sloth, their pride: and in the case of St. Peter he is identified with Satan himself in his arrogant rejection of the crucial way to God. But always the recognition of the obstacle is the beginning of its removal. There is no question of a judgement which is merely avenging. The sin is uncovered in order to be removed.

53

This is an important feature of the Transfiguration. It is an act of contemplation which reveals obstacles but also a means by which they are removed. In the cloud of glory, even though it is the shadow-side for the disciples, they see the Lord more clearly; in his nearness their fear is overcome. Their isolated and conflicting selves are assimilated into the divine Self of Jesus so that as they look round they see Him in all things. This is the basic healing which comes from all forms of contemplation. Sin is not a final obstacle to those who have the courage to persevere. In the revealed glory of God sin is consumed, in the fire of His love the dross of self is burnt away. The contemplative family descends the mountain not only renewed with the glory seen but with Christ in their midst, able to communicate the divine power and glory and healing to the disordered world. The Transfiguration states the fact that contemplation reveals sin. It states with even greater emphasis that contemplation removes it. Our attitude to sin therefore as contemplatives in these uncertain times must be one of fearless recognition combined with a courageous and persevering penetration into God who through the state of contemplative awareness destroys all forms of sin at its roots and takes it away for ever.

2. THE OBSTACLES TO CONTEMPLATION IN THE YOGA TRADITION OF PATANJALI. If we are going to use Patanjali as an Eastern guide to contemplation we must begin by using him as a guide to the obstacles of that contemplation. And here he is particularly helpful as a complement to our Western traditions. For Patanjali is free from our inherited theological controversies and gives us a new approach to a shared experience.

Patanjali does not divide the obstacles into the clear-cut division of original and actual sin. For him all obstacles are partly inherited and partly made. Under the conception of karma he sees everyman the victim of inherited defects and abilities and in his personal life continuously adding to them. There are many advantages to this more flexible approach and it certainly is more true to general experience.

Again, Patanjali divides the obstacles into degrees of intensity. The less fundamental obstacles he calls distractions (vikshepas). The more fundamental he calls the hindrances (kleshas).

In describing the distractions Patanjali refers them to physical causes. There are nine such physical states and each produces its own corresponding distraction. These are: disease, languor, doubt, carelessness, laziness, worldly-mindedness, delusion, non-achievement and instability. He goes on to point out that the presence of these distractions is indicated by certain symptoms: mental pain, despair, nervousness and irregular breathing. What he does not do is to mention anything approaching blame or judgement on the person suffering from any of these states. He is much more concerned with removing the distractions than to waste time on finding a scapegoat.

He prefaces his discipline for removing distractions with the basic rule that mastery of the heart for contemplation is brought about by two things: persistent, repetitive practice and indifference to results (cf. Yoga Sutras, 1 : 12). He then gives the following disciplines:

the constant practice of one pattern of life, what we should call the
    observance of a rule of life.
concentration of a life pattern around certain controlling points.
the regular cultivation of friendliness, compassion, gladness and
    indifference.
the practice of some form of breath control.
cultivation of the higher senses, such as the sense of seeing
    through art and the sense of hearing through music.
concentration on the inner light in the heart.
Meditations on: any of the saints
    dreams and sleep.
    any other helpful subject.   (cf. Sutras, 1 : 32–9)

Patanjali's teaching about the hindrances deals with much more fundamental obstacles to contemplation. Here he goes to the root of the matter in a way which very much resembles the Bible and the Christian approach. He names five such hindrances: Ignorance (avidyā), egoism (asmiti), desire (rāga), aversion (dvesha) and over-attachment to life (abhinivesha). He elaborates what he means by each of these hindrances. Ignorance is the error of confusing the non-eternal, the impure and evil with God. This hindrance is, like pride, the source of all others obstacles to contemplation. Egoism is the identification of the power that knows with the instrument through which he knows. Desire is absorption in pleasure. Aversion is being obsessed with pain. Over-attachment is an overclinging to life and a fear of death.

In Christian teaching these hindrances are all included in the seven capital sins and St. Paul gives a general description of them in this quotation from the epistle to the Romans: 'For this reason God has given them up to the vileness of their own desires, and the consequent degradation of their bodies because they have bartered away the true God for a false one, and have offered reverence and worship to created things instead of to the Creator' (Romans 1 : 24–5).

In this passage there are references to the basic ignorance which is the source of all other obstacles to contemplation in Patanjali's teaching and also to those emotional disorders which disturb the heart from its contemplative work. It is worth expanding these similarities between the two traditions.

Ignorance most nearly resembles the capital sin of pride which sets up the artificially made self as the true self. It leads men to find in the visible world all their satisfaction and to look for nothing beyond. Pride causes angels and men to turn from God as their true end to an idol of their own making. Although each man chooses his own way of ignorance he does not do so entirely. He is born into an environment where the majority accept a state of ignorance as their form of truth and pressurise everyone to do the same. He is born with inherited tendencies towards this hindrance. The sin of pride, the state of ignorance, is part of an inherited defect which is increased with every chosen act of pride and ignorance made during the journey through life. He is in darkness because, as our Lord puts it, 'he loves darkness rather than light'.

Bernard Lonergan calls ignorance by his own coined word, *scotosis*. By this he means 'an aberration of understanding' which takes the form of refusing to accept certain insights which are unacceptable in their implications. This is a state of mind which refuses to move into new modes of thought, which shrinks from passing through the material into the spiritual world, which clings to an old self and rejects the new self offered instead (c.f. Bernard Lonergan, *Insight*, p. 191, Darton, Longman and Todd, 1973).

All these examples are contemporary forms of the ignorance which Patanjali sees as the root hindrance to contemplative health.

Egoism exists in both true and false forms. True egoism is the awareness of the little child and this our Lord taught was essential for contemplation. 'Unless you turn round and become like children, you will never enter the kingdom of Heaven. Let a man humble himself till he is like this child and he will be the greatest in the kingdom of Heaven' (Matthew 18 : 3–4).

This kind of egoism makes an ego which is a receptive, cooperative instrument, capable of union with God. False egoism is the same ego, inflated with pride, contemplating the reflection of itself in all things. This egoism obstructs the contemplative from his goal and leaves him the centre of himself. This particular form of ignorance is the most deadly of all.

Desire and Aversion are disorders of the emotional faculties. They represent the extremes of emotional changes, from total aggression to total withdrawal, from lust to servile fear, from over-activity to sloth. The contemplative state requires a balanced tension midway between them, or, as Patanjali puts it, a state of stillness (sattva) between the extremes of activity (rajas) and passivity (tamas). In the Christian tradition a variety of human emotional temperaments is

56

recognised. These vary between the lethargic and the choleric, the sanguine and phlegmatic. Part of the art of the contemplative is to recognise his emotional bias and then to apply those corrections he needs.

Attachment is a clinging to life rather than surrendering to the Creator. It is expressed in forms of amassing wealth, clinging to life when death has clearly made his demands. Such attachment occurs in prayer, as Patanjali recognised, when certain supernatural sensual powers are attained and a man is tempted to hold on to them rather than pass through them in his journey to God. There is only one way of escape and this is the one taken by our Lord: 'Begone, Satan; scripture says, "You shall do homage to the Lord your God and worship him alone"' (Matthew 4 : 10).

Just as Patanjali gives advice for overcoming the distractions so in much greater detail he shows how the hindrances can be reduced and eventually overcome. He divides this way into a preliminary and advanced discipline. We shall consider this in greater detail. At this stage we may note the wise gradualness of his plan. It does not lead to over-strain and shock and the faculties are not destroyed but healed. Like the description given by our Lord of the healing of the vine, it is done by pruning and not by amputation.

Chapter 3

Preliminary Contemplative Training

In the gospels there are different names for those in different stages of following Christ. There are the beginners who are called followers; then the learners or disciples; and finally the proficients or apostles. These names describe three stages of growth: the call, the response and the fully trained. In Eastern spirituality similar stages are recognised: the *chela* or follower; the *shishya* or learner; the fully trained or *guru*.

These stages indicate the need for training and also suggest a graduated system measured to the different capacities of the pupils. Such wisely graduated teaching is especially needed in training for contemplative prayer. Too much too soon can easily lead to discouragement; and a supply of milk when meat is called for is equally fatal to perseverance. What is needed is at least two forms of training: a preliminary one for beginners and an advanced one for the mature.

This distinction was recognised by our Lord at the time of His Transfiguration. He had already chosen the twelve disciples. He had already given them preliminary training. Now He selects those mature enough for a further contemplative experience and these He takes with Himself to the mountain.

In all His training our Lord followed the classic pattern of combining experience with theory. And always in this order. Experience first and then explanation. He used what today would be called the empirical method. The disciples were to come and then to see. They were to experience the Transfiguration and it would be explained later. Like our Lady they were to have deep contemplative experiences which would mature in them as they afterwards pondered in their heart. The purpose of our Lord's training was not primarily to communicate facts but to lead to a shared contemplative insight.

This shared contemplative insight was not the end of His training but a stage in the process. It led to another shared contemplative insight of deeper intensity and prepared for yet another. They left all and that set them free to follow. They followed and came to see more clearly. They saw more clearly and then found union with Him.

The Church in her training follows her Master's example. Her

58

teaching is given in two main stages: the preliminary stage of the catechumenate during which the candidate is trained for the initiation rite of baptism, confirmation and first communion. And then the more mature stage of study and prayer. The preliminary stage in some ways corresponds to the period before the Transfiguration. The mature stage corresponds to the Transfiguration and the experiences which followed. This training is continuous. The teaching of the initiation rite is repeated each year during Holy Week through the ceremonies of the feet washing, the watch on Maundy Thursday, the veneration of the Cross, the lighting of the New Fire on Easter Eve, the renewal of the baptismal promises and the Easter communion. The mature training is given through teaching and the deepened use of the prayers of the Office and the practice of contemplative prayer.

Patanjali distinguishes different stages in training for contemplation. His main distinction is between training for beginners and training for the mature. He describes the preliminary training and its purpose in the first two sutras of his second book in this way:

11 : 1   Physical training (tapas), self-study (svādhyāya) and devotion to the Lord (Ishvāra pranidhāna) are the forms of active contemplative union (kriya yoga).

11 : 2   This training leads to contemplation (samādhi) and reduces the hindrances.

This is a minimal description of the elements of his preliminary training. It is a training of each of the faculties of our human nature: the body, the mind and the heart. It is in his description of the goal of this training that Patanjali throws a vivid light on the whole process of spiritual training. In the West this has so often been concerned with negative forms of self-control and repression. For Patanjali the purpose is contemplation and the reduction of the hindrances to this prayer. In his teaching there is no question of the training being an activity apart from contemplation. The training is in itself a form of contemplation. There is no question of the pupil having to wait until the higher rungs of the ladder of training have been reached before contemplation can begin. Contemplation starts with the first rung and each step is a further development of this contemplative activity. This teaching returns us to the New Testament where the disciples start contemplating Christ from the moment they turn to Him. It is true that this contemplation was for beginners and destined to develop. But it came at the beginning of their discipleship and grew to Transfiguration proportions later. This is an essential point to bear in mind as we consider in detail the three stages of preliminary training outlined by Patanjali. They are not merely stages of training. They are forms of contemplation as well.

1

PHYSICAL CONTEMPLATION

The pre-Transfiguration training given by our Lord was a balanced training of body, mind and heart. He did not make the mistake of many spiritual teachers of training one faculty at the expense of the others. From the Desert Fathers onwards there has been a tendency in Western spirituality to train the mental faculties at the expense of the body, to exaggerate the work of the spirit in contemplation and to belittle the part of the body in this work. Under our Lord's training His disciples became strong in body, mind and spirit and on the mount of Transfiguration contemplated His glory with all these faculties in healthy balance. The training of the physical came first. It began with the demand to leave all and follow Him. This was primarily done in terms of physical goods and physical response. It left a lasting impression on the disciples. That was what they most remembered of those early days when later on they questioned Him: 'We here have left everything to become your followers' (Mark 10 : 28). Their bodies were trained through long walks. Work went on, toiling all night and catching nothing. There was training about meals, recreation and sleep. All these activities assumed a contemplative dimension because they were shared with the Lord.

This physical side of our Lord's training was based on a special attitude to the body. Our Lord saw it as an embryo destined for future development. Death was not the end: there was to be the transformation of resurrection, anticipated by the glory of the Transfiguration. Always he stressed the importance of the body. He healed its sicknesses and renewed its faculties. He used His own body for His work. Through the touch of His hands He healed. His voice was a marvellous instrument, at one time speaking to crowds so that all could hear, then reassuring with gentleness those who were afraid, then lifted up to rebuke the winds and waves and compel their obedience. His movements had a message of their own. He could dominate crowds with a gesture and pass through them so that none dared to touch Him. He could groan from the lower centre of His being and after the resurrection had the power to breathe the Spirit into others. All this was momentarily revealed at the Transfiguration. It became a permanent state of His body after the resurrection. It was in this body in all its forms that the Lord prayed and communicated with the Father. It was not a hindrance: it was an instrument of spiritual and contemplative power. His teaching was full of reminders about a future change through death and resurrection. The embryonic body was charged with the seeds of immortality. All this teaching received greater precision at the hands of St. Paul who distinguished between the natural and spiritual body and insisted that the human body through faith in Christ was destined to share His glory.

1. THE BODY. Patanjali's teaching about physical training is based on a similar attitude to the body and its part in contemplation. He belonged to a tradition which included the teaching and practices of that form of physical discipline called hatha yoga. In this tradition there was a greater detail about the body and its functions than we find in the New Testament and of course nothing about the relationship with our Lord's body which comes through faith.

The yoga tradition thinks not of one physical body but of many. These bodies are thought of as sheaths. They are used up and replaced. Within is an inner core which corresponds to St. Paul's idea of the spiritual body which is eternal and indestructible. This body is sometimes called the subtle body and is destined for future growth and glory.

The subtle body has special centres of sensitive consciousness through which particular forms of contemplation take place. To our Western ways of thinking the idea of these centres is strange but some of them are in our own tradition, even though they tend to be ignored. There is the solar plexus centre and the heart centre. The ancient sarum prayer:

> God be in my head and in my understanding:
> God be in my eyes and in my looking:
> God be in my mouth and in my speaking:
> God be in my heart and in my thinking:
> God be at my end and at my departing.

is an example of this tradition firmly embedded in prayer.

In the Eastern tradition to which Patanjali belongs these centres are located in the spiritual body and related to particular forms of contemplation. To understand the physical training of the East for contemplation it is essential to take them into consideration.

The mūlādhāra centre is situated at the base of the spine. It is used in all kinds of movement and is connected with the sense of smell and the activity of deep breathing.

The svādisthāna centre is near the generative organs. It is used in movement and breathing and connected with the sense of touch.

The manipūra centre is at the solar plexus. It has emotional qualities and is connected with the sense of taste.

The anāhata centre is at the cardiac plexus. It is used in acts of concentration and meditation. It is connected with the sense of sight and imagination.

The vishuddha centre is at the throat. It is the centre for discursive thinking and is connected to the sense of hearing.

The ājnā centre is near the forehead. It is a centre of insight and silence.

The sahasrāra centre is at the crown of the head. It is used in imageless contemplation.

Closely related to these centres is the teaching about the kundalini or vital energy at the base of the spine. This is an allegory of the transformation of physical energy into spiritual insight by means of movement and breathing. Unless properly understood and carefully supervised this technique is both undesirable and dangerous but when linked with the Christian teaching about the new man and the Spirit it can be an effective means of sublimating sexual energy and redirecting it into prayer. All this is part of laya yoga which consists of opening the centres and practising forms of consciousness in each of them and growing in union with God in the higher stages of consciousness. It is an application of the mystery of the Transfiguration to the human body in the totality of its being. But always there are dangers and these have been well summed up in these words of Swami Prabhavananda: 'Hatha Yoga was designed to prepare the aspirant for spiritual experience by perfecting his body; but it has been condemned by spiritual teachers because it tends in practice to concentrate the mind upon the body itself. In the West it is found in a completely degenerated form as a cult of physical beauty and prolonged youth. As such, it may be effective certainly, but also dangerous. Over-indulgence in breathing exercises, just for the sake of the agreeable "oxygen jag" which they produce, may lead to hallucinations and possibly insanity. And, even at best, an excessive occupation with our physical appearance and well-being is obviously a distraction causing us to forget, in silly vanity, our proper purpose' (Swami Prabhavananda and Christopher Isherwood, *How to Know God*, p. 44, George Allen & Unwin Ltd., 1953).

All this is intended primarily for misuses of Hatha Yoga. It is even more applicable to Laya Yoga and the many variations of Tantric Yoga. It must be kept in mind as we examine the forms of physical training in terms of posture, breathing, recreation, sleep eating and work which make up the ingredients of a wise form of preliminary training for contemplation.

2. CONTEMPLATIVE MOVEMENT AND STILLNESS. There are quite a few references to our Lord's physical movement and stillness in the gospels. His eyes are frequently mentioned, sometimes looking outwards, sometimes up to heaven, once on Peter with such power that he repented and wept. So with His hands. Various physical postures are described. He sits, stands, kneels and in Gethsemane uses what we should call a prostration. He never used His body casually. There was an intention and power behind all His movement and stillness. In this He shared the attitude towards the body and movement of the Eastern traditions. In them bodily movements and stillness have a profound significance. They not only express inward thoughts and states through the various hand and eye gestures called mudras but they induce these states and intensify them. Robert Bridges in the Testament of Beauty emphasises this use of the body in prayer when he writes:

'Now every motion hath the bodily expression
beseeming each; and since the body cannot be
without some attitude so prayer will hav its own:
and here just as in any athletic exercise
ther be postures and motions foolish in themselves
and often undignified, so too the posture of prayer
may shame our pride of spirit, which would grudge the limbs
warrant of entry upon her sacred solitudes;
albeit the body came ther in full abject guise
to do submission and pay fealty to the soul.'
(Robert Bridges, *Testament of Beauty*, IV, 1164–73, O.U.P., 1930)

Bridges rightly stresses the fact that every physical movement can be associated with prayer. But this involves doing them in a special and contemplative way. They are not just physical exercises, performed with a physical expertise. They must be done with the following conditions fulfilled: (i) The mind should be emptied of distraction. (ii) The attention must be fixed on God in the form of what Patanjali calls (the endless). (iii) There must be no strain. Any form of pain must be treated as the red light. (iv) Breathing and movement should be co-ordinated. (v) Each movement and posture should be succeeded by an equivalent relaxation.

Once these conditions are fulfilled then every physical movement becomes a form of prayer and the wider and more varied the movements used the better. In a school in Bombay it was possible to combine some parts of Western gymnastics, running, team games like cricket, hockey and football with the use of some Yoga postures. This proved a very satisfactory combination. An even wider variety

63

is possible by the inclusion of such physical exercise as playing a musical instrument, or such other activities as swimming, golf and squash. And of course always walking and if possible some form of the dance. Of the use of the dance in prayer Ted Shawn has written: 'Religion and the dance were, at the beginning, one and the same activity—the form was the dance and the context was religion. There is no religion but that its essence and belief were originally far better expressed through the dance than could be done in words' (Ted Shawn, *Dance We Must*, p. 31, Dennis Dobson, 1946).

One of the most effective contemplative forms of the dance is the T'ai Chi Ch'uan, a dance of Chinese origin which combines sophisticated movement with that co-ordination of breathing and eye movement so essential for contemplation.

All these principles of movement and stillness should be confirmed by experience. Many young people have their first Transfiguration experience in some kind of physical movement. Roger Bannister is reported to have referred to an experience of 'switching on the Holy Ghost' towards the end of his four-minute mile and there are many others who have been transfigured in this way. Others have found new insight by turning from more vigorous movement to the gentle yoga postures or the T'ai Chi Ch'uan as the slowing down of middle life overtook them.

The yoga postures are a special series of movements and stillness which are particularly valuable in correcting physical errors of the body and preparing it for contemplative stillness. They also train the body for the experience of death; and they prepare it both for transfiguration experiences in this life and the resurrection. They effectively complement all other forms of physical training and bring them to a contemplative level. But they must be chosen with care and learnt under expert supervision.

The yoga postures are described in that form of yoga called hatha yoga and the classic exposition is in the Hatha Yoga Pradipika. Some 84 postures are described. There are many variations of them though most are irrelevant for stimulating contemplation. The following selection will be found adequate for this purpose and they should be thoroughly mastered. This involves not merely doing the posture but learning to relax in it and coordinate the breathing with the movement and subsequent stillness. The contemplative postures are:

The obeisance (padhahasthāsana)
Surya namaskar
Shoulder stand (sarvangāsana)
The plough (halāsana)
The backstretch (paschimottānāsana)

64

The snake (bhujangāsana)
The headstand (shirshāsana)
The meditation walk
The tree (vrkshāsana).

Each of these postures can be linked with a symbolic meaning. For instance, the obeisance symbolises self-denial; the surya namaskar, turning to Christ; many of the others are a physical expression of the sacrifice of the body to Christ. Not only are they training for contemplation and contemplative in themselves, but they can be built into the eucharist and the T'ai Chi Ch'uan used as a contemporary expression of the Way of the Cross.

When Mrs. Gandhi was asked whether she practised any form of yoga she replied that she did but that her yoga was a yoga of the eyes. In the Indian dance and in yoga postures the eyes play an important part in bringing the whole body to relaxed stillness and they have an equally important effect on the mind. Where the eyes are, the mind and body follow. The eyes can be used in contemplative prayer in three ways: for concentration, for relaxation, for communication.

The eyes can be focused on both outward and inward objects. When focused on an outward object they provide the raw materials for forming the image needed in the preliminary forms of contemplative prayer. Out of the visual material communicated to the brain the imagination builds the inner image. The eyes should be trained to look long and steadily at a particular object in order to enable this image to be made. The eyes can also focus on an inner object. The object most often used in contemplative prayer is one of the centres. By directing the eyes towards them they come under control and can be opened. We watch our Lord lifting His eyes to heaven, the head centre, and opening His whole being to the divine presence. We also find Him groaning as He directs his eyes towards the lower centres of His being. Looking at the inner centres in this way comes from patient practice. When it is achieved these centres of consciousness can be used at will in prayer.

The eyes when relaxed bring relaxation to the whole body. Relaxing the eyes comes from putting them out of focus. This is done by looking towards the tip of the nose and then closing the eyes and holding them relaxed. By steadily looking towards any tense part of the body relaxation follows. In the T'ai Chi Ch'uan the eyes are used throughout the dance to bring all the limbs under constant and relaxed control.

Through the eyes the soul speaks. During the Passion, our Lord looked on Peter and at once he realised the enormity of his denial and the certainty of the Lord's forgiveness. Through his eyes the contemplative shares with others what he has seen and known of the Word of life. To do this the eyes must be trained to be open and relaxed. In India the contemplative teaches prayer by showing himself in what is called a darshana and the most significant part of this showing is through the eyes.

3. CONTEMPLATING THE SPIRIT. The Spirit is manifested in the form of personal energy. He overshadowed the Mother of the Lord and she conceived. At the Transfiguration He is present in the form of the *shekinah*, the cloud of glory, overshadowing Jesus and the disciples, manifesting the divine presence and developing the capacity of the human senses to penetrate to the place where God is. The most revealing symbol and model of the Spirit is the act of breathing. It has been well said that God is revealed in the Bible as the God who breathes. And He breathes the Holy Spirit. This is implied in the use of the word spirit with its double meaning of Spirit and breath and in the Eastern tradition by the word *prāna* with its even wider meaning of energy.

The main actions of the Spirit in human life are cleansing and energising the heart. This is summed up in the prayer: 'Cleanse the thoughts of our heart by the inspiration of thy Holy Spirit that we may perfectly love thee and worthily magnify thy holy name.' The preliminary training for mature contemplation is mainly confined to learning to respond to His cleansing action. In terms of the Western tradition this involves concentration on the ways of purgation.

Breath is a symbol of the Spirit and breathing is a model of His movements. Our training is a question of losing our own breathing rhythms and coming into harmony with the rhythms of the Spirit. It means losing our own breath control and surrendering to the breathing of the Spirit within us.

Breaking one's own breathing rhythm begins with the mastery of certain postures. The most effective for this purpose are the upright standing posture with the back straight and the centres relaxed and the sitting posture with the weight on the spine. Other postures can be used but not for long enough to be as effective as these two basic ones. In this posture the eyes are directed to one of the lower centres.

The breathing rhythm is broken by controlling the breath with the abdominal muscles and reducing the rate of breathing, making a clear distinction between the in and out breaths and prolonging the period of suspension between them. Some may find this easier by controlling the nostrils with the finger, but this is not essential. Some five or ten breaths in this slower rhythm should be enough to break with the natural rhythm. The control is then removed and the breathing allowed to find its own pace. If the attention is kept on one of the lower centres and the body held firm and relaxed the rhythm that now takes over will be outside of personal control and under the control of the Spirit. God will be breathing within the obedient and responsive person. When this happens it will be possible to begin to respond to the three forms of breathing.

These three forms are inhalation, suspension or holding and exhalation. These are not self-induced; they are the supernatural movement of the Spirit. We are called to respond to the cleansing work they make possible.

Inhaling or inspiring the Spirit is a process of drawing the Spirit into the centres of the body, starting from the centre at the top of the head and moving down to the lowest centre at the base of the spine. As this is done we can think of ourselves as a potential mount of Transfiguration, waiting to be renewed and made glorious. This inhalation of the Spirit takes place in both stillness and movement. We can watch it happening to our Lord and his disciples as they climbed the mountain for climbing is a technique which emphasises this form of inhalation. The good climber must climb with his body upright, with the centres open and he is compelled to use the abdominal muscles for drawing in the breath. Unless breathing is done in this way climbing is either a very unpleasant experience or becomes impossible. It was realised in the form of stillness at the top of the mountain when our Lord entered the glory and the disciples thought to intensify the stillness by building three shelters.

Work done with recollection is another effective way of inhaling the Spirit. The same physical relaxation and mental concentration are needed as for movement but there is also the mastery of a skill of movement which effectively helps the mind to control other distractions. The T'ai Chi Ch'uan is another form of this kind of inhalation where the attention must fix itself on a demanding form of movement, even more complicated than most kinds of work and the breath is drawn in through both legs and the spine.

Suspending or holding the Spirit is a process of directing His energy to special places. Internally these places are located in the different centres of the body. Externally they are people and places. The bodily centres for the practice of preliminary training in this contemplation of the Spirit are the lower ones, the mulādhāra, the svādisthāna and the manipura. Our Lord gives two images of this action when he compares the Spirit to a well of water bubbling up into eternal life and to rivers of living water, and in both cases locates the Spirit in the lower centre of the belly. This holding of the Spirit to

67

a particular place requires great concentration, especially when it is applied to an outside point. Here it takes the form of a demanding act of intercession during which the Spirit is directed towards the person or place requiring His help. A symbol of the Spirit held in the place of concentration is always helpful. These symbols are abundant in the Bible and a selection will have to be made. We have found this series of symbols used cyclically helpful: water, dove, wind, incense, wine, oil and fire.

Exhaling the Spirit in this stage of training is essentially directing the out-breath to a point where His healing and cleansing work is needed. This differs from the suspended breathing which is concerned with holding the Spirit at one place. This is a question of applying the movement of the Spirit both within and outside. Within, it means directing the flow of Spirit to the cleansing and renewing of each of the centres of consciousness, particularly during the early stages to the three lower centres. Outside, it means directing His energy to a person or a situation and sharing in the movement of His energy at that place. Words help very much in this process and it is here that the Office can supply the concentration we need for this process of exhalation.

We may ask for more details of the impurities the Spirit cleanses as He breathes in us and we respond. Some of them can be described as has been done in the seven capital sins in the Christian tradition or in the analysis of the distractions and hindrances given by Patanjali, but a great many of the imperfections removed by the Spirit are in the unconscious and defy description. They are like the black karma of the Eastern tradition. Partly inherited, partly self-committed but mostly too deep even for tears. To this St. Paul refers when he writes of the work of the Spirit as a pleading of the Spirit within us (Romans 8 : 26).

Our Lady has in the Christian tradition been given the title of 'shrine of the Spirit' and in the mysteries of her life we have a model of the way the Spirit works when life has been surrendered to Him. Gerard Manley Hopkins describes this in a poem entitled 'The Blessed Virgin Compared to the Air We Breathe'. In this quotation writes with remarkable insight of the Spirit as reproducing the mysteries of Mary in each responsive person.

> 'He does take fresh and fresh,
> Though much the mystery how,
> Not flesh but spirit now
> And makes, O marvellous!
> New Nazareths in us,
> Where she shall yet conceive

Him, morning, noon, and eve;
New Bethlems, and be born
There, evening, noon, and morn-
Bethlem or Nazareth,
Men here may draw like breath
More Christ and baffle death;
Who, born so, comes to be
New self and nobler me
In each one and each one
More makes, when all is done,
Both God's and Mary's Son.'

The mysteries of Mary, especially the Conception, the Annunciation, the Visitation, the Presentation, Standing at the Cross, the Assumption and the Coronation provide an effective series of models of the way the Spirit works in human nature and enable us to co-operate with deeper understanding as He reproduces these mysteries within ourselves. Contemplating the Spirit is largely a work of breathing in harmony with the Spirit-rhythm and allowing Him to form the substance of these mysteries in our hearts.

In both contemplative movement and stillness and in the breathing method of contemplating the Spirit the imagination plays an important part. In what are called the postures the name gives us a hint about the work of the imagination. They are called after different creatures or plants: the tree posture, the snake posture, the plough and others. In doing these movements an image of the posture should be first formed and then this image used as a controlling instrument for the movement. The result is a greater control of the movement and a freedom from inhibitions which restrict both the body and the imagination from a complete response to the Spirit. The imagination is similarly used in the contemplation of the Spirit through breathing by means of a symbol of the Spirit. By holding this image in the lower abdominal centre it becomes an instrument of control for the breathing rhythm. This use of an image of the movement is not by any means limited to contemplative forms of prayer. It is used in the other arts. The painter works under image control. The musician plays the score in his imagination as he reproduces it on his instrument. All this trains the mind for the inner acts of contemplation through stillness which come when movement and breathing have been mastered.

MENTAL CONTEMPLATION

The second form of preliminary contemplative training Patanjali calls self-study. This is the training of the thinking faculties, not merely in their discursive and rational activities but in their capacities for insight. For the mind in its total activity is much more than a thinking instrument. It has the power to see secret things as well and the education of the mind aims at developing this faculty.

Our Lord's training of his disciples had this end in view. He trained their minds to think clearly and was infinitely patient in ridding them of prejudices and shallow thinking. But he also led them on to insight experiences. Having first trained the three disciples in the intellectual understanding of the life He was describing He then took them to the mount of Transfiguration where their minds were opened to see the glory of Himself and the kingdom.

The object of the mind is always the Word of God uttered in 'fragmentary and varied fashion'. The fragmented and varied utterance of the Word is not because He speaks in this way. He always utters His full being. What happens is that this utterance is only partly understood because the hearing and understanding faculties of man are inadequate. The training of the mind for contemplating the Word is therefore concerned with removing defects of hearing and sharpening the mind to grasp more perfectly what is spoken. This requires a varied training for the Word speaks in many ways. He speaks in words, written and spoken. He speaks through the symbols of creation. He speaks through the experiences of life, especially of eating and sleep. The training of the mind is therefore a training in study, in meditation, in assimilation and in the use of sleep and dreams.

Patanjali describes the essence of this training as a study of the self. It is not merely the collection of facts and the ordering of these facts into a coherent system, although this is needed. The facts are not ends in themselves. They lead to self-knowledge and to knowledge of the true Self, the Lord. The process is contemplative.

1. CONTEMPLATING THE WORD. In the Transfiguration Christ is revealed in two forms: as the Word of God and as the Image of God. We hear Him speaking to the disciples and we overhear that secret conversation with Moses and Elijah. We watch His form and clothes shine into dazzling whiteness and we follow the glorification of His body within the cloud. This is a summary of the way God reveals Himself in the Bible. He speaks as the living Word. He reveals Himself through creation and above all through the bodily image of the incarnate manhood.

This verbal and visual manifestation of God is part of the Eastern tradition as well. Patanjali describes God speaking through words and God revealing Himself through images.

This twofold manifestation of God requires a double response and training. There is the response of listening to the Word and studying its meaning: there is the response of contemplating the images and becoming identified with them. The first is the preliminary training for the second and more complete contemplation of the Word.

Patanjali calls the study which leads to the contemplation of the Word, self-study. By describing it in this way he emphasises that it is not merely the mastering of a subject of study. It is an exploration into the self. The self in the form of the ego and the Self in the form of the Lord. This is no mere accumulation of facts in order to pass an intellectual test. It is the mastery of knowledge in order to contemplate the Word. This goal controls both the materials of this study and the way in which they are used.

There are three ingredients for this study: physical experience, reasoning and the mastery of a sound tradition. Physical experience comes from the senses making contact with external, sensible objects. Sound reasoning is based on the laws of logic. The tradition is made up of the scriptures. All this requires persevering study which must be repeated for a long time with an indifference to results.

The use of the senses in the study of the Word involves what is called the empirical method. We find it being used in the Bible in the Old Testament by the use of historical events as the material for the study of the Word. Both the Law and the Prophets use this method. Isaiah begins his account of his vision of God in the Temple with the words: 'In the year that king Uzziah died' (Isaiah 6 : 1). The historical books of the Bible draw conclusions about God and his working from the study of events. So it is in the Psalms and in the Writings. There is a close contact between the teaching and the physical experiences from which it is drawn. This is even more apparent in the New Testament where the physical events of our Lord's life and the life of the early Church are the materials for the teaching and our Lord's parables are based on the technique of analogy which leads Him to make comparison after comparison between the mysteries of the kingdom and the events of daily life.

So the study of the Bible involves us in this way of contemplating the Word. But this should not be confined to the Bible. Science and the arts supplement and enrich the Bible material for contemplating the Word. A book like Bishop Butler's *Analogy of Religion* is still a classic example of this method. Equally important is the study of history and above all of biography in the study of the self. The wider the material used the richer will be the penetration of the mystery of the total self and the more intense the contemplation of God.

In using all this material a form of sound reasoning is needed. Without it wrong conclusions can so easily be drawn from sense experience and reading. When reason is applied to this material for the purpose of contemplating the Word it results in a theology. This need not be the same for every tradition or for every member within the tradition. In India there are six main theologies: the Vaisheshika, the Nyaya, the Mimansa, the Vedanta, Sankhya and Yoga. There are many things in common between these differing theologies. They are logical in that they follow the rules of sound reasoning. But they differ about the interpretation of many mysteries. This is a healthful thing and we find it reproduced in the many theologies of the West. It is not necessary to work for an artificial synthesis between differing theologies before using one of them for the contemplation of the Word. Each has its own help to give and ultimately the desired conclusion should be the construction of one's own system of sound thought, of the building up of his own theology by each mature contemplative. This may seem an anti-ecumenical programme but when used for the contemplation of the Word it can lead to a greatly enriched understanding and to a unity of life and a tension of thought much more alive than any committee-framed and majority-accepted formula.

The materials of a sound tradition to which Patanjali refers as a necessity for the study of the self come most soundly from the tradition to which each person belongs. This does not mean accepting the ideas of one's inherited environment without criticism but it does suggest that it is sound to use them first before going to outside sources. This is what Jung means when he deplores an uncritical borrowing of oriental systems of thought by Western people. He describes the result as 'a stultifying of the intellect', and this is only too clear. For Western Christians the main materials of their tradition are in the Bible, the creeds and the forms of prayer. These provide a rich source of raw material for the study of God and the self. On the other hand, there are many enrichments and insights of this tradition from other sources. Science can be used with its deepening awareness of the creative mystery. This was the contribution Teilhard de Chardin made with such powerful results in his life and writing. The poets have even more to contribute. In this generation and in the Western tradition there is the work of such leaders as T. S. Eliot and Kathleen Raine who not only deeply understood the thought of their age but made so many illuminating comments upon it. And then there are the insights of other traditions, at this time especially from Eastern sources. Here we need to go to primary sources and not be misled by versions specially adapted to suit present demands. As Thomas Merton saw so clearly, this influence of one tradition upon another is a long and slow process and must not be hastened and over-simplified.

It may well be that in the account of the Transfiguration, where Moses and Elijah are shown in converse with Jesus, we have an illustration of this inter-change of traditions at the deepest level. These leaders represent the two great traditions of the Old Testament, the Law and the Prophets. Our Lord did not hesitate to borrow from both as He proclaimed His own gospel of the kingdom. He borrowed however, not as a mere imitator but as a master, altering and correcting where necessary and building His borrowings into His own teaching so that it was a living and original whole. When we take from other traditions it is in this way that the borrowing should be done.

All this study of creation, all this training of the mind in correct thinking, all this assimilation of tradition is a work of a special kind of study which in religious communities is given the description of spiritual reading. It is something more than intellectual reading, the amassing of facts and the arranging of material into a system. It is primarily a way of contemplating the Word and is a discipline of many parts. We shall consider some of them. The rest can be learnt by the way of constant practice and contemplative growth.

St. Thomas Aquinas gave this valuable instruction about the way of study to one of his pupils which has a general application to us in carrying out the preliminary training of self-study. He wrote: 'This is my admonition and your instruction. I exhort you to be chary of speech, and to go into the conversation room sparingly. Take a great heed to the purity of your conscience. Never cease the practice of prayer. Love to be diligent in your cell, if you would be led to the wine-cellar of wisdom. Ever be loving towards all. Do not bother yourself about the doings of others; nor be familiar with anyone, since too great familiarity breeds contempt and easily leads us away from study. Do not join in the doings and conversations of the worldly. Above all, shun roaming about outside the monastery. Consider not from whom you hear anything, but impress upon your mind everything good that is said. Make an effort thoroughly to understand whatever you read and hear. In all doubt seek to penetrate to the truth. Try always to store away as much as possible in the chambers of your mind. What is too far above do not strive after for the present.'

In this excellent advice is stored up the principles needed for sound study. There must be mental training, a training of concentration and selection. A system of regular reading, of detachment and of arrangement is essential. The humility which keeps the mind to those areas of thinking for which it is at present strong enough and the patience to wait, often holding contradiction in tension until strength grows is always needed. One could almost find in this advice of St. Thomas the suggestion that a filing system would be an advantage when the chambers of the mind become too full and the memory is unable to hold all its information. Without a plan of this kind study can so easily become a drug, a soporific, a meaningless accumulation of knowledge which obscures the self and smothers the heart for its true work of contemplation.

In reading the Bible some form of selection is essential. This is done by the Church in the form of a lectionary and in an emphasis, through the liturgical festivals, on certain important parts of the book. There is a primary summary of the great teaching of the Bible about the self in what are called the mysteries of our Lord and our Lady. These main mysteries in the case of our Lord are: the Nativity, the Epiphany, the Temptations, the Transfiguration, the Crucifixion, the Resurrection, the Ascension. In the case of our Lady they are: the Conception, the Annunciation, the Visitation, the Presentation, Before the Cross, the Assumption and the Coronation. In these mysteries are summed up so much of the Bible teaching and in mastering them, first of all by knowing the verbal text of the Bible where they are described and then by repetitive meditation making them part of one's own thought they become what St. Thomas calls 'a wine-cellar of wisdom' and open the heart to the deepest knowledge of the self.

This method of using the Bible was the basis of that great training in study of the self given in the *Exercises of St. Ignatius*. It was also the basis of the training given by Father Benson to the members of his own community. In the early days of the Society it was his custom to hand to each of the brothers an outline of the subject to be studied with directions of the themes for meditation and in this way he formed the spirit of the community. This repetitive use of the mysteries is equally effective used individually by those who are engaged in preliminary training and it follows the liturgical themes of the Church in her weekly cycle of prayer.

The preliminary contemplation of the Word is primarily a study of the verbal text of the Bible. As St. Thomas and others teach, the literal meaning is the basis of all others. This is a very different thing from fundamentalism which is a kind of idolatrous approach to the words of scripture. It is more like the approach of the accurate scholar who is concerned with language and meanings. The foundation of this study is language and therefore it is a great help to use the original languages of the Bible for it and to make one's own translation. This may seem a daunting task but the discipline of it wonderfully concentrates the mind and even though the language may be no more than superficially mastered the effort involved is of the greatest value in training the heart for contemplation. This is a very different approach from the merely critical use of the text for the answering of a particular problem. It is a way of using the words to discover the self and its weaknesses and strength and it also wonderfully sharpens the image of the true Self Christ who is the subject of every part of the tradition.

Side by side with this treatment of the Bible is the accurate study of the main parts of the theological tradition to which the student belongs. The approach should not be controversial but historical and objective, a search for what really happened and what really is being said. Here the study of the decisions of the great General Councils and the historical situations which made them necessary is invaluable.

Charles Davis has pointed out that the way in which the Christian tradition is most effectively communicated is not so much by dogmatic statements as by symbols. He writes: 'Each concrete, social form of religious faith is centred, so it seems, not upon a list of propositional beliefs, but upon a set of symbols. A complex of symbols lies at the heart of every religious tradition, and the formation of religious groups, with their unities and divisions corresponds to similarities and differences in the principal symbols in which religious faith has been embodied' (Charles Davis, *Christ and the World Religions*, p. 104, Hodder and Stoughton, 1970).

This is an important reminder for students of the tradition. Words are not the only way in which the Word is communicated. There is an artistic tradition both in the Bible and in the Church and in the literature of each. Understanding one's own tradition in this form helps to the understanding of other traditions. And the attempt to select one's own symbols and construct one's own images reveals significant truths about the self. Part of the study of the tradition should therefore be concerned with this mode of expression and that involves a training in what might be called art appreciation. The lack of this in many intelligent Christians deprives them of a valuable corrective to an over-emphasis on words and opens the mind to new and more complete penetrations into truth. Austin Farrer used to insist that the language of true theology was much nearer poetry than prose and that the theologian required as much of the sensitivity of the artist as he did of the scholar's semantic accuracy.

Meditation of a reflective kind is the way this material is assimilated in the preliminary stages. This is a mode of contemplation which corresponds to what in the Eastern tradition is called discursive contemplation (*savichara samādhi*). It leads the mind into a state of questioning and often of doubt. This is healthful and the learner should be prepared to live with his uncertainties without anxiety and resist the temptation for instant solutions. Patanjali calls it 'a flow of thought' around a mental subject. This makes great demands on the steadiness of the mind and comes from constant practice. When this can be maintained it leads to the kind of experience which is referred to in the Zen meditation leading to the use of a koan, in an experience of insight or satori in which the problem disappears through an act of vision. This is not something which can be ordered and controlled, but it is a mental state for which the other preliminary training prepares. We can watch our Lord leading His disciples to such an experience as He teaches and shows and leads them to that moment of insight at the Transfiguration.

Self-study finds its completion in self-expression. Just as the self-study is about the ego and the Lord so that self-expression is about the same mysteries of the total self. We can watch this taking place in our Lady in the mystery of the Visitation. Our Lady expresses both herself and the Lord. She is 'the lowly slave girl of the Lord'. He is 'The Lord, the one who is mighty, the one whose being is holy' and who acts as she describes in the magnificat. Our Lady's self-expression is complete in that it is more than verbal: she expresses in her own being the mystery she verbally describes. This we see happening at the Transfiguration. Our Lord's body shines with the glory and the voice gives it verbal expression. 'This is my beloved son.' The self-expression which is a process of the training of self-study must be similarly complete. It must be verbal and it must be in terms of personal transformation. We are to become like the Lord we describe. This is not an achievement of less than a lifetime. There must be what T. S. Eliot has called 'the intolerable struggle with words'; there must be the disciplined training which transforms the self into the receptive likeness of the Lord. For many the verbal expression will not be in words but perhaps in music, in the dance, in painting. The signs of a new consciousness are seen most clearly today in the variety of new forms of expression. There should be no question of limiting expression to the traditional forms and styles. One needs the originality of an Elijah as well as the traditional accuracy of a Moses. This requires a recognition of the Spirit within the tradition, especially in terms of the Bible and the formulations of faith. Searching for Him develops faith and in the power of faith the self can utter the mystery of its being. The Visitation and the

Transfiguration were both experiences of the Spirit and expressions of His power.

The Word contemplated in this way forms Himself in the heart as Manley Hopkins so vividly described and when formed He must be brought forth in whatever way the contemplative is able. The full faith as St. James taught is more than intellectual assent or intellectual insight; it grows complete in the action of works and the works of faith are the loving and worshipful expression of the Self we have seen.

2. OTHER MODES OF CONTEMPLATING THE WORD. The Word speaks through all forms of life and action. In the New Testament we find Him speaking with a special clarity in the daily actions of eating and sleep. This is recognised in the East where worship is so often the offering of the elements of daily food to the God and sleep is recommended by Patanjali as material for contemplative prayer.

(*i*) *Eating.* In the fourth gospel St. John gives a special emphasis on the miracle of the Feeding of the Five thousand as an experience of contemplating the Word. His description of the sign makes it clear that the crowd were being prepared for more than an ordinary meal. It is the time of the Passover which would mean that their thoughts were already turned towards the great events of their deliverance. Our Lord used a particular care in the feeding. He raised his eyes, a sign that He was dealing with mysteries beyond the reach of the ordinary senses. He first prepared his disciples so that they were ready to co-operate. His question to Philip was not for information but to test him. Then the arrangement of the people was to induce relaxation. The disciples were told to bring them to a state of calm (anapausis) a term used by the desert Fathers for a calm of heart. Care was taken over the collecting of the fragments and the end of the sign was not merely the feeding of hungry people but their enlightenment: 'this must be that prophet that was to come into the world' (John 6 : 15).

The account of the sign is followed by the discourse in the synagogue at Capernaum. In this discourse our Lord makes the fullest revelation of Himself that is given in the whole of the gospel. It is a revelation which is by no means limited to His manifestation in the eucharist, although this is certainly a part of the teaching; it is a revelation of Himself in creation and in the mysteries of man's share in its life. Further, He leads on to reveal the interaction of the Spirit with Himself and His words: 'The Spirit alone gives life; the flesh is of no avail; the words that I have spoken to you are both spirit and life' (John 6 : 63).

The contemplation of the Word through eating is manifested in both the eucharist and the daily meal of the contemplative family. Each relates to the other and the truths of one are the truths of the other. Both meals require a stylised presentation and both result in a communication with the Word.

The eucharist in its revised form is a much more effective instrument for this contemplation than in its earlier and more detailed form. It makes quite clear that the contemplation is through the ministry of both the word and the sacrament. The Word speaks through the scripture readings, the sermon and the creed. There is thus brought together all the ingredients of self-study we have already considered. The sense experience is provided by the living presence of the minister of the Word who is its present instrument as he speaks. There is the reasonable presentation in terms of the selection of the readings and the summing up of the teaching in the collect. There is the utterance of the tradition in the scriptures and the creed. All that is so often lacking is any idea of the way to respond to this material contemplatively. Although in the revised rite there is provision for silence after the gospel little time is given and so few know how to reach that harmony and relaxation in the heart which was the condition for our Lord's manifestation during the feeding of the five thousand. But the conditions are all rightly provided for a contemplation of the Word through the words and it is for people through persevering practice and detachment to master the art of using them in this way.

The second part of the eucharist provides the material for contemplating the Word through symbols of the Word. The symbols are the bread and wine and there is a contemplative use of them. They are shown. Like the icon they are named in their full significance, the body and blood of Christ. They are meditated on through the act of anamnesis or remembrance. They are broken and then they are assimilated in order to lead the communicant to that intimate feeding on the Word Himself, in his heart by faith with thanksgiving. Here are all the techniques for that contemplation of the Word through symbols which we shall later consider in a more mature form when we come to the advanced training for contemplation. Here the techniques are given with basic simplicity so that even children may begin to contemplate the Word through this form of eating.

All these principles we find when we return to our model of the Transfiguration. The gospel account is given against the background of the Old Testament story of Moses and the elders meeting God in the mount and eating and drinking with Him. The Transfiguration story does not mention the act of eating but it clearly assumes a mental assimilation which is eating in its most intense form. Again in

78

the Transfiguration there is the illumination of Christ as the visible symbol of the divine presence, there is the verbalisation of His real significance in the voice from the cloud and there is the concealment of the sign leading to an even more intimate participation in His presence.

So the eucharist carries on the way of contemplating the Word through eating which is assumed in St. John's account of the sign of feeding. But it does not exhaust the meaning. There is certainly an implication in this story that Christ is the food of every form of eating and that the meal properly arranged provides conditions for an act of contemplative prayer. These conditions may be summed up as a recognition of the presence of the Lord as the centre of the meal, the hearing of the Word and the feeding on the Word through the act of eating.

The family meal becomes a feeding on the Word when shared in faith by those who are united with each other in Christ. This union can be symbolised by a central object on the table, either a bowl of flowers or a lighted candle or any other object which has connections with Him. The symbol of the theme of each day's meditation may well be reproduced in miniature for this purpose. The table then becomes a holy place, like the centre of the chapel and training room for the members of the body of Christ and the Head. Around this centre the family should be arranged in order so that a state of relaxed stillness is reached. The reverent serving of the meal helps this and silence during the meal is also a great help. In order to intensify the silence music may be used but this should be carefully chosen. Heavily orchestrated music or music with aggressive rhythms should be avoided. Chamber music or piano music is most conducive to the development of the inward silence.

Simplicity should be the keynote of a meal used as an act of contemplation on the Word. Bread and fish were the ingredients of the Lord's meal or bread and wine. The food should also be the best obtainable and this means that the bread should be home-made if this is possible. On the other hand there is no need to be over-scrupulous. The crowd ate what the Lord provided and this should be the attitude of His guests at all times. Dietary fads hinder the unity of the meal and the self-forgetfulness of the occasion. In eating the mind should be centred on Christ in the heart and all distractions and anxieties should be repelled.

The activity at the end of the meal is the opportunity for the most intense contemplation of the Word. This includes both the washing up and the recreation. Washing up like the gathering up of the fragments is not a regrettable interference with the meal and the fellowship. It is a way of communion with the Word and care should be taken to plan it as carefully as the meal itself. This means dividing out the work so that everyone has something to do and organising the work so that it is done in harmony. It is one of the occasions when work can become most powerfully a way to contemplation and the art learnt together makes possible an extension of this skill to all other forms of work.

But most important is the period of recreation when this work is done. At Taizé this recreation is most carefully planned and nothing is left to chance. The group is limited to some eight members and there is a discreet leader or stimulator of the conversation. Here again there should be a centre to remind the group of the presence of the Word and the conversation should be guided as an act of intercourse with the Word through His members. This requires great skill on the part of the leader who chooses the subject and takes care that all are involved. Conversation is one of the most effective ways of contemplating the Word after a meal but there are other ways too. Sometimes a piece of work may be discussed and shared. Sometimes one person may share a particular skill. Sometimes reading or Bible study can be done. The recreation period should be limited as with meditation and it should only be lengthened for very good reason. It is in fact a corporate meditation with each member contributing his part and all receptive to the Word speaking through His members.

Through eating in this way we contemplate the Word but we can also do this through fasting which both prepares for the reception of the Word and enables the Word to be received more deeply into the heart. This is why prayer and fasting are often brought together in our Lord's teaching. The fasting needs to be planned with the same care as the meal. It should be moderate and under the control of Christ and the family. Individual fasting which tends to divide the family like special diets should always be avoided. The motive of fasting is not physical but spiritual. It is a way of developing the desire for God. 'My soul is athirst for the living God'. And our Lord's cry on the cross is the cry of one using fasting for this purpose. The form of fasting most effective is not so much total abstinence from food for long periods as periods of fasting on certain days and the regular practice of moderation at all times. The Indian teaching is that the stomach should never be more than three-quarters full so that room is left for correct breathing. This is obtained in the Christian tradition by the practice of monastic simplicity and the discipline of the refectory.

The balance to fasting is the religious feast. Festivals and fasts go together in the spiritual life. Our Lord not only fasted: He was also called the friend of publicans and sinners and a gluttonous man and a wine-bibber which at least implies that He was at home under festival conditions. So Easter follows Lent and the vigil should be followed by the festival. We can contemplate the Word under both conditions and the well-trained contemplative is at home in both.

(*ii*) *Sleep*. In the account of our Lord's prayer in Gethsemane we see a form of contemplation taking place through sleep. Our Lord takes the three disciples who were present at the Transfiguration into the garden and there commands: 'Pray that you may be spared the hour of testing' (Luke 22 : 40). He also tells these men to watch. He Himself carries out the command as he concentrates on the image of the cup and aligns Himself to the Father's will. The disciples have no concentrating image to steady their minds and so they sleep. But sleep is for them a form of contemplation though compared with the developed contemplation used by our Lord it is inadequate and incomplete.

There are two forms of sleep: deep sleep or what is sometimes called 'slow-wave sleep' and shallow sleep. The first kind of sleep usually comes during the earlier part of the night's rest and is without recognised images. The second kind of sleep comes later in the night and is the time when images are recognised in the form of dreams. Both kinds of sleep are needed and both experiences can be transformed into a contemplation of the Word. But for this, practice and knowledge are required.

Patanjali tells us that certain contemplative experiences can be induced by drugs but he warns against them for they have dangerous after-effects and so often end in fantasy or some form of schizophrenia. The barbiturates are the drugs which bring a form of sleep but their effects are particularly dangerous. They gradually destroy natural sleep and the sleep they bring is sleep without the deep, slow rhythms which are so valuable. They also damage the dream mechanism, nature's way of dispersing mental strain. This has further repercussions on the mind and makes it unable to practice contemplative prayer outside of sleep. Such drugs should only be used in special emergencies and addiction to them should at all costs be avoided. It is much better to endure sleeplessness than to get caught in this short cut to insomnia.

What we have to do is to use the sleep we are given contemplatively. This is a physical experience and as Patanjali teaches is an experience which must be mastered by all the senses. In considering how this is to be done we shall use this letter of Father Benson's to Father O'Neill written when he was in India and suffering from insomnia. It is full of wise practical advice which we shall see the disciples illustrating in Gethsemane. We can use it in planning our own sleep.

81

He writes on 9 June 1874 as follows: 'As for the mode of spending wakeful nights, it is difficult to advise. Sometimes the bodily state is so restless during a wakeful night that it is impossible to give the mind to continued devotion. Sometimes a little quiet reading may be the best means of tranquillising oneself for sleep. Of course you ought generally on such occasions to try to get to sleep. It would not do to turn these times of nervousness into vigils for spiritual purposes. The frame wants sleep all the more because it rejects it. You should do that which you find most helpful in disposing you to sleep. Sometimes a little quiet bodily exercise, a gentle turn in the compound, or a bath, may be useful. If you find you are able to give the time to any religious exercises without increasing nervous excitement, then you may take such opportunities as great occasions of thankfulness. I remember my mother during a long illness found the study of the Italian poets physically very helpful. There was just enough difficulty about reading a language with which she was not very familiar to give her the occupation which her mind wanted, and so much of the difficulty was merely mechanical. Anything more immediately touching the affections would have been too much for her to bear at that time. If you are able to turn such waking times to account, whether for linguistic or spiritual purposes, well and good. The simple reading of Holy Scripture, not for study, but as having a sacramental power to soothe the soul, may bring much comfort, and it tends imperceptibly to form the thinking habits according to the mind of God, so that it is very profitable. It is often disappointing to find when one is wakeful how utterly incapable one is of going through any religious exercises. The same nervousness which destroys the power of sleep destroys very often the power of tranquil thought and simple loving devotion. It seems to be such loss of time, void of profit both for this world and the next. But it is not so really. We give up ourselves to the will of God, and the acceptance of His will is the true way of sanctification. We learn our nothingness by such helplessness, and that is the greatest lesson we can learn' (*Further Letters of Richard Meux Benson*, p. 12, Mowbray & Co., 1920).

This is a masterly analysis of the technique of sleep and the treatment of wakefulness and deserves full quotation. It recommends the use of gentle exercise, the avoidance of anything mentally definite like a centre of concentration and above all that loving surrender into the hands of God. All these things make up the path to deep sleep and we find them being used by the sleeping disciples in Gethsemane.

They shared the walk with our Lord from the Upper Room to the garden. In the garden they allowed their minds to empty, they were heavy as the account of St. Mark describes it. They had no mental point for concentration like the Master whose attention was focused on the cup of the coming passion. And as a result they slept, not just ordinary sleep but the deep, dreamless sleep which refreshed them for the coming ordeal.

This is the path to deep sleep for us all: some form of preliminary movement as walking or one or two simple postures, a deliberate emptying of the mind from all structured thinking and images, and the surrender of the whole being into the hands of God. This is the way mapped by the office of compline and if a few physical relaxing exercises are added it is a sure way to deep sleep.

Deep sleep is in itself a form of what Patanjali would call imageless contemplation. It renews the whole of our nature, spiritual and physical. But there are also the dreams of shallow sleep which have a great importance.

The Bible recognises the importance of dreams. In the case of Joseph, the foster father of our Lord, his dream revealed himself and God's will. He saw himself as essentially a fearful man. The angel in the dream told him not to be afraid. And he saw God's will in the command to take Mary as his wife. This is what lies behind all dreams: knowledge of the essence of the ego-self and knowledge of God, the true Self. Some dreams may not be immediately evident in their meaning and require later meditation but if they are used as ways into the self and God they have much to reveal to us. They are contemplation with an image, a very real and fruitful form of prayer. In dreams, images are the usual form of communication and in dreams, because words are rarely used, there is every opportunity for the full exercise of the emotions. Some training is needed to enable the dreamer to give full play to his emotions in his dreams because in waking life his emotions are mostly under the strictest control. But in dreams it is healthful to give all the emotions unlimited scope and, as a result the contemplative prayer enters into that stage which Patanjali calls *sananda samadhi*, contemplation with joy, which is a most liberating experience. Through unlimited exercise in dreams the emotions become harmonised into a balanced joy which is communicated into waking life.

Sleep is one of the ways we use the night: waking is the other. Father Benson's advice about the use of the waking experiences of sleep is very important. He discourages anything too cerebral or energetic: he recommends tranquil thought and simple loving devotion. This is sound advice for ordinary conditions of wakefulness but there is another use of this time which can be most valuable. This is to use some of the waking time to play over the problems and events which have to be faced during the next day. This should not be done with any anxiety but if situations can be gently imagined and rehearsed it is then possible to live them with confidence when they

83

occur in the life of everyday. This applies also to what might be called replaying past experiences in such a way that mistakes can be remedied and sins forgiven. It is a kind of what psychologists would call abreaction and is one of the ways in which the sleeplessness of the middle years of life can be used for the remaking of the soul. This use of wakefulness needs practice to master it without anxiety but used in this way it becomes a form of contemplating the Word in the self and of co-operating with the re-creative work of the Word in that self.

God and man communicate with each other through sleep and dreams. The disciples in Gethsemane failed to keep awake and practice the prayer our Lord was using but they did not fail completely. Their deep sleep was a form of contemplation and in that prayer they shared a part of the Lord's prayer and were strengthened to live through the events of that night and the next day and to come through the disaster of forsaking to the resurrection. What we practice in sleep and dreams becomes for us the substance of our waking life in Christ.

The Transfiguration reminds us of the equally important truth that sometimes when sleep is resisted and a state of wakefulness maintained there is a rich contemplative reward. For in St. Luke's account he says that on this occasion the disciples did not give way to the desire to sleep: 'Now Peter and those who were with him were heavy with sleep but kept awake'; and their reward was great.

'And they saw His glory and the two men who stood with Him' (Luke 9 : 32).

So both sleep and wakefulness can be used to enter contemplative prayer.

3

CONTEMPLATIVE WORSHIP

The Transfiguration is not merely a model of contemplative insight. The contemplation of this event is alive and personal and moving. It all takes place in an atmosphere of worship. The object of this worship is clearly revealed, and also the place of this worship and its form.

1. THE OBJECT OF WORSHIP. During the first part of the Transfiguration the object of the disciples' worship is Christ transfigured. It is not the Master the disciples had been accustomed to know, so ordinary, so concealed, but the Lord in shining raiment manifesting His glory. Christ glorified is the object of contemplative worship, not the Christ of the hidden years although of course there is no break between this form of Christ and the Christ of glory. The hidden Christ was for a time only and in a state of humiliation. The glorified Christ is for ever and for the whole universe. He is all that St. Paul describes in the epistles to the Colossians and to the Ephesians: He is the cosmic Christ who is the head and Lord of the universe. But during the second part of the Transfiguration Christ as the object of worship is taken up into the fullness of God, and the fullness of God is the Father, the Son and the Spirit. We hear the presence of the Father as the voice proclaims Christ as the beloved Son. We see the symbol of the Spirit's presence in the overshadowing cloud. So the object of worship develops into the Trinity of Father, Son and Spirit.

In many contemplative traditions the object of worship never develops beyond an outstanding human figure. Much of what is called bhakti yoga is concerned with God in this form. The manifestations of Him are people who have developed outstanding insight into His truth and been transformed into His likeness. They are called avatars of the Lord and they arouse the deepest contemplative devotion. Many Christian contemplatives worship God in this way. Much of St. Teresa's writing suggests that she had an intensely human and emotional content in her contemplative worship. She writes with familiarity about the Lord and talks to Him almost as an equal. In bhakti yoga many of the hymns have this same endearing human quality with the result that it is a very popular way of worship and prayer among the simple people of India.

But worship of this kind eventually leads to something more mysterious and profound in its conception of God. Jesus is taken up into the fullness of the Godhead and some kind of Trinitarian formulation becomes essential. We can see this happening in the New Testament. We can see it happening in other traditions. For instance, the Buddhist conception of nirvana is an attempt to intensify the mystery of God and to deepen the worship of His people. He is unlike all that the human mind can conceive and a kind of apophatic approach to Him is seen to be the best way of describing Him as the object of worship. This developed approach is in harmony with the Transfiguration experience and becomes essential if the worshipper is to keep pace in his prayer with the insight into God which comes from growing contemplation. God is not simple in the sense of being easily understood. The richness of His being requires an image greater than human thought can itself conceive. In describing the God of contemplative worship there must be room for a 'cloud of unknowing', there must be plenty of cloud shadow which only faith can penetrate. When God becomes too easily understood then worship becomes shallow and ineffective. This is the great danger of a presentation of God on the lines of *Godspell* and *Jesus Christ Superstar*: it is too human to be true and too obvious to evoke worship. Only the numinous in the conception of God is strong enough for the practice of worship.

The preliminary training of the contemplative in what Patanjali calls devotion to the Lord must therefore be concentrated on forming satisfactory and growing images of God. This begins by using His invisible attributes in creation as means of sharing in His 'everlasting power and deity'. A great deal of effort must be used in meditation on natural objects for this purpose. Painting and poetry are especially helpful exercises in growing able to use the imagination in this way. Like the disciples we first learn about God from His creatures and from the humanity of Christ as shown in his most transparent children, in the Gospels and in all the things He has made. From this exercise comes the power to make satisfactory images of God in the heart to evoke worship. The sacraments are examples of the way this is done by the Church. But the sacramental signs are not the only instruments for this work. Every creature can be used in this way. Even our Lord practised this art and it comes out in so many of His parables where He compares God to ordinary things and events of daily life. Making and storing these images of God are vital activities in the preliminary stages of worshipful contemplation.

But the image is not enough. At the Transfiguration the image of the Lord the disciples knew was transformed and then taken into the cloud. Both experiences are part of contemplative worship: the change of the image and its replacement by the cloud of silence.

Images of God should never be opaque and changeless. They must grow increasingly transparent and always they must be alive and moving. Learning to make and live with such images is a great art and makes heavy demands on the energy and imagination. The heart is always naturally inclined to congeal insight into some kind of containing structure as St. Peter wanted to with his three tents. But images of God are like the things He creates, transitory and renewable. When an image has done its work then it must be cheerfully replaced by another. This is detachment in a particularly demanding form and is mastered with long and painful practice.

Between the loss of one image and its replacement there is a period of silence; the cloud comes down and there is the shadow and silence. This is a particularly difficult experience to handle and success comes from long practice. Our Lord in Gethsemane summed up what was needed in the command, Watch. It is a hard form of faith and is exercised by the will. In this exercise the emotions of fear and hope and joy and grief are brought into harmony. The Indian description of this emotional balance in in terms of the balancing of the gunas of inertia (tamas) and activity (rajas) until they reach the state of sattva, a condition of stillness. We can watch the disciples moving into this state before they hear the divine voice and reach the climax of contemplative insight.

2. *THE PLACE OF CONTEMPLATIVE WORSHIP.* The Transfiguration shows the disciples practising contemplative worship in many places. There was the difficult countryside around the alien towns of Caesarea Philippi. Then the glory of the natural beauty of the mountain. Then we find Peter struggling to make the tents for worship which were a recollection of the tabernacle in the wilderness. And then they entered into the cloud and were identified with the body of the Lord. These were all places in which worship and contemplation of various degrees took place and they are symbols of the places where this worship must always be done.

The world is a place of such worship. The preliminary training of the contemplative takes place in the world and under these conditions he must train himself to find God and offer Him true devotion. This is by no means an easy task but it imposes less strain than other more intense places of worship and should not be despised. A tradition has grown up which implies that comtemplation requires a special environment known as the enclosed life. This is not so. True contemplation can be practised in the world and it is there that it must first be learnt. The Western tradition is that the training of the active life in the world is the essential preliminary to the life of contemplation. This tradition is also found in the east where the four stages of life lead to liberation or kaivalya. First the youthful stage of continence, then the stage of manhood, then the householder, then the stage of withdrawal and the practice of union with God. Each stage of life is important and prepares for the next.

Nature provides another and more intense place for contemplation. Away from the man-made environment nature reveals more strikingly the presence and work of God. This was recognised by such groups of contemplatives as the early desert Fathers and later by the monks who built their monasteries in places of supreme beauty. But nature is not the only place of beauty: there are the arts and music and dancing. These are also ways to God and environments to be mastered. It is in the practice of the arts that the heart is trained for worshipful contemplation and some skill in at least one of them is necessary training for the fully balanced contemplative. This has been recognised in all traditions where music is one of the primary adjuncts of worship and architecture and painting and poetry have played such a general part in training men to find God and to express His beauty. Keats summed up this use of beauty when he wrote:

'Beauty is truth: truth beauty.
That is all you know on earth and all you need to know.'

The world is filled with evidence of man's conviction that this is true and in adding to that beauty through his own crafts he has found God.

So preliminary training for contemplation must be training in the arts. This means first of all choosing the form which most suits the particular person and then patiently mastering its technique so that he can use it as a means of exploration and expression. For the contemplative this is even more important than learning a profession. We find this understood in the early monasteries where such crafts as lettering and architecture and music were the main activities and in India there is similar evidence in the existence of such buildings as the Taj Mahal and the great Buddhist caves and the musical tradition and the dance.

Peter has been too easily despised for his misunderstood suggestion that three tents should be built for the three chief figures in the Transfiguration. But what he was feeling after was the need to make a dwelling place for God where he could be contemplatively worshipped. What he did not fully understand was that God did not dwell in temples made by hands but in hearts prepared to receive Him. And it is the shaping of the heart for this purpose which is one of the main acts of preparation with which the contemplative is concerned. It involves the work of cleansing the heart and then building it into a sanctuary of God. The hesychastic discipline goes into the way of doing this in some detail. A place is needed, the anachoresis, where external distractions can be reduced. Then there is the need to practice silence (siope) and internal harmony through work and prayer and study (anapausis) and finally the heart is guarded in a state of receptive stillness (hesychia) by the use of vocal prayer so that it can recognise and respond to the divine presence. A similar teaching is given in the Eastern discipline. Patanjali requires the making in the heart of an enclosure (desha bandha) and he prescribes the activities of meditation and contemplation in various degrees to prepare it as the place of meeting between the contemplative and God. All this takes place in various stages and it is for the student to find out what stage in this building he has reached and to go on from there. For beginners the early stages are primarily concerned with purgation. In the later stages more emphasis should be placed on illuminating the heart, responding as the eastern spiritual writers say, to the light in the heart (jyotis) and then learning to grow in love through exercises which unite the heart with the Spirit of love. In these ways each contemplative builds his own tent for God within the boundaries of his own heart. It is a life-long work in which death plays an essential part.

At the closing stages of the Transfiguration the disciples passed out of themselves into the cloud and into a deep union with the transfigured Christ. It was a kind of death to the individual self and a rebirth into the body of Christ. They ceased being a group of individuals and became one body in Christ. This was the supreme place for worshipping God. There they heard the voice of the Father and shared the energy of the Spirit and became one in the Son. So transforming was this experience that when they emerged from it they were enlightened and saw Christ in everything.

The body of Christ thus shared is the chief place where God is worshipped and contemplated. It begins as a local Church, a congregation of faithful people, and then it grows to include the departed members of the body, Moses, Elijah and the whole company of heaven and then it becomes a participation in the very life of God. The edifying of this building is the work in which all Christians are engaged and the more they respond to contemplative worship the more they can share in the work. In the preliminary stages they are mostly concerned with learning to live with others. This demands the keeping of the commandments and above all the practice of love towards others. When these are mastered then one moves on to the more intimate experiences of the body and to more demanding ministries. The work of sharing in this building is eventually some form of sacrifice, the offering of soul and body for the building up of the body of Christ. This is the theme of the eucharist and it is the motive behind all work. Christ is making all things new, He is the head of this growing organism, and it is as each contributes to its building that it moves to become a more perfect 'habitation of God in the Spirit'.

3. FORMS OF CONTEMPLATIVE WORSHIP. Few details are given us of the forms with which our Lord and His disciples worshipped God. No doubt they used the Jewish prayers but when our Lord gave the model of prayer He simplified this tradition and laid down a few principles which left much freedom for variation. We are not given any details of formal worship in the account of the Transfiguration beyond the hint that in thinking of building tents Peter must have had a larger idea than that of merely enclosing the divine glory. Some worship must also have been intended.

The present-day contemplative inherits a large tradition of what might be called liturgical worship with which to train himself in this vocal prayer. This is given in the West through the divine office and in the East through the many forms of what are called bhakti yoga.

The divine office is made up of scripture readings, the psalter, prayers and the eucharist. Its origin lies in pre-Christian forms of worship and it was taken into the life of the Church and modified to suit its needs. It is no static system of prayer but subject to constant revision as it changes to meet the needs of changing people. In the present generation the divine office in all churches has gone through radical revisions and now stands in a much pruned and simplified form, still waiting for a more adventurous use than it has as yet received.

For the contemplative the divine office is not the end of his contemplation but an instrument for training him in this prayer and one through which he can manifest some of his discoveries. His problem in these days is to find how much of the divine office he needs for his particular purpose and how it can be most suitably used in his present stage of development.

Certain principles hold good for this prayer in all its forms:

(i) It is essentially a corporate prayer. Most of the divine office is not suitable for private recitation since it presupposes a dialogue situation requiring at least two people. Using the divine office privately as was done until recently can be harmful to the contemplative since it involves him in reciting far too many words in an atmosphere of unreality. He has been in the position of a single actor trying to take all the parts of a play.

The present form of the divine office encourages experiment with the materials provided both in local churches and in smaller groups. Through this experiment the material suitable for such groups will be discovered and when found it should not be made too rigid. Also there should be room for improvisation. This prevents the prayer from becoming dead and makes it able to respond to the present.

(ii) The divine office is the main form of vocal prayer. Vocal prayer is an essential complement to mental prayer and when wisely arranged both supplies the material for mental prayer and also prepares the heart for this prayer. In devotion to God the energy of all the centres is needed and this includes the throat centre which is activated by sound and words. For this reason parts of the divine office should be sung or at least intoned. This activates the throat centre to its fullest capacity.

(iii) The divine office is a way of sanctifying time. Whether it is used in its completeness or in part it provides a way of setting aside regular times during the day for prayer. The full divine office comes at significant times through the day and enables work and recreation and meals to be brought under a regular rhythm.

(iv) The divine office and contemplative prayer can best be practised together, one being the preparation for the other. This means taking about half the time given to prayer for each of its parts and working in at the beginning some of the postures and breathing as an introduction, using the psalms as a breathing exercise and taking from the scripture readings images for the meditative part of the prayer. The end must always be silence, a silence deepened by the exercises which lead to it. Of all the forms of the divine office the services for Holy Week are most valuable for use in this way. In these services are set out the total mystery of our faith and by using them with all our faculties they can provide a pattern for contemplative prayer throughout the year, not only in terms of themes but in terms of symbols and ceremonial acts. The ways for doing this are suggested in the contemplative exercises in the final chapter of this book.

(v) The eucharist is the heart of the divine office and provides opportunities for practising more completely than in the other parts of the office all the principles which have been considered. In this worship the essence of corporate prayer is expressed, for not only are two or three required to make the service possible: this congregation is also gathered in its deepest significance. Each present member has a function and place, either as a layman or minister and Christ is the manifest centre with the energy of the Spirit recognised at the beginning in the prayer that He will inspire our hearts. The whole action of the eucharist is based on this structure of unity and each member of the body not only finds his true place in the whole but has also a vital function to perform. In this worship there is the full material of vocal prayer with opportunity to use it in a variety of ways so that the throat centre is fully opened. Thanks to the present freedom in modifying the eucharist there is also the chance to improvise and make the service what is needed by those sharing in it. We have taken long to reach this freedom and it will be some time before many will be able to use it without self-consciousness, but we can now experiment and learn and this will enrich all our ways of contemplation. Above all the eucharist provides for actions as well as words, for corporate movement and for silence. When these arts have been mastered the eucharist will become what it was in the New Testament, a technique for coming to a knowledge of the risen Lord, a way of manifesting His presence, a road to the deepest communion between the Lord and all His members.

(vi) In many ways our use of the divine office never leaves the preliminary stages. We are always learning to do it better: there are always new lessons to learn. But so it is with every art. The musician and the artist are always *in via* and striving to attain. What is important is that at all stages our use of the divine office shall be planned to help us grow towards perfection of contemplative prayer and not merely to the rendering of words and music with the greatest measure of technical skill. In order to do this there must always be present in our recitation of the divine office these ingredients:

(a) Self-denial. One of the advantages of a given liturgy is that it minimises the use of the self in devotion to God. Using given words and entering into a traditional prayer is the greatest safeguard to mere self expression in worship. But the words of the tradition have to be used for this purpose and not for self. This means learning to lose self in the worshipping congregation, accepting objective standards of worship as regards both voice and movement, identifying with the emotions of others. In the practice of these things the psalms are of the greatest help. They enable us to share in the thoughts and feelings of others; they stretch the self beyond the limits of its own boundaries and train us to identify with the masters of prayer and ultimately with the Lord Himself.

(b) Surrender to the Spirit. The energy of prayer is the Spirit. In vocal prayer we surrender ourselves to the Spirit. This is part of the exercise of what Patanjali and his tradition call *prānāyāma*, the assimilation of the divine energy into our own. In the preliminary stages this can be done by the use of breathing which harmonises the rhythm of our own breathing with that of others and through the rules of music. Later on with practice this becomes instinctive. The Spirit controls not only the use of the voice but also the growth of the emotions and the faith which makes true prayer possible. In this exercise the senses of touch and taste are used and the centres below the heart are the places where this is done. In the orthodox Church where singing forms such an important part of prayer the production of the voice from the abdomen ensures that consciousness is mostly in this centre and the controlled breathing demanded by this singing leads to a specially intense harmony with the Spirit. The Western forms of plainsong are also an instrument for achieving this same intimacy. The Eastern way of singing through the head centre also leads to a physical relationship with the pranic energy and directs the attention to the Spirit. Therefore in saying the divine office much care should be given to the recital of the words and the music used. Even if the full plainsong is impossible the use of a reciting note can be an effective substitute.

(c) Movement is an important part of worship and contemplation.

In the divine office certain postures, such as standing, sitting and kneeling are prescribed, but others may well be added from other traditions. Most important is the sitting posture. This should be firm and steady. There should also be preliminary movements which may take the form of part of the Tai Chi Ch'uan or some of the yoga asanas. The simplest asanas are those of standing and walking. As a preparation for the office slow walking is excellent for it breaks the over-active movement of daily life and imposes a slower and more suitable rhythm for prayer. In a small group it is not difficult to find a series of movements to prepare and introduce both the divine office and the contemplation afterwards. Even simple hand gestures can play their part and the use of the eyes in concentration and relaxation is valuable.

(d) The divine office is a combination of sound and silence. The achievement of silence in the office is as difficult as the achievement of sound. It involves stillness of body and mind. The body stillness comes from the firm posture; the stillness of mind from the elimination of distractions. This takes time and practice. To begin with care should be taken to listen with attention to the scripture readings, and to observe a silence after them.

4. CONTEMPLATIVE WORK. One of the main ways of practising devotion towards God is work. This is common to all religious traditions. In India there is a form of yoga called karma yoga which is specially concerned with this way of worship and the classic text is the *Bhagavad Gita.* In the Western Christian tradition the active life of work is recognised as the raw material of contemplative prayer. But both the *Bhagavad Gita* and the Western traditions insist that work must be done in a special way in order to stimulate contemplation. Not every kind of work done in any kind of way will do this. In fact, one of the tragedies of the present industrial society is that it has developed work which is contrary to the service of God and to contemplation and that the motive for so many jobs is not the glory of God but merely financial gain.

Work may be divided into two kinds: manual and intellectual. A well-balanced form of active service will combine both kinds. Manual work is needed to counteract the effects of sedentary work and intellectual work rests the body and directs its physical activity. In religious communities care is taken to provide both kinds of work. The caste system in India when properly controlled also helps towards a balanced activity. But mostly people have to discover their own balance. If they are working with their minds during the day then their recreational activity should be some kind of manual hobby. And if manual work is their daily activity then their leisure should be some kind of mental work. Above all, work in all its kinds should be chosen in response to God's will and accepted as a call, a vocation from Him. Only work received in this way can become the raw material for His service. We find our Lord in the temple at the age of twelve discovering the Father's will and then going down to Nazareth to work it out in obedience for the next eighteen years. This recognition and obedience are essential from all who would use work as a form of God's service and the material of contemplative prayer.

In the *Bhagavad Gita* there is detailed exposition of the way work should be done in God's service. Krishna insists that the work shall be suitable to the individual. 'Even a wise man acts according to the tendency of his own nature.' And when the work has been chosen he teaches that it shall be done 'with faith in the heart'. Doing work in this way means that it must be used as material for meditation and that from meditation the way it shall be done must first be understood. That is best done by means of a plan or symbol. As the mind flows around the work to be done so this plan will form and when formed it becomes the controlling centre of the work. In the wilderness and its temptations we see our Lord meditating in this way on his ministry and coming out to preach with confidence the gospel of the kingdom. Arajuna and Krishna engage in the same kind of meditation before the battle and here again the plan is formed.

Work like contemplation involves movement and mastery of movement is the result of repeated practice. So work done for God demands the mastery of its movements. This mastery comes from a balance between theory and practice. The movements must be imprinted in image form in the heart and then the limbs must be exercised so that they move from habit, as the movements are carried out. It is the same procedure as learning the movements of the dance. They must be seen in the heart and absorbed by the limbs and then they flow out in instinctive action leaving the mind free to dwell in stillness on God. As Krishna says to Arajuna: 'the truly admirable man controls his senses by the power of his will. All his actions are disinterested. All are directed along the path to union with Brahman.' In the Christian tradition this idea of working with God is expressed in even greater detail and St. Paul sums it up in his advice to the Philippians where he writes: 'You must work out your own salvation in fear and trembling; for it is God who works in you, inspiring both the will and the deed, for His own chosen purpose' (Philippians 2 : 12–13).

Such inspired movement can only come from close union with the Holy Spirit. The discipline of *pranāyāma* develops this union in prayer and the same practice has to be extended to the work outside of prayer. The practice of rhythmic breathing in harmony with the movement helps to bring this about. The athlete, Roger Bannister, described it as 'switching on the Holy Ghost'. Krishna reveals to Arajana this same truth by acting as his driver during the battle. An artist like Kipling described it as waiting for his daimon. It comes from a growing sensitivity to the Holy Spirit in prayer and in action. It is like the feeling which enables people to sing in tune or the instinct which gives the musician the ability to tune his instrument and then to play it in perfect harmony with the other instruments of the orchestra under the control of a conductor. Team games develop this sensitivity. So does work which requires the co-operation of many individuals. Often in India this kind of work has to be done and the harmony is intensified by the singing of songs especially composed for the purpose. Tolstoy gives this wonderful description of a reaper which illustrates this state of harmony in work most vividly: 'Levin experienced those moments of oblivion when it was not his arms which swung the scythe but the scythe seemed to mow of itself, a body full of life and consciousness of its own as though by magic, without a thought being given to it, the work did itself regularly and carefully. These were the blessed moments' (*Anna Karenina*).

This is the work which is both a form of devotion to God and a contemplation of God as well. It happens of its own and we can only be thankful when it comes and meditate on it when absent and prepare to receive it again.

Our Lord constantly preaches that the end of work is not a monetary reward but the gift of God Himself. This is what lies behind the mysterious parable of the labourers who were hired for a penny a day and at the end had a wages' dispute with the Lord who was offering them Himself. The end of all work is the loving contemplation of God. This is the theme of the *Bhagavad Gita* as well as the Christian tradition. Krishna says:

> 'Work is holy
> When the heart of the worker
> Is fixed on the highest'
> (p. 47).

And our Lord brings His life's work to a triumphant conclusion with the words: 'It is completed. Father, into thy hands I commend my Spirit.'

Pottery provides a wonderful model of all these principles in action. It consists of four acts: wedging the clay, centring it on the wheel, opening the centre and raising the clay into the object already imagined in the heart. The physical movements correspond to the wedging; the other acts reproduce that turning to Christ and identifying with Him through which the whole being is transfigured into His

95

likeness and offered to Him. All work when done in this way reveals something of the mystery of ourselves in God.

In India there was a muslim wheelwright who lived outside the All Saints' Convent in Bombay. Every morning, after saying Mass for the Sisters, I used to meet him sitting outside his workshop near an unfinished wheel, intoning the Qur'an. He was for many a symbol of the Eastern balance between work and contemplation, between the labour of the hands and devotion to God. In all stages work done in this way can train the contemplative for his life of contemplating God.

The men who shared the Transfiguration were all workmen: three fishermen and one carpenter. They were not engaged in their trades when they had this experience but their trades made them ready for it. The fishermen were used to waiting and responding to signs: the carpenter had the precise obedience to the capacities of various materials which years at his trade had given Him. Their work had been a preliminary training for this supreme experience and they were able to enter into it and taste it to the full. Our work either prepares us or hinders us for a similar experience. Work and prayer are inseparably united, work and contemplation develop side by side.

Chapter 4

Advanced Contemplative Training

The mountain of Transfiguration rises up from the plain and marks the distinction between the beginners and the mature contemplatives in the gospel story. In the plain are the people and the disciples who have already been led through a preliminary training. They have mastered certain physical controls, they have been trained to understand some of the mysteries of life, they have been disciplined in some basic kinds of prayer. But above them soars the mountain and up that mountain the Lord leads his most responsive disciples to further training so that they may be able to respond to the greater contemplative experiences which await them at the top.

This distinction between beginners and proficients is recognised in both the Christian and Eastern traditions. In the Christian tradition there are those in the way of purgation who have mastered some of the main obstacles between them and the contemplation of God. They have yet to pass through what St. John of the Cross calls the dark night of sense and spirit. Their faith has to be tested and developed. In the Eastern tradition there are those who have completed their training in preliminary yoga and are now ready for the more demanding training of the eight limbs of raja yoga.

This preliminary training may be described as mainly external and negative. It is about the physical body and the formal techniques of prayer, the formation of the contemplative family and the mastery of certain truths about God. It is the discipline through which the disciples had been when they stood before the mount of Transfiguration. The advanced training is about other things. It is largely concerned with internal things, the spiritual body, what St. Peter calls 'the hidden man of the heart' (1 Peter 3 : 4) and with the penetration of the truth beyond the many ways of its formal expression. This is summed up by Patanjali when he writes that the purpose of the eight limbs of yoga is: 'the destruction of impurities and the growth of spiritual illumination, developing into awareness of the divine presence' (2 : 28).

The experiences on the mount of Transfiguration illustrate the achievement of this purpose in a vivid way. Our Lord's body is changed and the whole creation shines with a revealed splendour. The barrier between the living and the departed is broken down and God speaks clearly. This is the positive goal of the training we are about to consider. It brings the contemplative into the higher stages of contemplation and intensifies his union with God. What takes place in the words of the Western traditions is the marriage between the soul and God. The Eastern tradition speaks of it in terms of absorption and identification between the soul and God.

In describing the training which prepares for this goal we shall use the teaching of Patanjali as our controlling source. Of all the writers on contemplative prayer he sets out the training most succinctly and with him as guide we shall attempt to build our own form of advanced contemplative training for our needs today.

Patanjali sums up the eight limbs in one verse as: restraints, observances, postures, regulation of prana, introversion, concentration, meditation and contemplation (2 : 29). The late Jack Winslow in his work on the Yoga Sutras describes each of these limbs in detail and summarises them as 'the pathway by which the spirit of man, created in the image of God, an effluence from the divine Essence, returns to its Source and Original—the road by which the pilgrim reaches that Home which is the goal of his long quest' (J. C. Winslow, *The Art of Contemplation*, p. 1, Association Press, 1931). Perhaps this goes further than Patanjali who is content to think of the eight limbs as ways of removing hindrances rather than as a road which leads to the divine goal. He was much nearer the Western view that God gives Himself and we not so much arrive where He is as prepare to receive Him.

The eight limbs describe not only training for contemplation but ways of contemplation; for the disciple contemplates as he trains and does not have to wait to master the training exercise before he can contemplate God. The disciples as they ascended the mountain were already contemplating their Lord though with varying degrees of intensity. So in examining the eight limbs we shall find ourselves dealing with different forms of contemplation. The first two limbs which Jack Winslow called the moral discipline we shall deal with under the heading of the Contemplative Life. The next three limbs we shall call Contemplation in the heart. And the final limbs will come under the heading of Contemplation with Images. We shall conclude this section with another heading, Contemplative Freedom.

CONTEMPLATIVE LIFE

A special life is needed for contemplative prayer. This has been recognised by all traditions and with an astonishing variety of forms. In the West it has included the free structure of the Desert Fathers and the strongly organised forms of monastic life. It has included the large Benedictine foundations and the small communities of enclosed religious. In the East there have been the large Buddhist monasteries and the almost structureless ashrams. And always in both traditions there have been the great individual contemplatives like St. John of the Cross and Ramāna Mahārshi who have gone their own ways in their own life styles. But it is certain that some form of ordered life is essential for contemplative prayer and in its earlier stages at least this includes both an individual and family pattern.

The individual pattern is concerned with man as he is, a divided person who needs an external pattern around which to build his life and a family structure to help him in the process. We have already watched our Lord provide for this in the conditions he lays down for discipleship, denying self and following Him. There is also needed a rough outline for handling the day by day problems of life, what would be called a rule of life. Side by side with the process of self denial there are needed ways of recognising the new self, hid with Christ in God (Colossians 3 : 3). This self is integrally part of Christ, a member of His body, embryonic and in its early stages hidden. It requires careful search to discover and leads to a face to face confrontation with God. H. A. Williams describes it as 'A discovery that God is in me ... immanent, yet in His immense transcendence'. This new self is gradually revealed. Internally it grows through meditation, externally through the study of Christ in the gospels, in the lives of the saints and in a life wisely ordered on their patterns. Its outlines have been summarised in the virtues of prudence, justice, temperance, fortitude, faith, hope and love. Its energies have been analysed in the gifts of wisdom, understanding, counsel, spiritual strength, knowledge, true godliness and holy fear. Its fruits in love, joy, peace, long-suffering, gentleness, goodness, faith, meekness, temperance. These are no more than outlines but they help in planning a life which will stimulate growth in these directions and cannot be safely ignored.

And then in the beginning stages the individual contemplative needs to grow in a family environment. In these days the Western traditions are being modified in the direction of the greater freedom of family structures found in the East. Unnecessary regulations are being discarded. There is much greater freedom to respond to the working of the Spirit in the family and like the original pattern given by Father Benson general directions are preferred to details. For instance, he was content to require that the conditions of Bethlehem, Nazareth and Calvary should be produced in the family and left the planning of the details to those who had that task. Living together for the purpose of contemplative prayer is more like sharing in a dance than a prison routine. We have still much to learn about this and our deeper contact with Eastern forms of contemplative life will be a great help towards the attainment of a wise freedom. One thing is certain: the guide of every true family is not a series of statutes or a written rule of life but the presence of the Spirit of Christ who He promised would lead us into all truth. Response to His presence makes demands on every member of the community who shares the responsibility for its health and life. It rests not merely with a few elected and criticised greater officers but with every member, from the most recent postulant to the oldest member in the infirmary.

1. THE CONTEMPLATION OF DENIAL. The three disciples on the mount of Transfiguration did not share at once in the illumination of Christ. It is true that they entered into the cloud of glory but it was the shadow of this cloud they first experienced. In other words they went into darkness before they came into light. This is an important part of the Western contemplative tradition: some form of dark night, some experience of a cloud of unknowing is a necessary way to full contemplation. This is a negative path, but it is also a growing period in the life of prayer during which the roots develop and the whole being becomes more able to carry the weight of glory towards which it moves.

Patanjali in his teaching about the restraints of the contemplative life lists five negative practices: non-killing (ahimsa), non-lying (satya), non-stealing (asteya), continence (brahmachārya), non-covetousness (aparigraha). He says that these five practices are part of a universal law and must be observed. He does not give any detailed description. This has been done by those who have tried to keep them, from the writers of the Upanishads and the epics to such great exponents as Ramakrishna and Gandhi. Each had his own interpretation and none so detailed as the interpretation of Ghandhi which was not only for his own private use but for all those who shared his great movement for independence. He would be the first to admit that there were few who have mastered his principles but this makes no difference to their truth. One of these most important principles was that the denials were much more than a form of law. He related them closely to prayer and taught that they were the means of preparing men both for political action and for the contemplation of God. One of the invariable practices of Gandhi throughout his life was the daily prayer with his followers and sometimes, as on the beach at Chowpatty in Bombay, these prayer meetings reached levels of profound corporate contemplation. Two million people practising contemplative silence with Gandhi himself as the perfectly still centre is an experience that none who shared it could ever forget.

These denials are part of a general pattern of discipline of the self, common to all traditions. It is what is called in the theology of the orthodox Church the apophatic way or the way of negation and it applies particularly to the mystery of God who is approached not so much by considering what He is like as by what He is unlike. In Eastern tradition it is called the 'netti, netti' way which similarly teaches a negative description of God and the way to Him. The Christian tradition has its own form of this way which we shall now consider.

Jack Winslow pointed out that the five restraints correspond to the five prohibitions of the Mosaic law: thou shalt do no murder, thou shalt not bear false witness, thou shalt not steal, thou shalt not commit adultery, thou shalt not covet. These have been developed in the Church catechism into this analysis of the duty towards God and one's neighbour:

2. To allow no created thing to take His place, but to use my time, my gifts and my possessions as one who must give an account to Him.

6. To hurt nobody by word or deed; to bear no grudge or hatred in my heart.

8. Not to steal or cheat.

9. To keep my tongue from lying, slandering and harmful gossip, and never by my silence to let others be wrongly condemned.

But none of these forms of denial is much good as material for contemplative prayer since they are little more than regulations to reduce hindrances. They become such material when they are seen as no more than regulations for the much bigger task of denying the old self, so that the new can take its place. When interpreted in this way they become an essential part of contemplative prayer.

The Upanishads teach that God dwells in the heart and that the acts of self-denial are for the purpose of allowing Him to reign. It is put in this attractive way: 'That being, of the size of a thumb, dwells deep within the heart. He is Lord of time, past and future, the same today and tomorrow. He verily is the immortal Self' (*Katha Upanishad*, p. 21).

101

Dr. Farrer in his seminal book *The Glass of Vision* writes in harmony with this teaching and then develops it into the essence of contemplative prayer. He writes: 'I would no longer attempt with the psalmist "to set God before my face". I would see Him as the underlying cause of my thinking, especially of those thoughts in which I tried to think of Him. I would dare to hope that sometimes my thought would become diaphanous, so that there should be some perception of the divine cause shining through the created effect, as a deep pool, settling into a clear tranquility, permits us to see the spring in the bottom of it from which its waters rise. I would dare to hope that through a second cause the First Cause might be felt, when the second cause in question was itself spirit, made in the image of the Divine Spirit, and perpetually welling up out of His creative act' (Dr. A. M. Farrer, *The Glass of Vision*, p. 8).

This is a glorious exposition of the mystery of the self and explains why there must be a way of denial which makes possible that communication with the true Self and can only be achieved when the glory of the true Self overshadows the false ego-structure and makes its transfiguration into the divine likeness possible. It is the negative form of contemplative prayer which we have now to consider.

Death is the climax and the model of this way of denial. Before it comes in its final form death is presented in many others for the sake of rehearsal and preparation. For the Buddhist death is contemplated in all its stark physical horror. For the Christian it is the death of Christ which is the matter of contemplation and that death shot through with the glory of the resurrection and Transfiguration. It is important to note that our Lord did not introduce his disciples to the mystery of his death until they had seen His transfiguration glory and even then He insisted that it should be contemplated as part of the total resurrection. Death is the shadow of the cloud of glory which overshadows us all. Most clearly is this full mystery set out for us in the eucharist which is the greatest of all symbols for meditation on death.

In a remarkable book called *The Moment of Truth*, Ladislaus Boros writes of death as 'the ending of our state of pilgrimage and the place of our fully personal encounter with Christ'. It is not only death which leads to these experiences but every meditation upon it and such meditations bring the opportunity to deepen our mastery of the way of denial.

Patanjali teaches that one of the hindrances to contemplation is aggression and the other aversion. These are emotional imbalances. It is not a question of reducing one and increasing the other; it is a question of developing both so that they can be fully exercised and may balance each other. We need more aversion and more aggression, more holy fear and more fortitude. Meditation on death increases our power to become perfectly passive to the control of the Spirit. Under the experiences of death we stretch to the limits our passivities and move towards that 'wise passiveness' which is the secret of contemplation. In this way the ego-self becomes more and more receptive to the true Self, the risen Lord, and more and more capable of assimilating Him. Its hunger for something more than its own creation is deepened. It hungers and thirsts for its true complement who is the Lord.

To respond adequately to the contemplative prayer opened to us by the limb of the denials much practice and repetition are needed. This comes from mediation not only on death itself but on all those other occasions when death is presented to us. The great moments are at baptism, Holy Week, every eucharist and sacramental confession.

Baptism brings death to us and resurrection in the signs of drowning and being raised to newness of life. Its symbolism of water and light are the essential materials for entering into the full mystery of death and resurrection. At least once each week this sacrament should be repeated in the heart. It is more than a moment of truth. It is the first moment of truth but through meditation it can be made present and become a continuous and present truth, controlling the whole of life and developing that passive faith in God which is balanced by the active service of the Lord in the heart and in the world. Baptism is the great communicator of Christian death and brings the grace of the Spirit into the heart which is the fruit of dying daily.

Holy Week expands the principles of dying in the sacrament of baptism against the background of our Lord's death and resurrection. During that week the events of the Lord's passion and resurrection are lived out in the heart, His death and resurrection become our own and we plumb the depths of self-denial. It is the great week of the year which sets a pattern for all the others. It presents the preparation for death and illuminates the way of resurrection to which it leads. The denials are fully lived through during a well-observed Holy Week.

Confession is another way of experiencing death. This is something much deeper than ego-analysis. It is more concerned with the examination of the Lord and His glory. It is the reception of His renewing grace. Sacramental confession is an important but occasional way of experiencing this kind of death. The contemplative use of this sacrament is like the meditation on baptism, a practice which helps in appropriating this death and applying its deepest principles to our life. This is also true of the eucharist in the heart where we can prolong the act of feeding on Christ and sharing His death and resurrection.

103

Other moments for experiencing death are sleep and silence. Deep sleep is a rehearsal for death and brings the grace of renewal. Only the mastery of silence can enable us to have this sleep at will. Sleep and silence are complementary passivities which bring both the physical and spiritual fruits of death to the whole man.

Death is a physical as well as a spiritual experience and so certain postures and movements help us to deepen our participation. The T'ai Chi Ch'uan is in some ways a dance of death, a complicated movement for renewing the ego and making it capable of union with the Lord. Its balance of yin and yang brings harmony to the opposing emotions of aggression and aversion and throughout the dance there is a movement towards a full response to the indwelling presence of the Lord who dances in the heart. Certain of the yoga postures are also helpful. Of these the obeisance posture and the corpse posture are most helpful. But in all these physical movements there must be the co-operation of the heart if they are to bring the full experience of death and resurrection and the application of the denials to the soul.

As we practice the five denials in these forms of contemplative prayer so their meanings grow. To begin with *ahimsa* is no more than avoiding giving pain. Then it develops into the deeper meanings it had for Gandhi and the still deeper meanings it had for our Lord. Self-denial begins as a form of self control and then becomes a response to the demands of our Lord to leave self behind. Aversion and aggression from being character disorders are found to lie at the root of our maimed relationship with God. And covetousness is seen as much more than a desire for the wealth of this world and something which puts alternatives in the place of God. But always we must be genuine and deal with the denials in the form we can see them at the moment and not as seen through the eyes of others. A false piety is of all evils in the spiritual life the most dangerous. We must be realistic in our self knowledge and deal with the ego as it is and not as we imagine and want it to be.

A very effective way of learning the state of the self is through a general confession and the advice of a wise director. This in many ways resembles the Eastern method of a guru–chela relationship and brings in an objective assessment which the individual is unable to achieve alone. But the guru–chela relationship should not continue for longer than needed. The chela should be trained to find his own way and eventually to become a guru to others. In Buddhist countries it is thought normal for a young man to spend some six months in a monastery for the purpose of finding himself and then to embark on his work in the world. A development of this method, using Christian monasteries for the purpose, is something which might well be used more often in the west, without any obligation being felt to join the order afterwards. In this way a period of intense contemplation of denial can form the preparation for the more positive contemplation of affirmation which we now consider.

2. THE CONTEMPLATION OF AFFIRMATION. Denial of the ego-self is part of a process of integration which must be followed by the contemplation of affirmation. We see this in action on the mountain of Transfiguration. The disciples pass from the shadow of the cloud into the nearer presence of Christ and are given the form of their affirmation through the voice which says: 'This is my beloved Son. Hear Him.' Having denied themselves and the old ego-self formation they are to be filled with the true Self, the Son of God. This affirmation is to be achieved by a process of listening contemplation without any visual reassurance, but it is under these conditions that faith will grow and through reflection on His words we are to come to the more complete vision of the future.

This listening to the words of the true Self is done in many ways by many traditions. The way of the catechism requires the fulfilment of those positive parts of the commandments and puts them in this way:

1. To worship Him as the only true God, to love, trust and obey Him, and by witness of my words and deeds to bring others to serve Him.
2. To reverence Him in thought, word and deed.
3. To keep the Lord's day for worship, prayer and rest from work.
4. To love, respect and help my parents, to honour the Queen; to obey those in authority over me in all things lawful and good; and to fulfil my duties as a citizen.
5. To promote peace among men; to be courteous to all; and to be kind to all God's creatures.
6. To be clean in thought, word and deed, controlling my bodily desires through the controlling power of the Holy Spirit who dwells within me; and if called to the state of marriage to live faithfully in it.
7. To be honest and fair in all I do; ... to seek justice, freedom and plenty for all men.

This is the way the Church teaches her children to listen to the voice of God. Patanjali gives a more simple teaching when he describes the five observances as: purity (shaucha), contentment (samtosha), austerity (tapas), self-study (svādhyāya), devotion to the Lord (Ishvara pranidhāna) (2 : 32).

105

In both these traditions we have positive approaches to the Lord-Self which involve us in the following actions: listening to His voice; emotional harmony; active service expressed in worship.

(*i*) *Listening*. Just as the ego-self is a talkative creation of ourselves, so the true Self, the Lord, speaks. The difference is that the Lord who speaks does so less frequently and in many ways. Before learning to make our response we have to be aware of the forms of this speaking. They are verbal, written and visual.

God speaks in the heart of man and through the lips of His servants. Samuel heard God speaking in his heart in the obscurity of the temple but God also spoke through him because he was also a prophet. In these ways God still speaks. It is not necessary to send missionaries to the heathen for God to speak to them. He has already spoken in their hearts and they have misunderstood His message just as effectively as those who have His written word and many prophets. Whenever the heart is silent the voice of God sounds. This speaking may be called the voice of conscience, the natural law or instinct. Through whatever of these ways man becomes conscious of a higher power, he hears God speaking.

And then in every civilisation there is a tradition, either oral or written, which brings together the wisdom of the great leaders. For the Western tradition this is most completely collected in the books of the Bible. Other traditions have other written forms. What authenticates them as the voice of the living Lord is their large measure of agreement. True, men have mistaken what they have heard and reported it incorrectly and this goes for the Bible as well as for other books, but when the whole tradition is used and compared the agreements are remarkable. There is for instance a clear measure of agreement between much of the New Testament and the *Bhagavad Gita* and the *Upanishads*; and the prophets of the Old Testament have much more than a similarity of historical period in common. They speak much the same language and witness to much of the same truth.

The Word of God, through whom all things were made, speaks through the images of creation which are signs and sacraments of His truth. Again this is common to both Eastern and Western traditions. In them all, God is witnessed as speaking to man in a garden in the cool of the day. Here His language is much more complicated and much more liable to misunderstanding. But for the contemplative God speaks through every part of His creation and reveals His glory. This is the first and the last utterance of the Word. The glory of creation precedes the verbal utterance at the Transfiguration and God goes on speaking in this way when the spoken word is silent.

It is to this rich and varied form of divine utterance that the

106

contemplative must train himself to listen. He turns all of his powers of awareness, away from the ego-self to the Lord. This is an act of re-direction and silence.

Much has already been written about silence and it is therefore not necessary to go into detailed explanations. What is essential is that silence that is both external and internal should be complete. External silence relates to place and time; internal silence to the heart.

It is sometimes possible to obtain a deep external silence in terms of a secluded place or a large and properly ordered building and this should be welcomed when given and is needed at certain crisis periods of life. But for the most part we have to be content with a simpler and more immediate condition of this kind of silence. It is possible by using a prayer mat which gives a small space of silence and when respected can go very deep. It can be obtained by the use of one room. Whatever is possible should be set aside for the purpose of silence only and not used in any other way. This applies particularly to the prayer mat and to the room. If this is done faithfully then the small place of silence becomes a centre of deep peace, always ready to receive the one who guards it. In this small space the voice of God can be heard. Such a simple external place of silence can be seen to be used on Victoria station in Bombay where in the midst of vast crowds the contemplative lays out his mat and at once enters a silence which is respected by those who walk round his self-made oasis.

The internal silence of the heart is a creation of the imagination. It needs an image of a silent place like a lake or a mountain and then the mind withdraws to that place and finds a deep, internal silence. This is what is implied by the psalmist who advises the contemplative 'to commune in his own heart and in his chamber and be still'. It is what our Lord referred to when he commanded his disciples to shut the door and enter into themselves in their prayer. The ability to do this comes with practice on a few carefully chosen images and also from slow movements such as the T'ai Chi Ch'uan. Walking can also bring one quickly to this inner silence.

Listening to the Word speaking in His many forms is the fruit of silence. It begins as internal reflection during which the reason is used and a state of colloquy encouraged. Slow reading is also helpful. But this is the beginning of the process of listening. It should develop into an opening of the throat centre and a passive attention to the Word who speaks. This is rarely a question of listening to words. The speech of the Word is both in sounds and in silence and is heard as much through the formation of images as in words. The verbal sound in the mount of Transfiguration came as the climax of other forms of listening. There was an attention to the glory of the

Lord, to the movement of internal thinking, to the recollection of the teaching of the law and the prophets and then the silence of the shadow of the cloud: all these experiences required a listening attention, a focusing of all the senses and then came the clarity of understanding in the verbal form. This kind of listening is not easy in an environment in which we are bombarded by so many babel sounds, but once the word has been recognised it can be distinguished in the heart speaking continuously in its many forms.

(*ii*) *Emotional harmony.* Patanjali says that one of the forms of affirmation is contentment. That implies a harmony of the different emotional faculties of the heart in union with God. These emotional faculties share the fragmentation of the ego and are found in a tension of opposites. In the Eastern tradition this takes the form of over-action (rajas) competing with inertia (tamas) and in the Western tradition of aggression competing with aversion and the unbalanced disharmony of grief and joy of hope and fear. So far from being a house of prayer the heart is what our Lord called a den of robbers, a place of conflict. In order to respond to the Lord who indwells the heart this war has to be converted into peace, into what Patanjali calls a state of contentment and this is a long process of response to the work of the indwelling Spirit of peace.

That is the fundamental principle. The achievement of contentment which leads to contemplative union is not the result of our unaided efforts. It is primarily the work of the risen Christ in the heart. He meets the disciples after the resurrection and his salutation of peace is His first gift to them. The Eastern symbol of the Lord of the dance teaches this same truth. The Lord dances in the heart and his creative dance brings peace when the heart itself allows the transformation to take place.

The human response to the divine work is a discipline of mastering the emotions by contemplating their presence and working in the lives of those who have most completely harmonised them. For Christians this means meditation on the Christ of the gospels and Christ in His saints. Other traditions have other personalities. This meditation differs from the ordinary meditation in which the external features of the character are considered. It penetrates to their emotions and practises making these emotions personal. The best example of this exercise in Western spirituality is the psalms where the whole range of emotions is expressed, and where they are sung these emotions can be absorbed with even greater intensity. Another way in which the contemplative use of the emotions can be practised is in dreams. Dreams provide an environment for uninhibited exercise of the emotions. In them the dangerous emotions like anger and

108

grief can be fully used and in this free use repressions are overcome and a more mature balance obtained. Dreams cannot be completely controlled but in proportion as the emotions are exercised in meditation so they will in dreams come more under control. Colour, sound, feelings are all raw materials for this kind of meditation and they should be used as alternative themes of meditation to the Christ of the gospels or the saints of tradition.

Meditation on the emotions is one of many ways of gaining control and harmony. This control is still further deepened in relationships with others and the actions of ordinary life. The contemplative must be unafraid of making the closest emotional relationships with others. He can practise this in corporate meditations and when mastered in this form he can further develop the relationship in terms of touch and other physical means. Even the closest touch, once emotional mastery is established, will lift the heart rather than the merely sensual organs into harmony. It is very important to undertake this kind of training with those who have the same end in view and then together emotional stability can be reached. Contentment such as Patanjali refers to is not the result of emotional withdrawal but of emotional engagement at the deepest levels with others. Contemplation does not reduce life in any of its forms: it intensifies every part of life and transfigures it into God.

(iii) Contemplative activity. In his summary of preliminary training for contemplation Patanjali includes the same three actions as are mentioned in the last three acts of the five observances, that is austerity, self-study and devotion to the Lord. But in this present context these actions take on another form. They are more positive and they penetrate deeper to the springs of action. It is no longer so much a case of self-induced activity as activity energised in members of the body of Christ through the Spirit. We see this taking place in the case of the disciples on the mount of Transfiguration. In the first part of the mystery much of their action emanates from themselves and bears all the marks of inadequacy. There is the confidence in St. Peter's suggestion that three tents should be built to confine the glory and then the fear and uncertainty. But when they enter into closer union with Christ which is symbolised by their entry into the cloud this inadequacy disappears and they come under divine control. The same transformation takes place as the contemplative at this stage of training loses his self-confidence and comes increasingly under the control of the Spirit as he performs the same actions he once did on his own.

This coming under the control of the Spirit is part of the general growth towards 'wise passiveness'. It can be stimulated by doing the same physical disciplines as have already been described with greater reliance on the Spirit. One of the ways of doing this is to make much more use of the breathing in each of the postures, using the breathing rhythm to control the pace of action and keeping the attention fixed on the Spirit as each movement is done. This can be transferred from the postures to every action of life so that whatever is done in word or deed is done in the name of the Lord Jesus. This usually results in a slowing down of the pace of movement and action and the practice of pausing before and after action to feel the movement of the Spirit. It grows especially in doing the T'ai Chi Ch'uan, no longer as a self-controlled dance, but as a co-operation with the Lord who performs it in the heart.

In self-study, especially the study of Scripture, the growth is towards a deeper understanding of the meaning behind the words. Having mastered the literal meaning the contemplative goes into the deeper traditional meanings described as the spiritual and moral meanings and passes beyond the work of the particular writer to the presence of the inspiring Spirit. This is not a denial of the preliminary form of study but a development of it. The disciples on the mount of Transfiguration were already aware of the written law and the teaching of the prophets. On the mountain they saw them in a deeper context, their relationship to Christ, and this led them on to the spiritual implications behind them which were fulfilled in Christ. Such deeper study applies to other materials as well. A new light shines on the old writings.

This new light does more than illuminate the material studied. It illuminates the mystery of the total self. The ego shows up more clearly. Its inadequate self-structures such as tents to contain the self are more quickly discriminated and the true Self shines with a dazzling clarity. It is not that the total self is more clearly understood but more clearly revealed and the contemplative finds himself going through the ego-self to the Lord-self with greater confidence. Faith grows from the dark night into the clear dawn.

One of the most significant developments in the mature use of the preliminary material takes place in prayer. Devotion to the words of the divine Office becomes less and more freedom exercised to meet the growing union with the Lord. We live in a significant stage of both corporate and individual growth in this modification of vocal prayer. The Church and its members have claimed their right to pray as they can and not as an old tradition decreed. There is still a great deal of courageous experiment to be done with this material but freedom to do this has been won and now it remains to enter upon it. In the east, in the bakti form of yoga this freedom has never been lost. Every man has been free to make up his own prayers and speak to God. We are beginning to learn how to use this freedom. It means that individuals must frequently examine their forms of vocal prayer and prune and reshape them. The Church and each congregation must do the same. In the use of this material we have to learn how to match our mood with the words we use. In the West the charismatic movement has opened new doors but we have still to learn how to go through them and use the freedom which lies beyond. True devotional freedom will never be mere license and the laws of art and beauty will still control our approach to God. But every form of prayer should be a venture into the unknown and there should be a new creation when it has been done. The inspiration of the theatre has still much to teach those who give themselves to the worship of God.

Preliminary training for contemplation is concerned with work done in a special way and this is true with the advanced training which more completely uses work, both as a means of contemplation and as a preparation for it. Perhaps this happens by changing the form of work. All work should be contemplative material but with growth some work becomes more appropriate than others. For instance, the musician can play any instrument but as his skill increases so he needs the finer instrument for his task. The disciples began as fishermen and as fishermen they found and began to contemplate Christ. But as they grew so this contemplation was done, no longer as mere fishermen but as fishers of men. Choosing the appropriate work for contemplation in its advanced stages is a great responsibility. It often means abandoning the work done until now. Many people in middle life should follow the example of our father Abraham and go into another land. Even before middle life younger people should be prepared to take this risk. In the East one's life's work is not unchangeable. There are definite changes required to meet different stages of life. The student becomes the householder and the householder becomes the sunnyasi and all because he has grown in contemplating God. It may be said that advanced contemplative work should be in the direction of increasing simplicity. Of all forms of work manual work is the most complete as a training for contemplative prayer. We find the disciples returning to this work after the resurrection and St. Paul never lost his skill as a tent-maker and under that discipline developed his most intense contemplative insights. It is important to be able to distinguish the signs for making the change and for choosing something else. When work loses its power to claim our full attention, when we can see through it and it no longer provides a kind of koan situation to stretch the mind, when our energies turn elsewhere then we should not too quickly reach for the energising pills but look towards new horizons and loosen the cords of our tents. The contemplative is essentially a pilgrim and not

111

a man of cities and city organisation. This is most apparent in his need for work changes and for wide horizons. We ignore these at the peril of our sound growth in contemplation and our mental and physical health.

2

CONTEMPLATION IN THE HEART

The description of the Transfiguration is introduced with the statement that the Lord took the three disciples into a high mountain, apart and alone. The preposition used is *eis* which can well mean into the mountain and always there have been at least two interpretations of the experience. It could well have been an external experience of mountaineering with a vision at the summit but equally well it could have been an inner contemplative experience shared with Christ in the heart. If we are to have this experience there is no doubt that the second of these experiences is the one we must look for. We must reproduce the Transfiguration in the heart.

The heart is the Bible word for the spiritual centre of man, the place where God dwells most intimately and is to be found. It also describes a nexus of spiritual faculties of emotion, insight and will with which this meeting with God is established. St. Peter goes further and speaks of the 'hidden man of the heart' (1 Peter 3 : 4), thereby implying that these faculties are organised into a new humanity. This is confirmed by St. Paul's teaching about the new man and the spiritual body. The heart is more than a centre, more than a nexus of faculties: it is the embryo of a new creation and it is with this organ that we share in proportion to its growth in the Transfiguration experience.

Finding the heart centre is one of the most important discoveries of every contemplative and is the essential beginning of his spiritual life. This discovery is not made through instruction from someone else, nor by mere rational and discursive methods. The heart centre cannot be geographically located. It is an action involving all the senses and emotions. This leads to deep experiences of grief, hope, fear and joy and comes to fruition in love. It is a discovery controlled by the Lord Himself who takes each and leads him into the mountain where the secret of His own heart is to be found. Of all the senses in this exploration the sense of touch is the most important. St. Thomas was ordered to reach hither his finger and touch the hands and to stretch out his hand and thrust it into the side and in this way He found the Lord's heart and the secret of His resurrection life. It can

112

be said that where the image of the beloved forms there is the heart; where the heart-break of grief is, there is the heart; where the throb of joy is, there is the heart; where hope is strong, there is the heart. All the experiences of life point to this centre and it is in enduring them in all their variety that this primal discovery is made.

Mother Julian in the tenth revelation of her *Revelations of Divine Love* gives a still deeper insight into the mystery of heart centre when she sees the human heart centre intimately connected with the heart of the Lord Himself. She writes: 'With good cheer our good Lord looked into his side, and beheld with joy; and with his sweet looking, he led forth the understanding of his creature by the same wound into his side within. And there he shewed a fair and delectable place, and large enough for all mankind that shall be saved, and rest in peace and love: and therewith he brought to mind his death worthy blood, and his precious water which he let pour forth for love. And with the sweet beholding he shewed his blessed heart cloven in two; and with his enjoying he shewed to my understanding in part the blessedful Godhead, as far forth as he would at that time strengthen the poor soul for to understand, as it may be said; that is to mean, the endless love that was without beginning, and is, and shall be ever' (*Revelations of Divine Love*, p. 63, Kegan Paul, 1902).

For Mother Julian going into the high mountain was entering into the Lord Himself.

There is a close parallel to this teaching in Patanjali's Yoga Sutras once it is accepted that the word corresponding to the Bible concept of the heart is his word *chitta*, often inadequately translated as the mind. For the chitta is the basic raw material of man, the instrument through which he makes a dwelling place for God, the eye through which he sees the Purusha and shares his life. Fortunately there is no need to argue either against or in favour of this interpretation. All that is needed is to share in the training of the heart and the chitta to make it capable of experiencing the Transfiguration and the in-dwelling Lord.

Before considering this training one further point needs to be made. For Patanjali and his tradition the heart is a centre of several focuses of consciousness. There are the lower centres relating to physical life, sexual life and the emotions, and the higher intellectual centres relating to reason, insight and union. The heart centre stands between them and draws on their life and energy. It can only function with full power when there is an unimpeded relationship between all these parts of human life. This may sound very foreign to our present way of thinking but it corresponds very nearly to the division of the parts of the spiritual and physical life of man as given by St. Thomas Aquinas. He writes of the vegetative, the sensitive, the appetitive and

113

the moving parts of the soul and over all the intellect. It is not difficult to see a close relationship between this picture and the picture of the centres given in the eastern tradition. What it emphasises is that into the heart centre are fed all the other experiences of life, that at this centre they are arranged and renewed and that through this reorganisation of the heart centre the whole man is remade and becomes capable of the vision of God.

Patanjali gives us a brief training of the heart for the early parts of its transformation. These are concerned with stillness and union with the indwelling Spirit. They come under the third and fourth limbs of the discipline of the eight limbs and are described as āsana and prānāyāma. There is much in his brief teaching applicable to our own training of the heart and we shall consider the teaching and its application. But more important still is the fact that this training is itself a form of contemplative prayer and raises the heart to a deep awareness of its indwelling Lord. One of the catastrophes of the modern cult of yoga in the West is the misuse of these two techniques for purely physical reasons and of practising methods of preparing the heart for contemplation as merely a way of prolonging youth and retaining a youthful figure. It is like the present-day use of Christianity as a way of social improvement instead of the road to the vision of God. The retribution which must follow this misuse is only all too clear. We shall consider these two techniques as taught by Patanjali under the headings of contemplative stillness and contemplative movement.

1. CONTEMPLATIVE STILLNESS IN THE HEART. The heart in its physical form is in continuous movement. When in health this movement is rhythmical and regular. In ill-health it is unrhythmical and irregular. But the admonition to the contemplative is to be still and the promise for this stillness is to know the Lord. This is one of the lessons of the Transfiguration. In movement the disciples came to a preliminary knowledge of the Lord. In the stillness of the summit they saw His glory.

Patanjali describes the way to this stillness in three brief sutras on the subject of āsanas.

The word āsana which is most often translated by the word posture means much more than that. It certainly does not mean a series of gymnastic movements. Āsana comes from the sanskrit word ās which means to sit. It is primarily a sitting posture for prayer and is only indirectly connected with what are called the postures of hatha yoga. There are many of these sitting postures: the lotus seat (padmāsana), the adept's seat (siddhāsana), the pleasant seat (sukhāsana), the auspicious seat (swastikāsana), the hero posture (virāsana),

114

the adamantine pose (vajrāsana). These are meditation postures because they can be held for a long time. It is about these that Patanjali writes in the three sutras we shall now consider. He says:

2 : 46   The sitting position should be firm and pleasant.
2 : 47   Sitting positions are achieved by relaxation of tension and meditation on the eternity of God (ananta).
2 : 48   When the sitting posture is mastered opposites such as heat and cold do not disturb the contemplative.

The sitting position is outwardly expressed by one of the meditation postures. It is essential to find one suitable and to master it. There are a variety to choose from and there is no need to limit oneself to the classic yoga postures which for some may be unsuitable. For instance sitting on a straight-back chair may be most effective for some people or the use of a prayer stool. The important requirement is physical stillness and the ability to hold the position for at least half an hour.

The more important aspect of the sitting posture is the inward stillness of the man of the heart. It is about this inner stillness that Patanjali is most concerned. At this stage of advanced training it can be assumed that a physical posture has been mastered: we are now concentrating on the attainment of this stillness of heart.

The experience to aim at is firmness and enjoyment. When the body and heart are in the right meditative posture these two experiences will be felt. Firmness comes from balance in gravity and in God: enjoyment from abandonment to environment and to the divine will. This experience does not come all at once and even when it begins there is still need for much growth. We grow into firmness and enjoyment by being ready to leave previous achievements and move into new ones. The man of the heart like the physical body will find this experience in the structure of the cross. In imagination it is necessary to see the cross as the essential shape of the spiritual body and to relax in its lines of support. This takes some time to become habitual but it is the lesson to master in reaching the first of Patanjali's conditions of contemplative stillness.

Patanjali gives two important actions for reaching the inner stillness: relaxation of tension and meditation on the eternity of God. Relaxation is the result of moving into tension. This may be physical pain: it will certainly be some form of preliminary inner conflict. These should not be artificially reduced or avoided but met like the athlete meets the difficulties of his course. What has to be discovered is the stillness at the heart of the pain. Discovering this place is like finding the peace at the heart of conflict. It is not merely an intellectual problem to be solved by asking and answering the

115

right questions. The point of inner peace is discovered by using all the senses and through the guidance of the indwelling Spirit. The way to it is through the pain rather than around it. But this journey is gradual and the contemplative needs to be sensitive to his 'pain ceiling' and not to go beyond it. He can be constantly probing the boundaries but without presumptuously going beyond the limits of his strength. In this way he advances the centre of balance between pain and relaxation. But there must always be a tension. The peace is found midway between the tension and the relaxation and never by the obliteration of either.

In this peace all the faculties are engaged. It is a peace of body, a balance of emotions and a control of mind. Patanjali understands that mind tension arises from trying to hold the mind tense for too long on a single problem. What is God like, why does He act in this way, what am I to become? And he cuts through all these limitations by requiring the mind to be emptied by contemplating the eternity of God. This eternity, because it cannot be envisaged, saves the mind from the exhaustion of trying to reach conclusions and like the koan teaches it to live with contradictions and the unknown. It is an exercise in emptying the mind and holding it open. To begin with it is often helpful to envisage large spaces such as a desert or the sky or the sea and then to move further into the endless. Putting the eyes out of focus by holding them on to the tip of the nose and then relaxing the muscles is also helpful. In this way the mind is gradually emptied and then held empty. This leads to a deep silence of the heart. It was the state to which the disciples were led when the shadow of the cloud covered them and the figures they had previously seen were absorbed into it. When they came out they did so with the brain completely rested and the eyes able to penetrate to the truth so deeply that they saw Jesus only.

Reaching the stillness of the heart is one thing: maintaining this stillness is another. Patanjali concludes his direction about sitting by showing how this is done. The heart is not shielded from distractions. Its stillness is tested by being once more exposed to them and in doing so it is strengthened to remain in an inner balance of stillness. So our Lord returns to the chaos at the foot of the mountain but His inner stillness is unshaken and so many of the Desert Fathers like St. Antony, having attained peace of heart, went back into the world to share it. Strengthening the heart in its stillness needs to be done gradually and without presumption. We should not look for tests beyond our strength as the Lord's prayer teaches us. We should not want to be led into tests beyond our strength for the sake of bravado. We should accept the tests given and use them to keep our heart in stillness. Sometimes these will take an inner form in terms of doubts

116

or anxieties: sometimes they will be an external demand on our peace. Like our Lord in the boat during the storm we should preserve the inner peace unshaken and use it not to leave our environment unchanged but to share with it our inner peace. Once true peace and stillness of heart have been achieved they cannot be shaken provided we keep our seat firm and centre ourselves in God. This is the supreme condition of contemplation. It is not a special environment conducive to peace and order but the world just as it is confronted by our heart trained in stillness through the mastery of this art of both physical and spiritual peace.

2. CONTEMPLATIVE MOVEMENT IN THE HEART. The man of the heart is alive and therefore moves but the movement is most often erratic and self-willed. The true movement of the heart is the movement of the Holy Spirit brooding over it and one form of contemplation is sensing His movement and responding.

We can watch the disciples beginning to do this during the Transfiguration. They pass through different emotions of hope, fear, grief and come to the harmony of joy within the cloud. These are all forms of heart movement. They are all the energy of the Spirit being used in different ways. The fourth limb of Patanjali's advanced training for contemplation teaches the way the heart may be trained to respond to the energy of the universe. He calls it prānāyāma.

Prānā is the sanskrit name for the energy of the universe. It is much more than we mean by breath and breathing, although breath and breathing are signs of this energy. In the Western tradition there is a similar relationship between the Spirit energy of the universe and breath with an identity of name for both. But this does not mean that prānāyāma is merely concerned with breath control. In its preliminary form this discipline is the mastery of good natural breathing habits but that is the beginning of the essential discipline which is that of bringing the heart into harmony with the Spirit. To do this we need to probe into the mystery of the presence and work of the Spirit and ourselves as His instruments and centres of indwelling.

St. John's gospel is as much the gospel of the Spirit as the gospel of Christ. In this mature account of the incarnation St. John reveals the Spirit in His relationship with the Lord and we find that this relationship is extremely close. He indwells the Word and is the life of the Word; He proceeds from the Word and communicates the Word to believers; He indwells believers and opens their hearts to understand the divine Word and transforms them into His likeness. All this goes on with increasing intensity as the heart responds to His presence and work.

We are the work of the Spirit. He comes to us, communicates the

117

risen Christ and transfigures us gradually into the present likeness of the glorified Christ. This we see Him doing in miniature to the disciples as they shared the Transfiguration. They share in the presence of the cloud which is the sign of the Spirit's presence. They enter into that cloud and are taken into the very being of Christ. They are so transformed that when the Father's voice proclaims the presence of the beloved Son the disciples are included in that mystery. All this work the Spirit now does inwardly in the heart. It is to be manifested outwardly through our own death and resurrection. Knowing this we have a present work of co-operation with the Spirit to complete and in doing this we can find much help from the instructions about prānāyāma given to us by Patanjali. He writes of this practice as follows:

2 : 49   When sitting has been mastered prānāyāma follows.
2 : 50   Prānāyāma is external, internal or suppressed modification. It is regulated by place, time and number, and grows in length and subtlety.
2 : 51   The fourth form of prānāyāma is a transcending of the ordinary in-out breathing.
2 : 52   Through mastery of prānāyāma the veil over the inner light is removed.
2 : 53   Then the brain becomes capable of concentration.

The discipline of prānāyāma for contemplation has been much misunderstood and exploited. One remembers an experience of an Indian, coming to teach methods of what he called yogic breathing, armed with instructions for the way to resuscitate a patient after heavy electric shock. In India there are wonder workers who practice forms of artificial breath control which slow down the pulse and reduce the breathing to the point of simulating death. None of these exaggerations finds any support in the sutras just quoted about prānāyāma. Patanjali links this discipline with the mastery of a sitting posture. He then names four ways of control: external, internal, suppressed and suspended. The results have nothing to do with spectacular forms of breathing control. These are not so much as mentioned. What follows is the illumination of the heart and the steadying of the mind for concentration. All this is very different from the excessive concentration on purely physical forms of breathing which unfortunately has obscured the reality of this training.

This does not mean that there is not in its preliminary stages a connection between prānāyāma and breathing. This has already been described in detail. It is a form of hygiene practised by every well-trained Indian in the early morning as part of the morning ablutions. This is a process of clearing the nasal passages and inducing deep breathing. In the West it compares with the open-window technique and the deep breathing exercises which conduce to physical health. Something of this kind is always necessary but it is not part of Patanjali's teaching in these sutras. Here he is concerned with a relationship with the energy of the universe, prāna, and the ways in which this relationship may be established and developed.

In the Western tradition the parallel to prāna is the doctrine of the Holy Spirit, the Lord, the Giver of Life, who proceeds from the Father and the Son who with the Father and the Son is worshipped and glorified, who spoke by the prophets. This identifies the energy of the universe with the Holy Spirit and then goes on to deepen the teaching by insisting that the Spirit is personal, divine and communicating. All this gives a deeper reality to the relationship which is possible with Him through the ways indicated in the sutras, that is externally, internally, by suppression and suspension.

The Spirit is present and works externally. He is the Lord of the living universe and can be seen through the vast system of creation He continually animates. He is also the Spirit of Christ in the gospels and can be seen working through Him. He is the power of the sacraments and sanctifies the Church. He energises the saints. Through all these external forms the Spirit is present and revealed and the first part of prānāyāma is to contemplate Him there. This comes from stillness of posture and concentration on one of the many ways in which He is revealed. It involves the study of the scriptures, meditation on the gospel images of Christ, on the mysteries of that shrine of the Holy Spirit, the virgin Mary, appropriation of the signs and spiritual graces of the sacraments and participation in the life of creation, sharing in the universal praise of all the creatures. This is both stillness and movement, for the Spirit we contemplate is living and therefore moves in constant rhythm between the Father and the Son and throughout all creation. The movement is the movement of perfect love and it is that rhythm we assimilate as we contemplate the Spirit present and working outside of ourselves.

But we are temples of the Spirit who lives within us and so another form of prānāyāma is making contact with the presence and life of the Spirit in the heart. In the heart He talks of the things belonging to the Lord and reveals them, and so part of our response to the indwelling Spirit is listening to His voice and assimilating His interpretation of the truth. This requires the most delicate receptivity. Again the Spirit works in the heart, carrying out an individual work of transfiguration. To this we have to respond and that leads to the need of understanding His methods of working, the virtues and gifts He infuses and the fruit His presence brings forth. The detailed

119

descriptions of the theological and cardinal virtues, the analysis of the gifts which occupy such a large part in the exposition of Christian truth in the second part of the *Summa* are of great importance and in some way they must be mastered if there is to be an intelligent co-operation with the Spirit. The tragedy of so much of the present charismatic movement is that the presence of the Spirit has been recognised in the heart by so many enthusiastic people without the training needed to take their share in His work. It is one thing to have re-discovered the inner power of God; the other need is to re-discover the knowledge of the working of this power which has been communicated to us through the old traditions. It will be a tragedy if the Church has to re-live the past mistakes of pelagianism, quietism, enthusiasm, jansenism because the experience of the past has been ignored by those who need it most or withheld from them. The obvious signs of a renewal of this form of prāṇāyāma brings with them the urgency of a return to the wisdom of the saints who taught how this inward co-operation with the Spirit-Lord could be achieved.

The suppression to which Patanjali refers as a form of prāṇāyāma is not a suppression of the divine Spirit but the subordination of the human spirit to Him. This is a very important exercise and without mastery of this relationship a most dangerous situation can arise. The history of contemplation is littered with the ruins of contemplatives who have tried to exploit the Spirit to their own ends. We see this taking place in the Acts of the Apostles when the sons of Sceva tried to impose their will on the Spirit (Acts 19). Aldous Huxley in his great book, *Grey Eminence* describes this same tragedy in detail. Only as instruments and not as manipulators must we live in the Spirit. We can watch our Lord training His disciples in the exercises of surrender. On the mountain they are reduced to impotence before being taken into the cloud. St. Paul says that when he is weak then he is most strong because most responsive to the Spirit. The right posture is a great help towards this surrender. All of the yoga postures can be used to make the will supple and surrendered. The more advanced forms of this training come inwardly by learning to surrender in obedience to the will of another, by identifying with the self-emptying of our Lord, by cultivating gentleness within and towards others. The exercise of 'waiting upon the Lord' both in prayer and before action is an effective training of the will in surrender to the Spirit.

The final and most complete form of prāṇāyāma is the transcending of all self-controlled action for action controlled by the Spirit. This is the state described by St. Paul when he writes: 'I live; yet no longer I. Christ lives in me' (Galatians 2 : 20). This is the state revealed by the Transfiguration when the divine voice recognises no one but the beloved Son and all are included in Him. St. Paul in his description of the body of Christ sees the whole body, made up of many members, all of whom have mastered their own will, coming under the control of the divine Spirit. In achieving this final state of prānāyāma some form of community life is essential, for the most subtle forms of self will can only be destroyed through the influence of other personalities on one's own; and the most developed forms of response to the Spirit can only be learnt by sharing intimately life with others. This is where regular acts of corporate contemplative prayer are so important. It is in this prayer that self-will is most intensely mastered and reaction to the wills of others achieved. All this prepares for the final death of the self in preparation for its resurrection in the Lord.

Doing the T'ai Chi Ch'uan is one of the most effective and practical ways of learning this transcending of self by the Spirit and when it is done with a few others it acts even more powerfully. From beginning to end this dance is a contemplation of the Spirit. The movements are entirely given and generated from the Spirit centre of the body and the maintenance of an inner stillness emphasises that total surrender of self-inspired movement which is so essential for this final state of prānāyāma. This is the most advanced form of training we have found for this stage of prānāyāma and one that most effectively produces the two results of illumination and strength.

In the Eastern tradition there is a recognition of the presence in the heart of what is called the uncreated light or the light of the heart (jyotis). This is part of the Christian tradition where St. John says that 'the true light enlightens every man'. This light is present in all and obscured in most. It is obscured by the pseudo-constructions of the ego-self. Prānāyāma is the discipline that breaks down these structures and trains the ego to be no longer self-willed but surrendered to the Spirit. In proportion as this is achieved the heart becomes translucent to the light. This is one of the important results of the Transfiguration. Our Lord's face and clothes shine because the impediments to the inner light have gone. This luminosity is a sign that contemplation has been realised and in the east it is sufficient for the contemplative to reveal this light to be believed. The practice of giving a darshana of the renewed self is all that is asked from a holy man. He does not have to preach long sermons or answer trivial questions. He uncovers the light. The world waits for this manifestation by the Church and only as the Church masters the whole of the discipline of prānāyāma will it be able to give what is so urgently needed.

Patanjali does not mention the kundalini allegory in the sutras but he does recommend the practice of meditation on the centres of

121

consciousness which is an essential part of the allegory. This allegory has unfortunately been dismissed by some as merely an attempt to allegorise the process of sexual sublimation. This is undoubtedly partly true and for the practice of continence or brahmachārya it is invaluable. But continence is no more than the negative side of the great positive concentration of all energy in the Holy Spirit which is the essence of prānāyāma. This concentration of energy in the heart involves the lifting of sexuality and all other energy forms into this centre and the instrument for this is prānāyāma. By directing energy into the heart the whole body is revitalised and strengthened. In the East such symbols as the phallic symbol are used to direct the attention for this purpose and the energy is often stimulated through the help of a really enlightened guru. This was the experience of Vivekananda and Rāmakrishna.

In the West the same process is undertaken under different symbolism. Here the symbolism of the spiritual marriage, of Christ as the bridegroom of the soul, of the Song of Songs replaces the kundalini allegory and it is much richer and much more apparent than in the ambiguities of the east. It is a great loss to normal spiritual development that so much of this great tradition has been hidden under negative interpretations of chastity and some practice of prānāyāma is needed to correct the balance. The greatest symbol of the Holy Spirit for this purpose is the tongue of flame and the most complete form of His energy is love. In the contemplation in the heart through movement much practice is needed in the art of the giving and receiving of love in all its forms in Christ. He is the master of love and His love is the Holy Spirit. His love takes all forms in proportion to our capacity to respond. There is in Him the fulness of physical love (eros), of brotherly love (philadelphia) of community love (sterge) and of divine love (agape). And all have to be mastered in their appropriate ways. This is the climax of contemplation in the heart, this is its supreme movement. There are many signs that the present so-called permissive Society is breaking free from the limitations of love taught by an earlier generation and whether it is able to move into the full form of love depends on how far the total doctrine of the spiritual marriage is practised and taught in this contemplation in the heart.

3. CONTEMPLATIVE DETACHMENT. The heart is a centre of conflicting images some of which arise from within itself and others from the contact of the senses with outside. Our Lord by taking the three disciples into the mountain removed them from contact with many of the sources of outside distraction and then through the cloud of glory burnt up many of those from within. Through these experiences they reached an intense state of contemplative detachment and saw the divine glory. Detachment of some kind has always been part of the Western spiritual tradition. In the early forms it was the desert of the Fathers; later the monasteries; and in the teaching of St. John of the Cross the experience of the dark nights of sense and spirit.

Patanjali and the Eastern tradition share this teaching in the exercise of sense-withdrawal (pratyahāra). He includes it under the fifth limb of the eight limbs and describes it in this way:

2 : 54   Sense-withdrawal (pratyahāra) is an exercise by which the sense organs are withdrawn from their outside objects and centred in the heart.

This is a twofold process: a withdrawal from outside and a concentration within. In the *Bhagavad Gita* the action is described under the image of a tortoise:

'The tortoise can draw in his legs:
The seer can draw in his senses.
I call him illumined.'

This is a withdrawal of all the senses: the eyes are withdrawn by putting them out of focus, looking at the tip of the nose and then closed; the ears are withdrawn from all outside sounds; the nose from smell, the hands from touch, the tongue from taste. This is a long and gradual process which in its early stages is stimulated by physical withdrawal through external silence and what is called the custody of the eyes. As more control is gained so the physical withdrawal becomes less necessary. It is a process which reaches completion at death. It is helpful to adopt a physical posture for a daily exercise in withdrawal and the hands folded across the chest is useful as a reminder that the doors of the heart must be shut. Then a period of concentration and withdrawal on each sense in turn increases the intensity of the detachment. In this way the outer senses are disconnected. The process has then to be transferred to the inner senses.

The inner senses are called in the East the tanmātras. Through them the sense stimulations from outside are converted into inner feelings. When outside stimulation is removed these tend to become more powerful and unless they are firmly controlled the practice of external withdrawal can do no more than increase the power of the internal images in the heart, giving them the proportions of fantasy and delusion. It may well be that some schizophrenic states are the result of disturbing the outer sense experiences without paying attention to the inner corrections this requires. For the purposes of contemplation this means paying serious attention to what St. John of the Cross writes about locutions and interior visions. These have to be ignored with at least as much resolution as the external sense stimulators. The process is very much the same: recognition of the stimulation and then withdrawal of the internal sense from it. This comes both from practice and from inner help. Just as the disciples were helped to withdraw by the shadow of the cloud so for the contemplative there is help in the form of the 'cloud of unknowing' or what Patanjali calls 'the rain cloud of virtue'. This reduces the power of the inner senses and overshadows some of the sources of stimulation. This should be welcomed when it comes in the form of a reduced power of the senses and as far as possible sense stimulators like spectacles and hearing aids should be used with the greatest economy. Perhaps some of the main discontents of middle life arise from this artificial stimulation of the external and internal senses and the failure to accept their diminishments as the opportunity for a more intense withdrawal and a more active contemplative life. This is a form of fasting which has been given too little attention in these days of the enlargement of the range of the senses through the invention of modern scientific instruments.

Sense-withdrawal both external and internal does not create a vacuum but an opportunity. The opportunity is the chance to centre more completely on the loving and indwelling Being of God. This Being is in one sense an absence of sense stimulation since God is without 'body, parts or passions' and it is only when the heart is most free from sense stimulation that it can most completely centre on God in the heart. This centring is rightly recognised by St. John of the Cross as a dark night and in the East there is much insight in the teaching that part of the experience of God is this negative darkness of nirvāna. What is important to remember is that although this darkness is without forms and images it is vibrant with life and love; for God is both perfect life and love. The heart centres around a cloud which to begin with is shadow but within alive with the love of God. In this state of undisturbed stillness the great emotions of love, hope, joy, grief and fear can be brought into balance and simplified into a state of loving joy. This is the most developed stage in this degree of contemplation, a contemplation of joy, what Patanjali and his tradition calls the insight of happiness (sānanda samādhi). We can hear this coming out of the cloud on the mount of Transfiguration when the voice proclaims not merely the Son but the beloved Son.

The contemplation of detachment is often forgotten or passed through too quickly and the result is that one of the important patterns of life is missed. St. Paul reminds us that we live in a rhythm of decay and renewal, the old man decays the new man is renewed day by day; and nowhere is this process more clearly manifest than in the rhythm of human life. Almost every ten years we are physically and mentally required to decide our attitude to the next phase of sense withdrawal as the senses change in their capacity to respond to outside stimulation and the feeling to their interior counterparts. Unless we master the art of sensitive response to these conditions we are exposed to nervous breakdown or mental illness. Not only is this a contemplative opportunity: it is also a serious danger which can only be averted by training in awareness of the symptoms and skill in making the needed adjustments. One range of sense experience ended as the disciples climbed the mount of Transfiguration and another opened for them as they came down. So with ourselves. Skill in handling this limb of the eight limbs of yoga will not only lead to deep contemplative experience: it will guard us from those breakdown dangers to which so many of the untrained people waiting for our Lord in the plain succumbed.

3

CONTEMPLATION WITH IMAGES

In his great book, *The Glass of Vision*, Dr. Farrer wrote: 'The stuff of inspiration is living images.... If we set about our quest in that way (hunting for theological propositions) we close our ears to the voice of scripture. The modern tendency is to seek after historical record, whether it be the record of events, or of spiritual states in apostolic minds; it is not surprising if it fails to find either the voice of God, or the substance of supernatural mystery. We have to listen to the Spirit speaking divine things: and the way to appreciate his speech is to quicken our own minds with the life of the inspired images' (*Glass of Vision*, p. 44).

Patanjali defines yoga as the control of the images in the heart and in the Transfiguration mystery we find this image-mastery taking place in the hearts of the disciples as they move into union with their transfigured Lord. So Peter moves from the image of the Lord in dazzling brightness to the image of the vessel to contain that brightness, to his own penetration into the cloud and union with the Lord. It is all a question of image and image control. This makes it of first importance that before we go on to consider the way to use and control images we shall be clear what those images are.

1. IMAGES. Patanjali distinguishes between true and false images. True images are formed by the action of the senses on an external object, by the use of right reason and under the guidance of a sound tradition (1 : 7). False images are based on a distorted sense perception, on the misuse of reason and through the influence of an unsound tradition. In the third book of the Yoga Sutras he gives a wide variety of sense objects which can be used for the formation of images, ranging from the body to every kind of created form.

When we come to the Christian tradition of images we find an even greater wealth of image forms and a more detailed analysis of the different image materials. The more important of these in scripture are given in this list together with their Greek equivalents and a short description of their forms.

Mystery (*musterion*). The most usual Christian image of this kind is contained in the sacraments. These are outward signs with inward meanings. In Christian practice there are two greater sacraments, baptism and confirmation and then five lesser sacraments, confession, matrimony, holy orders, holy unction and confirmation. This does not exhaust the meaning of sacrament, for every action which combines an outward sign and an inward meaning, such as the use of the body to express spiritual truth, can come under the meaning of sacrament.

Sign (*semeion*). This is a key word in St. John's gospel and is used to describe what in the other gospels would be called a miracle or wonder. St. John uses it to describe an action which reveals the glory of the Lord. All the ingredients which make up this kind of image are contained in the miracle at Cana of Galilee when the water was changed into wine. We have here the outer materials and the inner manifestation of the secret of the Lord.

Myth (*muthos*). This in the Bible is used to describe a story which has no basis in historical fact. Usually it refers to the legends of other religions. It is a great pity that this suspect word should have been used to describe what some modern critics have found to be the essence of the gospels. A more careful choice of word would have avoided so much suspicion and misunderstanding and would have made a deep insight much less liable to be rejected.

Parable (*parabole*). This in some ways is the New Testament equivalent to the word myth. It describes a story used to convey a truth of the kingdom. It is much used in our Lord's teaching but is found in other parts of the Bible as well. It is a form of analogy by means of a narrative.

Image (*eikon*). This is the general word in the Bible for image. It describes a creation, often the work of the imagination, through which spiritual truth and life are revealed. The great image is our Lord who is described by St. Paul as 'the image of the invisible God'. Man is also an image of God though much less adequate.

126

Idol (*eidolon*). This is a false image of God used for the purpose of worship. It was the iconoclastic controversy from A.D. 725 to A.D. 842 which forced the Church to define her attitude to the image as distinct from the idol. This was done at the second council of Nicaea (A.D. 787) where it was defined that 'the honour paid to the image passes to its original, and he that adores an image adores in it the person depicted thereby'. This means of course that not every image is suitable for the purpose of depicting God in this way and there are many rules in the Eastern Church about the form images used in this kind of worship should take.

Phantom (*phantasma*). This describes a mental misconception which arises from a distortion between the object in the mind and the senses. We find the disciples sometimes making this kind of image of our Lord and having it corrected by a sense experience such as He gave when walking on the sea or after His resurrection.

There are other words relating to images in the New Testament such as miracle (dunamis), wonder (teras) and type (tupos) but these are of lesser importance and do not add much to the image material of scripture. The words already considered in greater detail are the ones which supply the material for making images, in the heart, of the Lord.

This leads us to make the important distinction between external and internal images. External images are objects and events which have a real existence outside of ourselves. Internal images are structures of the imagination made in the heart from these external materials. They are true or false in proportion as the material used by the imagination is objectively true and the imagination operates within the limitations of sound reasoning and a valid tradition. When this happens the image in the heart is true and can be used as the Eastern Church so clearly teaches, as an instrument for making the deepest relationship with the Lord. In other words such images are the instruments of contemplative insight. To reach this state through an internal image requires a special form of control which has been described in both the Western and Eastern traditions. We shall consider this control with reference to our Transfiguration model and the teaching of Patanjali. It leads to the deepest contemplation in the heart which we have called insight contemplation.

2. INSIGHT CONTEMPLATION. At the Transfiguration the disciples were confronted with a variety of images. There were the Lord, the figures of Moses and Elijah, the cloud and the voice. These they used to fix their attention, then they tried to understand their meaning and eventually they were taken into the meaning and heart of the images as they were caught up in the cloud. These three actions, concentration, reflection and insight are to be found as the subjects of the last three limbs of Patanjali's teaching about contemplation training. He brings them together under the one word, samyama, which may be translated as a centring of the heart. We shall consider each action separately and in detail. In practice they always take place in sequence and should never be separated in making the full act of centring. They are three parts of one integral process of contemplative insight.

(i) *Concentration.* Patanjali defines concentration as 'a holding of the heart in one centre' (3 : 1). The Sanskrit phrase is desha-bandha which is literally an enclosed space and this links up with the Western images of the garden of the soul, the enclosure, the anchorhold. It is a limitation of the heart within a particular point of interest, a centring of the heart around one thing. This can be any one point, but in an act of Christian contemplative insight it will usually be one of the external images or symbols of the Lord. This external image may be visual, verbal, tactual, relating to taste or smell and drawn either from the great wealth of such images in the Bible or in the tradition of the Church. There is so great a variety to choose from that it is essential to make a limited selection and to use a small number of such centres repetitively. As such images tend to wear out it is wise to change them when they lose their power and to replace the worn-out ones with others. We live in an age of rebirth with regard to some of the older images and we should be sensitive to this movement remembering that there is a resurrection as well as a death among the images we have been accustomed to use.

The way of binding the heart to one image is both external and internal.

The external binding is done by bringing all the senses to bear on the image; the eyes, the ears, the touch, the taste, the smell and holding them in an act of strong awareness for as long as possible. This is what is done at the eucharist when the bread and the wine are elevated and it is a great mistake to end this too quickly. Sir John was wiser than sone people realise when he urged his priest to raise the host higher. The sign that the maximum physical concentration has been reached is the failure of the senses to remain at that pitch of concentration. The eyes then tend to water and the other senses fade. This is the point, not for greater effort bur for internalising the act of concentration.

The first step towards this internalisation is to close the eyes and remove the other senses from the object to the centre of the heart. At that centre an internal image of the external image will begin to form. This is work of imagination and memory and is largely outside one's own control. It is certainly not a photographic reproduction but a creative work of art which will tell much about the ego and the intensity of one's self-denial. As the internal image forms so the inner senses are concentrated upon it together with the emotions. If this is done seriously the image will become illuminated as at the transfiguration and alive. It is important to work seriously to bring about this animation of the image. The intensity of the ensuing contemplative insight depends upon the degree of life in the internal image. An inner breathing of the Spirit upon the image will help to quicken it into life. In many ways at this stage the contemplative is acting like the artist who through his creative imagination brings into being a new creation. As he makes the inner image the contemplative is exercising powers which build up the renewing of the ego-self: he is constructing that mysterious body called the spiritual body which eventually will become the new environment of his prayer, the dwelling place of his resurrection life. When Peter asked to be allowed to build three tents his insight was greater than many commentators have allowed. He was feeling after this new body which the sight of the Lord's transfigured body was inspiring him to create. In creating the imaginative image in an act of concentration the contemplative is making his contribution to that building not made with hands to which St. Paul refers in his second epistle to the Corinthians.

The climax of this stage of contemplative insight is what Patanjali describes as one-pointedness (ekāgrya) a state of undistracted attention in the heart.

(ii) *Meditation.* When the heart is centred the discursive reason is free to work. It is a great mistake to try and by-pass this mental activity by trying to reach a state of thoughtless vacuity too quickly. Some of the instant forms of contemplation imported recently to this country from the East have ignored their own traditions of logical thinking and endeavoured to simplify contemplation to the recitation of a meaningless mantra while the mind is allowed to decay. Already there are enough signs of ensuing mental disturbance to convince the discerning that this is not the way. It is quietism under another name. The mind must be fully exercised before it can use its higher powers of insight and this exercise is through the practice of discursive thinking.

We can watch the disciples using this mental activity during the Transfiguration. Having seen the Lord in glory they begin to associate Him with the other great spiritual leaders of their tradition,

129

Moses and Elijah, and they watched him in his relationship with that teaching. It is an act of discursive meditation using not words but complementary images.

Sometimes the mind is well enough furnished to do this kind of thinking on its own but more often it is wise to follow the great leaders of this kind of thought, the writers of the New Testament and especially the evangelists. This means using the internal image as a centre of thought around one of the great gospel mysteries. We can see it done by the iconographers of the Eastern Church, by the medieval cathedral builders, by the makers of the great stained-glass windows. They are all thinking the thoughts of men greater than themselves after them and expressing these old thoughts in their own new ways. This is part of that way of thinking which is called the making of remembrance (anamnesis) in the liturgy. It is worth considering carefully what this involves so that the same principles may be applied to this part of contemplative insight.

The two great moments of remembrance are the eucharist and the events of Holy Week. In both of these moments certain events of the past are recalled in order to make them present and ourselves capable of sharing in them as if they were taking place now. It has been rightly said that the act of remembrance makes the past present. Under these conditions the past is more than made present: it is made available so that the events re-presented may be shared by those who remember them. This is most obvious in the eucharist where Christ is made present in order to be shared, and in the Holy Week ceremonies the events of that week are recalled in their resurrection transfiguration so that we may share not only in the events of His passion but in the victory of His resurrection as well. In this case the events are re-enacted in the heart which through the resurrection has become the place for the indwelling and present work of the risen Christ and His Spirit.

It is with this approach that the mind meditates on the mystery symbolised by the image. The image becomes a centre of action in the heart where the mystery is made present in order to be shared. So the heart is transformed into Nazareth, Bethlehem, the mount of Transfiguration, the Upper Room, Gethsemane, the Praetorium, Calvary, the tomb, the Garden of the Resurrection, the mount of Ascension, heaven itself and the throne of the Lord; and in this heart the events are reproduced through the meditative act of remembrance to be seen and shared and to be transformed by the power of the Holy Spirit through such participation. We do not so much think past thoughts as listen to the Spirit speaking divine things and doing works of power—now. This meditative method of remembrance is an act of immense importance and should not be by-passed because it makes sometimes painful demands on our concentration and seems to hinder the simpler insights of contemplation.

Patanjali defines meditation as 'an uninterrupted flow of thought towards the object of concentration' (3 : 2). This describes meditation in its developed form. In its earlier stages the flow of thought will be far from uninterrupted and until the flow is established such helps as the repetition of a short phrase (mantra) or reflective reading will be a help. But when the mind begins to flow then these supports should be withdrawn and even the use of supplementary images dispensed with. The flow is inwards towards the object of concentration and as this object is ultimately the Word made flesh it is a constant movement towards Him as He now is. This means that the mode of thinking becomes increasingly less realistic and more imaginative and the imaginative images grow in the forms of signs and mysteries. It takes time and perseverance to train the mind to think in these ways but once mastered it is possible to lift the heart towards abstract modes of thinking which increase its capacity to make contact with the ascended Christ in what St. Teresa would call 'intellectual visions' and St. John of the Cross dispensing with images. This leads us on to the most intense form of contemplative activity, the activity of insight.

(*iii*) *Contemplative insight*. A stage is reached in the Transfiguration experience when the disciples no longer move actively towards the truth. They are taken up and led, the truth is infused under the image of the cloud which overshadows them and the voice which enlightens them about the true mystery of the Lord. Through these given experiences they are enlightened and penetrate into God. It is this kind of experience which follows the meditative activity of contemplation and leads on to what Patanjali describes as 'a union between the ego and the object of contemplation' (3 : 3).

In this brief description is summed up the essence of contemplative insight. It is more than an external looking at the Lord. It is identification with Him, what St. Paul refers to when he says, 'I live, yet no longer I; Christ lives in me'. It is a transformation of the ego structures of self and self-consciousness into union with the Lord as the true Self. This happens gradually and through various stages. They may be described as the shadow, the waiting and the identification.

(*a*) *The Shadow*. The disciples at the Transfiguration began this experience by being covered with the shadow of the cloud of glory. This is something which they accept rather than achieve by their own efforts and as meditation develops this is the experience of the contemplative. His taste for discursive thinking and images dries up and he finds himself entering into a silence without images. Patanjali divides this experience into various degrees: first there is the drying up of images (nirvitarka samādhi) then the silencing of discursive reflection (nirvichara samādhi) then the harmonising of the feelings (sānanda samādhi) and finally the experience of entering a cloud (dharma-megha samādhi). All this corresponds to the western tradition expressed in its classic form in St. John of the Cross and his teaching about the various dark nights in which certain functions of the heart are changed and transformed. This drying up of the natural faculties is an inescapable experience and often coincides with physical periods of life such as middle age and the menopause. It is something to be welcomed and used.

The important thing when this experience is reached is not to make any effort to delay it. To do this is to run into the danger of arrested spiritual development. This can have the most serious consequences. If there is no response to this inevitable growth, or opposition, then certain forces come into play and the prayer dries up or regresses. The important response is to enter into the cloud.

Entering into the cloud is first of all an act of acceptance. We permit the experience. We learn to do without images and to live with the mind still. It is a state of deep inner silence. Within this silence we should continue to practice the routine ways of vocal prayer and the physical exercises of the spiritual life should go on. These become even more important during the period of life in the shadow of the cloud for they give the contemplative something he can still do and are immensely beneficial. They balance the increasing inner stillness in which it becomes necessary to live.

(b) *Waiting*. The timing of an insight is outside human control. We can only wait for the light which brings this experience. But there is an art in the waiting. This is what tests the stillness of posture in the heart and the surrender to the Spirit. The disciples had to wait in this way. Patanjali describes a form of contemplation which is without seed and image (asamprājnata samādhi) and this is the result of waiting with the heart empty of all images and thought. It is an experience often described by the poet and artist. T. S. Eliot speaks of it as the 'still point of the turning world' and it is that point which the contemplative must occupy with inexhaustible patience if he is to move into union with the Lord. This is no aimless waiting. It is a waiting patiently for the Lord as the psalmist describes it. In this waiting the contemplative enters into that experience of God which the East describes by the word nirvāna and the West by its apophatic theology. It is God without attributes in the fullness of His loving Being. It is both emptiness and fullness, an emptying of the ego and a purifying of all emotional desire for God only. This happened when the disciples were overshadowed by the cloud. It happens at every eucharist when the outward sign is fractured and then eaten. It is then that the Lord is assimilated in the heart by faith with thanksgiving.

This is a period when the emotional life may be disturbed and some when the author resolves that 'at midnight will I rise to give thanks unto Thee'. And this is the one action that can be undertaken during this waiting. It was the action used by Christians during their vigils before the festivals. They filled in the time with singing and readings. A sound focus is here most helpful to keep the mind centred. Often some form of singing will help. In a corporate meditation it is at this stage that singing, such as plainsong alleluias, can be used. But most important is the energising of the will to acts of praise and thanksgiving. Only these are strong enough to overcome the darkness of this waiting period. It is here that the Divine Office supplies the material needed for thanksgiving which alone can overcome the depression of waiting for an unknown period in otherwise a state of complete inactivity. Some form of reading may also be used but not so that it interferes with that emptiness of mind which is the essential preliminary to its being filled with God.

(c) *The identification.* The climax of the Transfiguration is when the disciples on turning round, that is on returning to their normal ways of perception, 'saw no man save Jesus only'. They saw the whole universe as an expression of the cosmic Christ and themselves as sharing in Him. This was the experience of St. Paul and is shared by all who come to the supreme insight. They see God in all things and themselves sharing in His life. In this state the ego becomes completely receptive to the Lord. It is what St. Augustine had come to see when he wrote that God had made us for Himself and that without Him our hearts were restless until they find their rest in Him. This comes as a temporary flash of insight in its early stages and then tends to disappear. The disciples had their moment and then they had to go back to the bottom of the mountain, holding the experience in their heart while they grew stronger for the permanent state of awareness which the resurrection would later on give them. To begin with the contemplative has to be content with his partial and transitory insights but once they have been given he can never be the same. He is then always homesick for the kingdom. So this experience can be given in the early stages of contemplation and then disappear while other experience is gained. We find St. Paul returning over and over again to his first insight and using it to keep himself steady on his course.

The important fact about this experience is that the vision and the images are now given and are not the result of imagination. The word used for this in the Western tradition is infused. The experience is a

133

free gift from God. This is what is implied by the phrase dharma-megha-samādhi. It is like a rain cloud which comes from outside the control of the contemplative. What is required is a receptive co-operation with the images as they are given.

Bernard Lonergan gives a careful analysis of the process towards insight as it happens to the scientist, using the story of Archimedes and his discovery of the principle of displacement and specific gravity as his example. He lays down the following exercises as the necessary prelude to contemplative insight:

(i) A period of tension and rational enquiry.
(ii) A sudden and unexpected insight.

This insight he explains is not a result of outward but of inner conditions. Such insights depend upon the endowment of intelligence, a questioning attitude of mind and an accurate presentation of definite problems. They are a process of pivoting between the concrete and the abstract, the world of sense and the world of imagination. What is experienced as insight can only be expressed in 'the abstract and recondite formulation of the sciences' and therefore it is often best left unexpressed. We find our Lord on the way down from the mount of Transfiguration earnestly enjoining the disciples to tell the vision to no man until the experience of the resurrection was there to help their description. Insight actually passes into the texture of the mind and becomes part of a series of insights through which we rise eventually to the presence and life of the Truth (Bernard Lonergan, *Insight*, p. 3, Darton, Longman and Todd, 1972).

The process of identification and insight is gradual and passes through well-defined stages. St. John of the Cross gives the classic account of these stages as he describes the following three signs:

(i) Meditation with reason and imagination is no longer possible.
(ii) An absence of desire to fix the mind or senses upon particular objects.
(iii) A desire to be alone, in loving attention upon God, without making any particular meditation, in inward peace and quietness and rest

(St. John of the Cross, *Works*, Vol. 1, cxiii, trans. Alison Peers.)

He goes on to advise the contemplative at this stage 'to learn to be still in God, fixing his loving attention upon Him, in the calm of his understanding, although he may think himself to be doing nothing' (ibid., p. 129).

It is in making this response that the direction of Patanjali is so valuable. For the postures and breathing lead to this required stillness and the practice of detachment and concentration are just what is needed when the normal forms of meditation are no longer possible.

The abandonment of the image and meditation is not a once-and-for-all action. It is something which has often to be repeated and in times of dryness it is essential to return to the image and the meditation. It is wise in most forms of contemplative prayer to begin with the image even though it may have to be discarded almost at once. It gives the mind direction and saves the contemplative from daydreaming and sleep, those great obstacles to real insight.

One of the most important moments of the Mass is called the fraction. At this point the symbol of bread is broken and the worshipper is invited to eat it and feed on the Lord in the heart. This is a summary of the experience of insight we have been considering. The symbol is removed and in its place the Lord of the symbol is offered no longer to be looked upon but to be shared. St. Paul puts it in another way when he writes: 'Wherefore we henceforth know no man after the flesh; even though we have known Christ after the flesh, yet now we know him so no more. Wherefore if any man is in Christ, he is a new creature: the old things have passed away; behold, they are become new' (2 Corinthians 5 : 16).

So we pass from concentration to meditation, from meditation to loving insight and on to union with the Lord. At this stage it is the Spirit who takes the initiative and we respond with silence and stillness. The silent stillness is primarily inward and has to do with the control of images in the heart. Eventually they are completely suppressed and the heart is held in an empty, receptive awareness. From this state develop those other contemplative experiences described by the Western tradition as union, the spiritual marriage, and the vision of God and by the Eastern tradition of Patanjali as freedom (kaivalya).

4

FREEDOM

The Transfiguration was not merely a manifestation of the Lord's glory. It led on to the descent from the summit to the crowd below, to the sick young man, the anxious father and the distracted disciples. Into this situation our Lord came with power. He exorcised the evil spirit and showed his disciples that the source of this power was the prayer he had just completed. The three disciples who had been with Him on the mountain had some share in this power, but to nothing like the same degree. We may say that our Lord's contemplation on the mount was much more than an experience of the glory of the Father; it was a sharing of His power and from that moment He began the process of His death, resurrection and ascension by which He came to the fullness of His glory.

This is the climax of contemplation. Because the contemplative has an insight into God this insight leads him on to a relationship and because God is love this is a relationship of love, a sharing of His life and power. The image used for this relationship in the Western tradition is the spiritual marriage which is an attempt to describe the fulfilment of man's quest for God in terms of a perfect and reciprocated union. We find this image used in the Song of Songs, often by our Lord and it is the theme of such contemplatives as St. John of the Cross and many others.

Patanjali describes it as a state of freedom and defines it in this way: 'Freedom (kaivalya) is the state of liberation when there is a balance of purity between the heart and the Lord' (3 : 56).

Under these conditions that full relationship between the Lord and the contemplative becomes possible. It is the fulfilment of the Lord's promise: 'Ye shall know the truth and the truth shall make you free (John 8 : 32). This is the real freedom and the meaning of eternal life.

Christian contemplative prayer like eastern contemplative prayer is a growth towards an increasing and loving freedom. In its early stages it is reached by means of the discipline of rules and the observance of a law: in its later stages these rules and laws are transcended by love. But the rules are a necessary beginning. As the contemplative grows so they should gradually be discarded. The growth according to Western tradition is first a purification of heart, then an irradiation of heart and then a union of heart with the Spirit. In this last stage the obstacles which separate from God are removed and there is a perfect union between the love which inspires the ego and the object of that love, the Lord. They come together in a single will, a single joy and single purpose.

The Transfiguration reminds us that the freedom of the Lord was possible in all conditions. His freedom was on the mount in the glory of the Father but it was equally in the plain with the sick man and the crowd. His freedom was inviolable. This is the freedom of the true contemplative. It is within himself and independent of the outside environment. No special place of withdrawal is needed, no special conditions of life. It is a perfect interpenetration of love.

1. FREEDOM IN GOD. In the Transfiguration we are given a glimpse of true freedom in God. It is revealed by the voice from the cloud. 'This is my beloved son, hear him.' The freedom is declared by

God Himself and this is an important insight. We do not win our own freedom. It is a gift from God. And it is not a relationship of complete independence but rather of filial obedience. 'His service is perfect freedom,' as the prayer book collect describes it. We take up as sons the freedom given to us by the Father.

This God-given freedom is bestowed as we grow more able to respond. In terms of contemplation this is expressed in an ascending scale of contemplative power: acquired contemplation, infused contemplation, quiet, union and the spiritual marriage. Patanjali with his much more limited view of the nature of God does not give the growth in such detail. He makes a broad division between contemplation with an image and contemplation without an image. He distinguishes between emotional union with God and that union when the emotions are in a perfect equilibrium. In his words it comes to fruition when the activity of the emotional energies, the gunas, are at rest. All these stages in growth towards contemplative freedom are clearly illustrated in the gospel picture of Christ and in the lives of the great Christian saints.

On many occasions we are shown our Lord agonising in His prayer to the Father. The prayer in Gethsemane is the classic example when in an agony he prayed more earnestly and the sweat was like great drops of blood falling to the ground. This was no easy contemplation. It was acquired by blood and tears and sweat. But this form of contemplation was exchanged for a more relaxed union when he lifted up his eyes to heaven at the tomb of Lazarus and could thank the Father for hearing Him always. We see Him in this stage of prayer during the Transfiguration. The prayer of quiet is seen in those periods of silence and stillness which he manifested in the boat during the storm and above all during the period in the tomb waiting for the resurrection. It was after the resurrection that He revealed a further growth in prayer when He spoke to Mary Magdelene of an ascent to the Father which was even then going on. The Spiritual Marriage was for Christ an affair between Himself and the Church. It is described in the Book of Revelation where it is made clear that this relationship is both corporate and individual. It is a relationship of love for which the Lord Himself prepares His Church. In the epistle to the Ephesians St. Paul uses the image of marriage as the supreme symbol of the relationship between Christ and the world He has redeemed. All the actions of physical marriage find their fulfilment in this mystery which is the theme behind the Christian marriage service.

Our freedom in God is a response to His presence in us. This grows from a disciplined effort to an inspired and almost effortless response. Like the musician, the scales have first to be mastered and the score learnt and then comes the free flow of music through every part of the being. All this comes to fruition in the state which is called the Spiritual Marriage and which corresponds to that identity of life which is implied in the word kaivalya. This is the goal of the contemplative and requires more detailed explanation.

2. *THE SPIRITUAL MARRIAGE.* The relationship between God and man implied by this description is common to many traditions. It lies behind the myths of non-Christian sources and is shared by all forms of the Christian tradition. Karl Barth writes of it with penetrating awareness in this comment on the Song of Songs: 'According to the Song of Songs, the Old Testament knows finally a proper meaning and seriousness of the sexual relation as such. That is why it ventures, in the voice of the prophet, to describe the connexion between Yahweh and Israel in terms of the relationship between man and wife. It knows equally well the disturbance to which the sexual relationship has fallen in historical reality. For this reason it can present the relationship between Yahweh and Israel as perfect on the part of Yahweh but only as devastated on that of Israel' (Karl Barth, *Church Dogmatics*, Vol. III, Part 1, p. 319, T & T Clark, 1970).

Here he recognises the state of matrimony as the perfect model of the relationship between God and man and also the fact that this relationship is impaired on the part of man but still complete with regard to God. It is because God remains faithful that a restoration is possible and this comes about as man grows in contemplation and likeness to God through His grace.

The most complete exposition of the model of matrimony is given us in the sacrament of Holy Matrimony where the principles which govern the fully developed union between a man and his wife and by analogy between man and God are expressed. We shall use the form of this sacrament in the Prayer Book as the model for describing the contemplative state implied by the Spiritual Marriage.

The bridegroom in this relationship is Jesus Christ, true man and true God. This has not always been understood in other traditions and with disastrous results. In some forms of Hinduism it has led to the concept of God as the Mother with all the enormities of Kali and her worship. In the obscurities of some forms of the Christian tradition it has led to a misunderstanding of the function of Christ towards the individual and the Church which has had equally devastating results on the development and freedom of man. Christ is the bridegroom by His own claim and as Karl Barth makes so clear in the prophetic anticipation of his role in the Old covenant. But He is primarily the bridegroom of the corporate bride, the Church, and it is only in fellowship with the Church that we share this relationship.

This implies that the Church and the individual are called to play the feminine role in relationship to Christ and in the teaching of the Bible the feminine role is first of all the acceptance of ourselves as we are and as Christ the bridegroom is making us. As we are, we are the sinful bride: Christ is engaged in the words of St. Paul in 'consecrating, cleansing so that he may present the Church to Himself all glorious, with no stain or wrinkle or anything of the sort, but holy and without blemish' (Ephesians 5 : 26). This involves those who respond to this relationship and work in an adjustment which is demanding in different ways as we are male or female. From the male it demands the development of the anima in his nature and the surrender of the animus to the Lord. From the female it demands the union of herself with the Lord through her relationship with the Lord in the male. It is the mystery to which St. Paul refers when he says that the head of every man is Christ and the head of the woman is the man. This is only possible as the individual is taken up into the life and being of the corporate bride, the Church.

Union of this kind with the Lord begins immediately there is a voluntary turning to Christ and from that moment the experiences of this relationship as described in the marriage service begin. The Christian life and the bringing forth of its fruits begin to take place. There is a capacity to transfigure the natural functions as energies for the life in Christ. The relationship of love between Christ and the believer develops as this relationship grows between the believer and other members of the body. So the Spiritual Marriage takes one form under the conditions of life in the Church militant here on earth and prepares for the completed form described in the book of Revelation where the bride comes down from heaven adorned for her husband and transformed from her fallen state into the glory of the heavenly city (Revelation 21).

The sacrament not only gives us this model of the state and life of the spiritual marriage but also the conditions under which it is to be lived and experienced in this world. It involves a relationship between the bridegroom and the bride.

The bridegroom who represents Christ undertakes to have the woman and to live with her. He undertakes to love her, comfort her, honour and keep her in sickness and in health and to remain faithful. The woman, who represents the Church and all its members, undertakes the same relationship and conditions but with the significant addition that she will obey. This is a fundamental condition of the relationship of the Spiritual Marriage. It ensures that the true relationship between God and His creature is maintained, no matter how highly God is prepared to raise him. He is still in a relationship of obedience which is intended to grow into loving obedience as between bridegroom and bride as the creature comes to know God.

All this is permanent. There is no question of God changing in His attitude to man and the Church. He remains faithful no matter how often His children fail Him. The marriage with Him is indissoluble. The Church and man on the other hand partly fail to respond and so the Spiritual Marriage is not an experience of better but also of worse, of poorer as well as of richer, of sickness as well as health and death eventually comes to transfigure the experience into conditions of eternal life. But although there is this variation in experience the Spiritual Marriage is not broken. Sickness and poverty do not break the union with God; they merely introduce new experiences. Again, the state of the Spiritual Marriage is not the reward of a life well-lived and of conditions fulfilled. It begins as a potential relationship, a covenant between God and man, between Christ and the Church and when man and the Church turn to Christ these conditions of union at once come into force.

Patanjali makes it clear that union with God in its early stages is spasmodic because the heart cannot remain long in a stable relationship but must oscillate from one image to another. This is the message of the Transfiguration. For the disciples it was a temporary experience of glory and then it became a secret to ponder while other experiences were lived through. But the relationship was there and on the part of our Lord it was already complete. Even though the disciples forsook Him and fled He remained faithful and after the resurrection He restored them to Himself. For them it was a growth to realise and the Acts of the Apostles and the epistles are the story of the way this was done. Death took away the variableness of the Spiritual Marriage and made the glory of it stable. Contemplatives are called to this relationship and to all the degrees of experience which it entails. They live out in their own lives the history of the Church and in their own lives they grow increasingly to realise this living union with God.

3. THE FRUITS OF FREEDOM. At the foot of the mountain of Transfiguration the limitations of the disciples are shown against the freedom of our Lord. The limitations of the disciples were a division between their awareness of a need and their ability to meet it. The freedom of our Lord was an awareness of need and a complete power to meet it. The sick boy and his father were frustrated by the weakness of the disciples and completely satisfied by the power of Christ. This is a model of the early stages of contemplation as compared with the freedom to which fully developed contemplation leads. It shows freedom developing from an awareness of weakness through intercession to complete power in Christ.

The three disciples who shared the Transfiguration show the first of these fruits. Unlike the other disciples who presumptuously try to take over the Lord's work they are content to wait in their weakness. They leave it to Him. This kind of humility is the early fruit of true contemplation. Those who have it do not talk about visions or other spiritual experiences. Unlike those who have surrendered to the attraction of the lesser spiritual powers they do not try to manipulate other people and they have no plan for the reformation of the world or the Church. They wait in silence and ponder the glory of the Lord. This is a true and powerful fruit of developed contemplation and one to be found in the lives of all genuine contemplatives. Patanjali warns the spiritual aspirant of the dangers of being led into a fascination for the spectacular powers or siddhis and insists that they are hindrances to the finest fruits of contemplation. This is warning constantly repeated in the other contemplative traditions. There are many warnings in the lives of those who have stumbled when confronted with these powers and Aldous Huxley in his book *Grey Eminence* records with unforgettable skill the disaster of Father Joseph who took this path. It is not difficult to trace the same mistake made by many leaders of our own generation.

Intercession is another genuine fruit of developed contemplation. Of this the father of the boy gives us an impressive example. He understands the needs of his son. He describes to our Lord a lifetime's anxiety and misery which was redeemed by love. He commits the child entirely to the Lord and responds with all his strength to the Lord's demands on his faith. As a result the fruit of the Lord's contemplation enters the child and he is healed. Here we have a model of what intercession becomes when united with contemplative prayer. There is the formation of the image of the person in need, an image which is animated by love and brought into the presence of the Lord in the heart. There is the patience to wait in faith for the Lord's action. There is the willingness to participate in the healing work. For after the child was exorcised the father had still his part to play as he worked on the long convalescence which must have followed the healing. All this the mature contemplative must be prepared to do. The fruit of his contemplation is not a cloistered indifference but the ability to take the world into his heart and there to hold it while the Lord does His work and afterwards to work with Him in whatever way is given in the continuous activity of renewing the world.

In Christ at the foot of the mount of Transfiguration we see the final fruit of contemplative freedom. This is not just a power to see

God and share His glory. It is the power to love perfectly and to work without hindrance the works of the God we contemplate. Our Lord does this towards the child, His glory now hidden; but the power is there and the inner vision of the Father undimmed. For the prayer to which he refers as the source of His power is the prayer just described, the prayer of Transfiguration. The true contemplative is neither indifferent to the needs of the world nor is he incapable of meeting them. In our Lord there were perfect sympathy and an absolute power. This has been the mark of all true contemplatives. They did not withdraw from the world for some selfish purpose of self-development. Their withdrawal has been for a time and for the purpose of renewing the world. In this world we are in obscurity about the life after death but enough has been shown us to suggest that the measure of spiritual insight and power developed in this world is the starting point of growth in the life of resurrection. This means that whatever is gained in this world is the raw material for the life of the world to come. Contemplative insight and power are therefore the most important assets that we carry with us through death and anything which increases them on this side of death is the most worth-while of all activities. We are all explorers, some into the mysteries of this world and the techniques of its control: others probe the eternal world and to them the rewards are also eternal. The vision seen in this world may very largely be secret and inexplicable but the Lord reassures us that in the resurrection what has been partly seen will then be fully known and proclaimed to all the world. 'You will receive power when the Holy Spirit comes upon you; and you will bear witness for me in Jerusalem, and all over Judea and Samaria, and away to the ends of the earth.' (Acts 1 : 8).

Chapter 5

No Means But This Prayer

The Transfiguration is not an isolated event. It may be seen as the heart of the gospel narrative, forming a climax to which the first part of the narrative leads and a point from which the second part develops. We have already followed the mystery to the climax. We now follow it as it becomes the expanding centre of the gospel and the centre point of contemplative prayer and the Christian life.

Our Lord himself connected the Transfiguration to his future life experience. He did this by linking it with the coming events of his death and resurrection and by tracing the power behind his work to this prayer. The Transfiguration was to remain a secret 'until the Son of Man is risen from the dead', not because there was anything inherently sacred about it which must be hidden from the gaze of ordinary people but because it could not be described until after the powers and insights belonging to the resurrection had been given to the disciples. After the resurrection the Transfiguration would be communicable and others would be able to understand it. It was a mystery until linked with the culminating events of the Lord's life.

Again, our Lord told his disciples that the power of his ministry was to be found in the Transfiguration prayer. 'There is no means of casting out this sort but prayer' and the prayer to which he refers is the prayer some of his disciples had just shared, the contemplative prayer of the transfiguration. All the great redeeming acts which followed the Transfiguration were rooted in this prayer. The greatness of their power was confirmed by the greatness of this prayer.

So it is with contemplative prayer of whatever intensity and ourselves. This prayer is not an isolated event, something which comes from a preliminary withdrawal and when experienced has no connection with life as it has to be lived. It is an integral part of life. It takes place in that life. That life is both the preparation for it and the raw material. This prayer is the power of that life and the energy by which it can be transfigured. Contemplative prayer is therefore no form of withdrawn quietism by which we can escape life and withdraw from its cares. It is the instrument above all others by which we penetrate life and overcome and cast out its enemies. This is the witness of the great contemplatives of all ages and particularly of that down-to-earth contemplative, Richard Meux Benson.

To understand the extent to which Father Benson penetrated his active life with contemplative prayer one has to live in the Mission House he built and absorb the tradition he left behind. The house is itself a sign of his prayer. It contrasts with the larger and more imposing building which replaced it early in this century. There is a simplicity and compactness about it which speaks not of an attempt to revive a past age of monasticism but of the ordinary conditions of life in his time. It must have fitted unobtrusively into that part of Oxford. And then there was the mixed life he lived in it. As Vicar of the new building development area of Oxford, with very little in the way of precedent to guide him, he provided for the spiritual needs of those people and worked out a plan of social life which anticipated and often surpassed the efficiency of the welfare state. There were schools for every kind of education, an allotment system, a large home for old people and in the porch of the Mission House a large trunk with baby linen ready for the next new member of the community. It was all a wonderful mixture of commonsense efficiency and spiritual insight: those marks of the true contemplative at all periods. It was indeed a bringing down of the essence of the Transfiguration to the plain and a sharing of its glory with the world.

This is the tradition which the present-day contemplative must be prepared to develop if he is going to share the power of his prayer with the world. Books will undoubtedly be necessary in order to share his vision with all men and now the great sufferings of the Lord have been crowned with his resurrection such books will always be necessary to lead others to the vision. But the life outside the vision is equally important and it is this life which authenticates the prayer. It is the pattern of this authenticating life we have now to consider and for us in these days it has to do with our Religious life as members of the revived community life which Father Benson did so much to rebuild, the way of proclaiming theological truth which he initiated in his methods of missions and retreats and in his writings, and the ways in which Christians are to be trained as messengers of the gospel both within and beyond the ordained ministry of the Church.

1

RELIGIOUS LIFE FORMS

Our Lord began his ministry with twelve men and he finished it with none at all. All through that ministry we see him avoiding any policy which would have resulted in a large and popular movement and after the Transfiguration he dissuaded others from joining the centre nucleus by emphasising the hardness of his demands.

This is in sharp distinction with the history of so many communities. They have started a handful and finished a world-wide institution. This was the story of the Benedictine order which achieved its maximum size during the great days of Cluny and from then onwards suffered the inevitable decline of all forms of dinosaur growth. It was the story of the Jesuit order and it is the story of the religious revival in the Anglican Church to which Father Benson contributed so much during the last century. From small beginnings there has been growth in the form of buildings, numbers, structure and central control. Already we are witnessing the decline which this kind of largeness inevitably brings.

Father Benson shows his awareness of the danger of excessive growth in this letter to Father O'Neill, written on 23 July 1874: 'I am sorry in one sense for your having to move, but I am not sorry at your getting away from those premises. I would much sooner settle in some smaller way. I think, however kind it was of the bishop to put us there, that large premises are a serious hindrance to poverty. It is not like the Bombay settlement of which we are only the nucleus. But I would much rather our mission should do its work— principally witness, prayer, preparation—with as little of external surroundings as possible. If I were in your place, I think I should pack up most of the things you took out, and leave them in a box. One could not refuse many presents, but I felt them to be in many ways grievous "impedimenta" to missionary life' (*Further Letters of Richard Meux Benson*, p. 16, Mowbrays, 1920).

This attitude to growth in the Religious Life is confirmed by experience of corporate contemplative prayer and is being once more asserted by some far-sighted teachers in our economic life. It has been found that there is a maximum number for a contemplative prayer group and that when this is exceeded the group changes and loses the intensity of its life. This has certainly been the experience of many religious communities. The enlargement of buildings, the revision of Rules of Life and Statutes have promised more life and efficiency but in practice they have absorbed the life of the organism and left a lifeless shell. Vatican II revealed the Roman Catholic Church very alive to this danger and already in the anglican communion steps have begun to be taken towards breaking up the large central body into smaller, independent groups with much greater freedom to operate outside the pattern of the written rule and statutes.

In 1973 Dr. Fritz Schumacher addressed the Design and Industries Association in Rome on the theme of Aristotle *Small is*

Beautiful. He quoted from Aristotle the teaching that 'To the size of states there is a limit as there is to other things, plants, animals, implements; for none of these retain their natural power when they are too large or too small, but they either wholly lose their nature, or are spoiled.' He has since published a book on this theme and it has been taken up by many thoughtful people. He challenges the accepted belief that growth rate is a necessary condition for the healthy life. What he has stated about our social and economic life has even greater application to the life of Religious communities and it is for those who belong to such bodies to learn from the children of this world and apply the lessons to their own problems. The questions we have to ask and answer are what for us is the right size and having achieved that shape what is right for us to do in that dimension.

The Right Size. Dr. Schumacher concludes his quotation from Aristotle with the remark: 'Small is beautiful but not at all easy' and with this we would all agree, especially those who are facing the present problem of cutting down so many overgrown Religious Life structures to size.

When Peter said 'Let us build three shelters' at the time of the Transfiguration he was giving a clue to future forms of the Religious life. They were to be expressed in simplicity. There were to be no such pretensions as the Temple which took forty years to build. The pattern was to be the tabernacle in the wilderness, something of basic simplicity and easily changed and moved. As we live in the buildings made by our predecessors; often imitations of medieval architecture, impossibly expensive to run and repair, designed to emphasise our present few numbers in comparison with the many of the past, we may deplore our heritage and agree with Father Benson that buildings so easily become sepulchres for the living. But we still have some freedom of movement provided we have a clear idea of what sort of buildings we shall aim at when the way opens for us to move.

The size and form of the buildings will be controlled by the shape of the contemplative communities we plan to put in them. The Transfiguration indicates the size. Jesus took three of his disciples. At another time he indicated the sort of community most conducive to manifesting his presence: it was two or three gathered together in his name. We may look forward to communities of this size as the authentic pattern for the future. And the buildings such communities will need should be no larger than an ordinary family house without any ecclesiastical ornamentation. When communities have cut themselves into these sections there is every chance that they will become free to live their true vocation and in doing so will grow again. It will then be seen that the present drying up of vocations was a blessing enabling us to take the way already marked out for us by a few courageous communities, of returning to the desert simplicity from which we all came.

But communities are more than buildings. They are also organisations and most of them have built up their organisation of statutes and rules and customs on the Roman Catholic patterns which have now been abandoned by most Roman Catholic communities since Vatican II. Recognising the irrelevance of much of these traditions is often as difficult for Religious as for the Indian Christians who have been asked to give up their Victorian forms of Christianity. At great cost they were planted and accepted and now that they have grown into large and permanent structures it requires much courage and sacrifice for people past middle age to give them up. Here again the Transfiguration has a message. It is true that our Lord spoke with Moses, the representative of the Law and to Elijah, the representative of the prophets, but he spoke not as one who had come to imitate and continue but as one who was to fulfil. And his fulfilment took all kinds of new forms, above all the form of discarding a great deal of ancient material and reducing obligations to the simplicity of love and guided by the Spirit he gave.

Some form of rules every corporate body must have. Even the well-planned Christian family has its customs and traditions. But Religious communities are faced with the obligation of deciding how much of their over-weighted organisation structure they need in the present world. Most of the detailed legislation can easily be left to commonsense under the influence of the Holy Spirit and very few permanent statutes are needed beyond the baptismal vows under which all Christians are already bound. Written constitutions have been rejected in our own country and have proved an embarrassment in others where they have been used. The charismatic movement is a recall to the true Christian legislator, the Holy Spirit and to train people to claim and use the prophetic freedom which has always been ours in the Christian Church. Of course, this presupposes a much more adequate period of novitiate training for such freedom but if we carry out our contemplative prayer to its full development it will lead us to a state of spiritual freedom not slavery and in that freedom we shall have to live. Most rules are for a kindergarten stage of life and at that stage are most necessary. But when grown up these childish things must be put away and we must be ready 'to run the way of thy commandments, when thou hast set our heart at liberty'.

Religious communities in the past have started with few commitments and then become overgrown with responsibilities. By the Middle Ages the Benedictine Order was practically responsible for

147

the education of Europe and supplied most of its Civil servants. The Reformation helped to put this right, but when that had settled, Religious Communities undertook the conversion of the world. All this involved complicated organisation and absorbing activity. The revival of the Religious Life in the Church of England soon led to a similar growth. Some communities undertook the training of the clergy, others ran schools, some went into the parochial ministry as experts in one particular form, such as the training of youth, and all went out into what was called the mission field. Very soon the work of Religious communities started to control their lives and Religious were trained for particular responsibilities before their special gifts had been discovered. We do not find our Lord treating his disciples in this way. They were to share with him a ministry which arose from a form of prayer, was made possible by that prayer and required no other organisation whatsoever. This was indeed small and beautiful but it was also effective and powerful and in the early years of the Church the one instrument needed for proclaiming the gospel throughout the world. As we think of the size of the work of Religious Communities this is an example which provides us with guidance about both the size and the forms this work may well take.

When our Lord did his first piece of ministry after the Transfiguration he took it over from what might be described as a committee of apostles. The man had brought his son for healing and he was handled by a community quite unable to heal. Our Lord took over the work and handled it as a person to person situation during which he established a relationship of trust and eventually cast out the evil spirit. Most spiritual work can only be done at this level. Team ministries and community ventures lack that intimate communication of Christ in his members which comes when the contemplative confronts the person in need and becomes an instrument of the Spirit.

If this is true then we have the guidance we need about the size of community work: it should not exceed what can be done by one person using the simplest equipment of the Spirit-filled personality. People can be excited and brain-washed by large numbers and mass media as Dr. McLuhan has so convincingly taught us, but they can only be led to saving faith one at a time by coming into living touch with one who believes.

This fact guides us in selecting community work. Most of the work previously done by communities has now been taken over by the state and it is foolish to attempt to compete with this organisation. Having decided on this point each community is then faced with choosing a new form of work which shall be suitable to its needs and capacities.

The Right Work. It is easier to approach this problem from a negative angle first and to decide what work is clearly unsuitable for Religious communities. It can safely be said that most of the work now done by the welfare state is of this kind. Hospitals, schools and welfare of that kind now need such large resources of staff and equipment that they are beyond the scope of any community. In any case they make such demands on the life of the Religious as to leave no leisure for his main activity of contemplative prayer. The kind of work that is suitable relates to this prayer and the special faculties it develops. These faculties are sensitivity to the Spirit, insight into the presence of God in men, awareness of man's deepest needs. These faculties are especially needed in making personal contact with people and evoking in them the response of faith. Such healing needs are not recognised by the welfare state but they are powerful when aroused and wisely directed. This is especially true in cases of mental illness which is where what are called the processes of spiritual healing are most effective. Here is an area of service for which the religious may be particularly equipped and outstandingly effective. But he will need training beyond what is concerned with prayer. Some of the skills of the good psychiatrist he will have to learn and apply in his teaching. There will be no compromise if he is trained in this with others who do not share his vocation. He can still add to what he learns from the children of this world all the insights of a child of light and make his ministry that much more effective. Such work will be intimate and personal and for that he may rightly claim the same freedom as the priest receives for his work as director and confessor. It is in effect an extension of this work, an application of the eastern conception of the work of a guru under the more restrained conditions of our Western traditions. This is of all forms of ministry most needed and most easily within the scope of the present-day contemplative.

All this was taught by Father Benson in a chapter of the rule entitled—'Of Missions'. Here he laid the foundation of all religious activity in contemplative prayer. He insists that for ministry it is 'necessary to be specially exercised in the prayer of affection and contemplation'. There is a persistent rejection of what are now called the mass media, and trust in the effectiveness of personal contact between the spiritually alive teacher and the people to whom he is sent. 'The results of the mission will be proportionate to the faith and prayerfulness with which the work is undertaken.' And then there is a remarkable insight into the essential qualities of the spiritual leader, the guru, which are common to the best in both eastern and western traditions. 'Be careful not, by any strained effort, to lead them to do acts which are beyond their own degree of contrition, lest by overdriving those that are with young, the true fruit of the mission be endangered. The firmness of a father must be combined with the tenderness of a mother in dealing with them.' Here are the principles of the right work for the religious, the way the work should be done. Should they be taken seriously again there will be need for a second reformation of the Religious life in the second century of its renewal. The contemplative will not be afraid to accept this task and as he does so his prayer will grow to meet the new demands.

Other Religious life forms. Our Lord left no plan as to the structure of his Church. It was to be centred on Himself and energised by the Spirit but its growth was to be free. The earliest description of the Church reflects this freedom: 'They met constantly to hear the apostles teach, and to share the common life, to break bread and to pray' (Acts 2 : 42).

There has always been a tension between those who have wanted to impose a centralised control over the Church and those who have striven to keep it free. In our country this struggle took its earliest shape as a struggle between the Celtic and Roman form of the Church and it still goes on between the independent churches and those who want them all united into what is called 'the great Church'. To this variety of churches has now been added a number of experimental forms of community living which resemble neither the traditional communities nor the present forms of the Church. Young people are experimenting with a commune type of corporate living which has much in common with the Indian conception of the ashram. In these the structure is kept very simple and members are left to make their own way of life within a common family. These new ways of common life are too new to assess their value. They often collapse and change from one form to another. But what has been said about the principles of Religious communities and contemplative prayer apply to them as well. To survive they need a foundation in some shared contemplative prayer. They too have a maximum size beyond which they disintegrate or harden into lifeless structures concerned with mere survival rather than life. And their work is not a duplication of other types of welfare already covered in this country by the National Health organisations but something in which a person to person relationship is essential and where people of trained insight have mastered the ways of penetrating not only to their own centres but to the centres of others as well.

Most of all, the Church needs this contemplative approach. It has become over-structured and in an attempt to free itself has adopted a democratic form of government which is out of keeping with its hierarchical origins. Democratic methods are well-suited to the secular government of this country but in a body where the Lord is

King they are unsuitable; and synods based on parliamentary methods of debate and procedure stifle the work of the Spirit who still operates through trained individuals and responsive groups. Voting and majorities have nothing to do with the action of the Spirit in the Body of Christ for He has so often worked through minorities and never hesitates to regard the lowliness of one person when it comes to decisive action.

This does not mean that the organisation we have inherited or helped to build can be irresponsibly jettisoned. Our Lord did not overturn the organisation of the Jewish Church. What He did was to set up the kingdom within it and manifest its freedom in Himself and the small group he chose and trained. This must be our action now. There is no point in opposing the democratic structures of the Church. Such opposition can always be mastered by the method of the democratic vote and the techniques of public debate. But the growth of small contemplative groups within the Church, sensitive to the danger of success and mere size, using the direct ways of the Spirit could bring down the walls today as effectively as in the past. It is for people dissatisfied with the present to take this way within their local Church and to pray through a day of small things to the achievement of their goal. This was the method of Christ and the first apostles and it has been vindicated by history.

Contemplative prayer is not withdrawal nor is it the acceptance of inadequacy: it is the way of deeper penetration and for those who persevere the most effective for changing the course of history.

2

CONTEMPLATIVE THEOLOGY

The Transfiguration was not an isolated mystical experience which had no effect on the practical thinking of those who shared it. St. Peter reminisces about it in his second epistle when he writes: 'It was not on tales artfully spun that we relied when we told you of the power of our Lord Jesus Christ and his coming; we saw him with our own eyes in majesty, when at the hands of God the Father he was invested with honour and glory, and there came to him from the sublime Presence a voice which said: "This is my Son, my Beloved, on whom my favour rests". This voice from heaven we ourselves heard; when it came, we were with him on the sacred mountain' (2 Peter 1 : 16–18).

It was one of the controlling influences of the earliest Christian theology and showed how powerfully contemplative experience could affect the thinking of the Church. This has often been so. The finest theology has been the work of contemplatives who have written of insight experiences against the received traditions of the Church.

Theology today is in a confused and often conflicting state. For this it is not fair to blame the wickedness of the world or the inconveniences caused to traditional thinking by the conclusions of Vatican II. A great deal of the blame must be attributed to the theologians themselves who have given up essential theological principles, sometimes in an attempt to win an instant notoriety or allowed themselves to be over-influenced by current trends of scientific and philosophical thought. This is one of the lessons of that admirable analysis of twentieth-century religious thought by John Macquarrie in which he describes the variety of influences which have played upon theologians during this century and made so many of them lose their grip and follow what Bunyan would call 'By-Ends', leading them and their readers nowhere.

The rise of many new universities both in this country and throughout the world has of course increased the theological output and with easy publication flooded the theological market with a vast number of ephemeral publications. This is not entirely a disadvantage. It has led to the growth of what Bernard Lonergan calls 'a pluralism of theologies' and he sees in this a symptom of the way theology will advance in the future. He writes: 'Such a pluralism or multiplicity is of fundamental importance, both for the understanding of the development of religious traditions, and for an understanding of the impasse that may result from such development' (Bernard J. F. Lonergan, S.J., *Method in Theology*, pp. 271–2, Darton, Longman & Todd, 1972).

He sees this pluralism replacing the massive structures of such a theological system as scholasticism and making it possible for other facets of the truth to be expressed. This is a good sign and the existence of many more independent theological faculties in the new universities may well encourage these new theologies to develop and make this contribution. It means that the old single standards of orthodoxy in terms of a single theology have now been discarded and that we stand on the threshold of a new freedom. It becomes all the more urgent that this new theological freedom shall be used under the control of sound theological principles. What these are in their complete form cannot be described in a work of this kind, but there is a place for certain principles derived from the experience of contemplative prayer which can make an important contribution to the total structure and some of these will now be described. They have to do with experience, formulation and communication.

Theological Experience. St. Peter in the quotation already used from the second epistle insists that his teaching was not based on 'tales artfully spun' but on evidence seen with his own eyes. And St. John makes the same claim when he writes: 'It was there from the beginning; we have heard it; we have seen it with our own eyes; we looked upon it, and felt it with our own hands; and it is of this we tell' (1 John 1 : 1). Both base their teaching on theological experience. In doing so they are in harmony with a strong movement in present-day theology which insists that the source of sound theology must be experience and so form a school of empirical theology. This is an advance on theology concerned merely with semantics or the arid regions of what used to be called higher criticism. It has brought theology into touch with life and with the living God. But this means that there must be a way to such experience which has to be taken before there can be valid theology about it. In finding such a way contemplative prayer has some essential help to offer.

The way of prayer which has here been considered assumes the presence of God in the heart and suggests ways for removing hindrances to the recognition of his presence. It also points to certain ways of experiencing this presence within the life of the Church.

Patanjali taught that sound religious insight came from an objective experience arising from the senses, from the interaction of reason on that experience and from the interpretative help of a sound tradition. We find St. Peter applying these principles to the Transfiguration and St. John to the incarnation. For them these were validly objective experiences not a tale artfully spun. It was something they both experienced with all the senses and then worked out through the play of sound reasoning upon it. All this was done against the background of their Old Testament traditions. And the result was that fundamental theological insight that the person they had experienced in this way was the beloved Son of God. To theologise with similar clarity the present-day theologian needs something of the same experience.

His experience begins with the Holy Spirit and is continued by the initiation rite of the Christian Church, administered with the fullness of an adult initiation and, where this is not possible re-experienced by way of anamnesis in the Holy Week observance of the Church. This experience develops in the sharing of the eucharist and the reproduction of the other gospel mysteries in the heart. All this is a part of that mind poise or samyama which has already been described and set out in the exercises which form the conclusion of this book. The fully equipped theologian will need to persevere in patient detachment until he reaches some measure of the experience contained in these mysteries and then he will be in a position to begin the creative thought of his theology. This requires something more

153

than intellectual brilliance for the making of theology. That is helpful but the first need is the experience which we should always remember was first given to men of no academic training whatever.

The experience is the beginning, the foundation. On this is built the work of sound reason and the integration with an inherited tradition.

Sound reasoning leads to sound theology but this reasoning is something more than what is required in scientific thought, although this is by no means to be despised. It is an intercourse between the human mind and the divine Word, speaking in the heart and recognised in a process of reflective thought. The movement of the mind will certainly be needed to do this, but it will be the mind under the trained control of the Holy Spirit, the mind illuminated by grace. Skill in this is the result of some kind of meditative thinking and that comes from mental discipline, the recognition of mental hindrances and a planned discipline for reducing them. Again this requires that the theologian should be more than a thinker. He must above all be a man of prayer.

And then the tradition within which the theologian must do his thinking and his harmonising is the Christian tradition. This does not mean an indifference to other traditions and ways of thought. It does mean accepting the Christian tradition as contained in the Bible and the mind of the living Church as the directing influence of thought. We see this kind of thinking in the great theologians of scripture. Peter and the rest bring Moses and Elijah into their thinking. St. John integrates his thought both with the teaching of the Old Testament and with the major theme of Greek thought of his time. All this involves a wide sympathy, an ability to see Christ as the centre of all truth, speaking through many traditions and yet with a special clarity in one's own. And all these traditions not as conveying truth of the past through documents of sometimes doubtful historical value, but living and contemporary traditions through which the Lord present continues to speak.

Theological Expression. Our Lord did not command his disciples never to tell the vision they had seen at the Transfiguration to any man. What he did was to tell them to delay the telling until they were more mature and the time ripe to describe their experience. After they had shared in the passion and the resurrection then they would be ready for the task of putting into words what they had seen. The early Church theologians were in no hurry to write anything until it had been tested and fully experienced. So we find the gospels being written some time after the event and a person like St. Paul spends much time waiting before putting pen to paper.

This is the first rule to observe in formulating a theology. It is the

154

result of an experience assimilated over a long time. Like poetry, good theology is emotion recollected in tranquillity. This is above all true of the theology of the contemplative. He must make it part of himself first. The truth has first to be heard, read, marked and inwardly digested before it can be shared with others.

Sharing theology with others is a question of discovering the language and ways of thought in which they live. Something like an act of contemplative intercession is needed to reach this depth of understanding. We find our Lord an expert in the art. With the scribes and pharisees he speaks with all the legal and controversial skill of the scribe. To country people he speaks as himself a workman and uses all the language of his trade to communicate his meaning. And to those skilled in prayer he speaks in yet another way suitable to their mode of insight. A skilled theologian who successfully communicates and shares his thought must be not one person but many; he must not merely have his own style but be able to reproduce the style of all to whom he speaks. Perhaps this is what St. Luke was trying to say about the gift of Pentecost. The Spirit inspired the apostles to speak in all the many ways of thought used by their varied audience.

Speaking with these kinds of tongues is an exercise in contemplative prayer where the mind is trained to deal with symbols and use is made not only of the mental parts of man but of all his other faculties as well. A theology expressed in these ways will not have a single style but many and will appeal to every part of man.

Austin Farrer used to say that good theology was more like poetry than prose. It uses all the arts of symbolism in the form of physical objects, mythological narrative, interpreted history or what Karl Barth calls saga, drama and movement of every kind. Scripture is full of examples of all these things. It is a mine of symbols. St. John's gospel is built around the seven I AM symbols of our Lord's discourses. The mysteries of our Lord's life are given us in a mythological form which makes them ready-made instruments of contemplative prayer. And the present and past are so skilfully interwoven that the resulting theology is an account of God present and working everywhere and at all times. And then there are the many forms of movement in sacraments and worship which are left so open as to invite imitation and development by all who grasp their style.

A theology as varied and exciting as that is needed to lead people into the experience of God through contemplative prayer. Such theology must be more than an academic subject, a theory about God: it must be a way of introduction to the living and loving God. The early disciples never merely talked about God. 'Men took knowledge of them that they had been with Jesus' (Acts 3 : 13).

Symbols, myth, saga, movement: these are all instruments for expressing a living theology. But the most convincing expression is the transformed lives not merely of individuals but of small contemplative groups of people. Father Benson saw this corporate expression of theological truth as the essential activity of the small community he founded. He wrote about it in this way: 'So let us realize that we are indeed called into a Religious community to carry on the work of spiritual instruction, but that that work is not at all to be measured by the mere extent of opportunity, nor are we to find any discouragement, if it is thwarted by the impediments of outward necessity. We are to be living ourselves in fellowship with Him, who is the incarnate truth; and He who comes to dwell in us will make Himself manifest in our lives in such a way as He pleases' (Richard Meux Benson, *The Religious Vocation*, p. 267, A. R. Mowbray & Co., 1939).

This suggests that the most powerful instrument for communicating theology is not the individual theologian but the contemplative family.

In the Old Testament we read of schools of the prophets and our Lord continued this tradition by selecting and training twelve disciples. The early Church was a loosely connected group of family Churches, meeting together for prayer and sharing the truth they had by incorporating others into their life. Theology, having moved away from the concept of a single statement of truth to which all must conform and recognising the legitimacy of a pluralism of theologies, is now free to encourage the growth of theological families grouped around certain leaders and learning in various forms of contemplative prayer to assimilate and communicate their insight into truth. This could result in a variety of expression based on a common doctrine and when achieved it will be an instrument for communicating the truth in that rich profusion which is one of the marks of Scripture and indeed of creation itself. There are many signs that this development of the Church is already taking place. One hopes that it will not stop short at house churches for the sake of house communions but become contemplative families for training in contemplative prayer and centres where through that prayer the truth of God may find more adequate theological expression.

The expression of theology under these conditions will most certainly lead to the multiplication of contradictions and paradox. These are marks of the New Testament theology and indeed of all truth which is partly apprehended and partly expressed. It is a mistake to attempt to iron out all the contradictions and paradox in one's own theology let alone in the theology of a group. The Church does not settle matters by means of a majority discovered by a democratic vote. Our own Church warns us that even general councils may go wrong when things are settled in this way. Truth is discovered and expressed in the Church by the growth of a common mind worked upon by the Holy Spirit. It takes a long time to form and during the waiting much patience is needed in order to live with our contradictions and accept the paradox.

The Athanasian Creed is an example of this state of theological contradiction and paradox. It piles them one on top of the other. But for the contemplative this is no obstacle to his prayer. Rather he carries the contradictions as the Zen Buddhist is expected to carry the koan and as he does so he grows into the heart of the truth and is led to the insight which is the satori reward of those who are prepared to wait for God to lift up the light of his countenance and enlighten the darkness of our ignorance.

Easy forms of theological harmonisation are like committee schemes of reunion: always premature and almost always wrong. In the presence of this kind of varied and often contradictory theology the contemplative family has to learn to pray. It means living much of the time with the vision in secret, waiting for the hour of enlightenment to dawn. It means loving with compassion those whose insight we cannot accept. It also means waiting and loving in a state of complete confidence that these are the conditions for the dawning of the daystar in the heart of all those who are faithful in their contemplative watch for the Lord. This is a great work of true theology and it is shared not merely by the traditional and long-founded communities but by those rapidly growing contemplative families who have been called into the mountain of contemplation and must find themselves sooner or later sharing the same responsibility as their predecessors of proclaiming what they have seen to the whole world.

3

TRAINING THE CLERGY

Among those most responsible for making and expressing a theology are the clergy of our Church. Their vocation is to be the messengers, watchmen and stewards of Christ and this work can only be done by men who have had a deep experience of Him and are skilled in communicating what they have seen and heard. One of the most perplexing situations of the present time is the uncertainty among the clergy about the essentials of their calling and as a result the confused methods of training they are being given.

It is in the training that the uncertainty begins. We find our Lord

157

avoiding such uncertainty at the beginning of his own training work of the disciples: 'Jesus went away to the lake-side with his disciples ... He then went up into the hill-country and called the men he wanted; and they went and joined him. He appointed twelve as his companions, whom he would send out to proclaim the gospel' (Mark 3 : 7–14).

His followers were to be his companions and they were to proclaim the gospel. All of his training was designed to make them adequate instruments for this purpose and his success in this work was one of the great achievements of his ministry.

In these days with so much uncertainty about whether the clergy are to be unpaid welfare workers or supplementary teachers or leaders of minor revolutions it is not to be wondered at that a good deal of their training is left to themselves and many teachers have relegated theological teaching to a project which students must do for themselves. This is a situation which cannot be tolerated by either the teachers or the students of the Church. It is an urgent duty of every Christian to give his time and prayer to the resolving of this confusion.

The problem is not primarily intellectual. It used to be thought that an improvement in the education of the clergy would be the answer. This was particularly so in a country like India where every effort was made to educate ordinands to a university level. But this did not increase their effectiveness as ministers of the gospel. In fact the reverse was the case and when an enterprising English missionary took over a small country estate and turned it into a math or ashram and there taught ordinands the rudiments of discipline, prayer and the communication of the gospel he trained an outstanding generation of priests who, although hardly literate by English standards, were apostolic in effectiveness. By all means the clergy of this country must have an adequate academic foundation which the new and older universities are able to supply but this can be no more than a foundation and upon it a still more important superstructure of asceticism, prayer and sympathy remains to be built. It is about this superstructure that we are particularly concerned and in its planning there is much that contemplative prayer and training have to contribute. We shall consider each of these separately and in more detail.

Asceticism. Ascetic theology is not often mentioned in these days of freedom but it plays an important part in character and ministerial formation. We find our Lord taking this part of the training of his disciples seriously. They were strong, physically and mentally, when they started on their mission and this was not by chance: we can watch our Lord training them to this end. Much new thinking needs to be given to new forms of asceticism when much of the old has been understood and rejected. Much of the old was negative and concerned with an approach to sex which was dangerous and certainly unacceptable today. The old ideas of chastity were based on denial rather than fulfilment and celibacy was approached in terms of withdrawal from important areas of human experience rather than a new and creative use of them. We may be thankful that much of this mistaken attitude has been emphatically rejected with the exaggeration which always accompanies a liberating movement. We have now the opportunity to go over the ground and reconstruct on a new pattern a contemporary ascetic pattern.

First we need to remind ourselves that there is nothing inherently repressive about the idea of asceticism. It has to do with training for an athletic contest and is essentially positive in its attitude to the body. Asceticism is practised, not to reduce the body but to increase its powers and our control. It has as its object a positive growth and the development of a number of powers which are usually found in a state of unbalanced conflict.

The purpose of Christian asceticism is both to integrate the body into the total harmony of man and also to make man able to act in his highest form which is the act of contemplative prayer. This means recognising the weaknesses of the body and repairing them but equally being aware of its undeveloped capacities and bringing them to maturity.

In the Western tradition the weaknesses of man are summed up under the one category of sin and this is subdivided under the seven capital sins which are the main sources of human sickness. In the tradition of Patanjali these weaknesses are contained in the hindrances of which the root one is ignorance or blindness. It may well be that both descriptions have something to contribute to the other. Certainly the first need in forming a sound asceticism is to have a clear idea of the obstacles it is designed to overcome. Even if we decide to retain the traditional sevenfold division of sin there will still be the need to formulate these sins in terms of the present and in doing this much help will be available in the teaching of a sound psychology.

And then the undeveloped capacities of human nature need to be again examined. In the scholastic theology which has had such influence on our Western tradition these capacities have been formulated under the headings of the cardinal and theological virtues and the gifts of the Spirit. There is much to commend this analysis. It is to be preferred to a vague form of goodness or imitation of Christ which may so well develop into self consciousness. On the other hand, the Patanjali teaching about the gunas or emotions goes to the

159

springs of action and has much to contribute. The question that must be asked and answered as adequately as possible is 'Lord what is man?' and the equally important question 'Lord, what is man destined to become?'.

Asceticism is a training of all the faculties of man. It is a mistake when in training the clergy an almost exclusively intellectual training is given. The result is a one-sided development which leads to many physical problems in middle and later life. There are now disquieting signs both among clergy and bishops of over-stress and physical breakdowns taking the forms of coronaries and ulcers and slipped discs. This all points to an unsound training of the body and emotions at the expense of the mind. There is an urgent need to develop some wise physical training of the body on the lines of Eastern yoga and movement to correct the imbalances of much of the present training of the clergy. Some forty years ago in at least one missionary theological college it was compulsory to spend Saturday mornings doing some kind of manual work such as carpentry. This was even in those days despised as a non-intellectual activity but those who planned this work were wise and it supplied an essential balance to the other kinds of training during the week. It should not be impossible to draw up a scheme of physical movement to develop the body for the strains of the ministry and especially for the stresses of middle life. Patanjali's teaching on posture and breathing is one of many possible systems which would meet this need.

And then there are the emotions. The ministry makes heavy demands in terms of emotional stress both within the home life of the clergy and in their relationships with their parishes. Western tradition recognises that the emotional life is a harmony of four basic emotions of fear, grief, hope and joy. In the East the principal emotion of joy is stressed and a balanced emotional life is one in which this emotion predominates. Karl Barth never tires of emphasising the need for gladness in the relationship of person with person and traces emotional health to the achievement of this goal. Such a balanced emotional life is the result of planned emotional training. It involves both internal and external discipline. Internally it involves the art of cultivating the emotional life and being unafraid of the dark as well as the light emotions. Externally it means learning to live in warm emotional relationships with others and for this purpose the recognition of the power of the sexual instincts and the ways of harmonising them positively with the emotional life are of first importance. The Eastern allegory of the kundalini and of the ways to raise its energy into the higher centres have much to teach us. Marriage and celibacy are both forms of chastity and chastity is an art of emotional living which can be of all forms of life the most fruitful. In losing this

160

art many Christians have dried up their emotional life and incapacitated themselves for the work of communicating the Word and the Spirit who is the Lord, the Giver of Life.

The mind is one of the human faculties which needs ascetic training if it is to be an instrument for penetrating to God and communicating Him to others. Our Lord teaches that the training of the mind for His purposes follows a different pattern from the ordinary training of the schools. He did not imitate the methods of the scribes and pharisees in teaching his disciples. They were taught by a system of spiritual experiences later explained and by a method of learning by doing. There is of course an important place for academic learning and academic methods but these are not the whole mental training of the man of God. He must be led to spiritual experience before the explanation will have any meaning and he must be given work which will open his mind to the divine presence. In the East this kind of training is done by what is called a guru–chela relationship. That means that an older and spiritually experienced man becomes the leader of the disciple and shares with him his experiences and points the way towards them. Ideally this is possible between the older priest and the man in training but such older priests are not easily found and almost always the man who comes under such influence has already been ordained and so has passed beyond the stage where training of this kind and decisions arising from it are any longer possible. Our Lord trained his disciples primarily by bringing the strength of his mind to bear on the minds of his followers. This is the essence of the mental training of the clergy. In the last century this was understood by such great bishops as Lightfoot and Westcott. We may need to examine their ways afresh and to observe how nearly they followed the ways of Eastern mental training and how successful they were.

Prayer. The fundamental activity of the priest is prayer and until recently an ordered prayer-life was an essential part of his training. Present theories about prayer and revisions of prayer forms have tended to change this priority and often where attendance at the offices is voluntary it is astonishing to find how many future priests have lost the conviction that prayer is their chief work and training for prayer the most important part of their apprenticeship. But this is not all. Contemplative prayer is hardly given any place in the training of the clergy so that it is not unknown to find clergy unaware of many of the methods of popular forms of oriental meditation as they are now taught and ignorant of the ways in which so many of them endanger not only the sanity but the spiritual life of their people.

Training in contemplation is one of the most important forms of

161

asceticism for the clergy. This makes it essential to compile such a form of training as will be suitable for present needs and be capable of development as the contemplative grows in this art. In the East such forms are available in great variety and detail. There are the Yoga Sutras to guide those who want to contemplate in that way. There are innumerable variations of Buddhist contemplation. And then there are the adaptations of these ways by the contemporary masters such as Ramakrishna and Ramāna Maharshi who have given classic expression of this prayer to their own living disciples. Our clergy in training have the right to insist that they be given at least that amount of help. They should have as clear guidance about training in contemplative prayer as they are given in their Bible study and they should not look in vain in the Church for living exponents of these methods. Whenever this kind of help has been offered, and this has been boldly given by some women's Religious communities, it has been warmly welcomed and used. Contemplative prayer has its rules and these are not hard to learn. But they need to be seen in action and their results confirmed in the lives of present-day contemplatives. Such people need not be Religious, although they will often be found in that form. Adult Christians should equally be able to supply this need. I can remember a gardener who practised this kind of prayer and a civil servant who made it the light and energy of his monotonous work. The Church as a whole is responsible for training her leaders. Training in contemplative prayer is not something to be left to a few teachers in theological colleges. They should be supported by contemplative families throughout the Church. Prayer of this kind will only become powerful when it is manifestly the prayer of the most alert parts of the Church.

Communication. One of the purposes of the ordained ministry is to supply the Church with messengers. The clergy must therefore be trained to communicate the gospel. Our Lord trained his disciples for this work but he did it not so much by making them fluent in speech techniques as by training them to be responsive to the Holy Spirit. A study of the sermons in the Acts of the Apostles confirms the success of this method. They have few of the skills of the practised speaker but they are alive with the power of the Holy Spirit and their results are dynamic. Training in this kind of communication is as an essential for an effective ministry as for a messenger of the Lord.

There has never been a time when the world has been more sensitive to the technique of communication nor had so many ways of persuasion. Through the mass media it is possible to bring almost world-wide impact for the spreading of the message. In doing this not only have the visual aids been mastered on a world-wide scale but the other senses can be appealed to and already certain subliminal techniques have been achieved which can bring the message to the unconscious faculties as well. It is a great temptation for the messenger of the Gospel to be caught up in these techniques and to be deceived into thinking that they are the ways for the most effective proclamation of the Word. Already some oriental forms of meditation are being communicated by American-sponsored methods and the effect seems to be success beyond the dreams of the most successful of advertisement campaigns. But we must be under no delusion: this is not the machinery for preaching the Gospel. The Word does not speak in this way nor is faith generated by a process of battling for the mind. The Word speaks through the instrument of the converted man and men are led to faith by the power of the Spirit. Training for this kind of proclamation is therefore intensely personal, far removed from modern hidden persuaders and dependent upon the powerful co-operation of the Spirit. We may venture a few suggestions about this training drawn from some of the principles of training for contemplative prayer.

(*i*) *Listening to the Word.* The Transfiguration teaches us that the preliminary condition for speaking the Word is listening to the Word. St. Peter emphasises that the source of the gospel is the voice and the sublime Presence seen and heard on the sacred mountain. And St. John reminds us that this listening to the Word is an exercise of all the senses: taste, touch, seeing, hearing and even the sense of smell has a place. It is an act of what is called in the Western tradition anamnesis and in the teaching of Patanjali samyama. That is the mind and all the senses are brought to bear on a single object, then there is discursive thought around that object and finally the listener identifies with the sublime Presence who communicates in this way.

In training to concentrate on the Word it is important to be alert to the many ways in which He speaks. Through the written word of the Bible, yes, but also through the truth written in every other form of literature. Through the spoken word of those who are His obedient instruments. In the heart as a deep silence. And also through every part of the creation. 'The heavens declare the glory of God' because by His Word they are created. If we limit the speech of the Word to the Bible we deprive ourselves of many other forms of His utterance and are unable to compare the speech of the Word with other forms which is such an important safeguard against misunderstanding His meaning. Our Lord taught His disciples to hear God speaking through nature, to recognise His Word in the teaching of a John Baptist and after His resurrection to listen to His speech in the heart. Those who are to speak the Word clearly must listen to at least as wide a variety of sound as that.

While being sensitive to the extent of the Word it is necessary to concentrate on those ways in which he speaks most clearly for particular people. Some hear the Word most clearly in nature. Wordsworth was one of these. Others hear the Word most clearly in the Bible and again in certain parts of the Bible. The contemplative as he develops comes to hear the Word most clearly in his own heart. Where the Word sounds most clearly there he must listen and concentrate all his attention. It is a process of most sensitive selection, like the painter who comes to specialise in a few subjects because through them he most deeply penetrates to the truth.

This listening to the Word in a limited place involves the application of all the senses and emotions and also that sense called commonsense by which we compare what we now hear with what has already been spoken and harmonise the total utterance into a single message. It is a process of meditation, a flow of mind towards the heart of the message. This requires persevering training and practice in complete attention. It brings into action the emotions as well for the message must be received gladly if eventually it is to be communicated like the magnificat from a joyful heart.

Listening, pondering lead beyond words to the voice who speaks. The Word speaks in order to draw us to Himself and in union with Him we are then able to become sensitive instruments for the utterance of Himself. Such an instrument was John the Baptist so that some heard him speaking and followed Jesus. That is the object of all the training of the true listener: so to receive what is spoken that it can be transmitted as the voice of the master himself.

(*ii*) *Uttering the Word.* The essence of uttering the Word is listening to the Word and so the vital act of communication is listening. If the training in hearing the Word is well done there will be little doubt that the Word will be spoken. Yet there are certain dangers to avoid in speaking the Word and certain skills which ensure that it is uttered clearly.

The main danger in speaking the Word is to think that the Word will be more distinct if we conceal or disguise ourselves. At one time this concealment may take the form of the parsonic voice: at another the imitation of the masters of certain secular techniques of communication, the fiction of 'the man's man' the attempt to capture the audience by becoming identified with it. These are snares and delusions. Sometimes they have an immediate success but in the long term they are easily recognised and rejected and the messenger who plays with his identity ends so often by losing his own soul in an attempt to win the world. Messengers of the Word must be trained to know themselves and in that knowledge to use that self for the communication of the Word.

Dr. Johnson observed that the success of Methodist preachers came largely from this genuine use of themselves. His explanation is worth repeating for it contains so many warnings and encouragements to ourselves as we train to become more effective instruments of the Word: 'Sir, it is owing to their expressing themselves in a plain and familiar manner which is the only way to do good to "the common people", and which clergymen of genius and learning ought to do from a principle of duty, when it is suited to their congregation; a practice for which they will be praised by men of sense. To insist upon drunkenness as a crime because it debases reason, the noblest faculty of man, would be of no service to the common people; but to tell them that they may die in a fit of drunkenness, and show them how dreadful that would be, cannot fail to make a deep impression. Sir, when your Scotch clergy give up their homely manner, religion will soon decay in that country' (30 July 1763).

The Word of God requires the co-operation of the real and genuine man if it is to be uttered with conviction and power. So arises the need to train the messenger in the art of embodying it in his real self and to let it speak without imitation or disguise.

The richness of the Word and the variety of his instruments of speech demands a similar variety of utterance in the messenger. The Word must be heard through his total personality and it will be heard in movement and gesture even more clearly than through sound.

In the East the teacher uses himself to convey his message. The realised contemplative will not hesitate to expose himself in the communication of his message. So with our Lord: 'Behold my hands and feet. It is I myself.' In this way He proclaims His resurrection. The Eastern contemplative speaks of making a darshana or manifestation by which he means using his body as a lantern in which the light may shine. It may seem presumptuous for a messenger to use his body in this way, but contemplative prayer transforms a man and he should be ready to show the Word in his own body by letting it speak with this transfigured power. Learning this art is in some ways like the craft of the actor who becomes the part he plays, the person he represents. In the past much emphasis was placed on the clothes of the messenger. John the Baptist wore a kind of uniform for his work: the Religious has also his uniform and until recently the priest had his. It is a great mistake to discard this symbolism. It certainly needs fresh thought and modernisation but not discarding. It is the frame in which the minister of the Word may most easily be seen, it is a sounding board for his message. There is an urgent need to experiment in new forms of this ancient principle.

And in this uniform the messenger of the Word speaks, not only with words but through movement and gesture.

Until the liturgical reform there was a whole series of expressive movements in the Mass which had to be learnt as part of the preparation for the priesthood and used with accurate precision. Through them the individuality of the priest was absorbed into the greater mystery of the Church and he spoke through movement. Perhaps the forms of this movement had grown over-detailed and communicated less clearly to the present generation than before but the principle of speaking through movement was sound and needed revision rather than demolition. It is to be hoped that there will be a renewed examination of this art of speaking in movement, applied not only to the Mass but to contemplative prayer as well. We have found that movement both expresses and makes possible the sharing of mental acts and that such arts as the dance are of great value in leading people of all degrees of mental development to a deeper hearing of the Word. Dr. Rudolf Laban has produced an important analysis of the principles of this kind of movement. He reduced them to 'The Sixteen Basic Movement Themes', which were the subject of his great book, *Modern Educational Dance*, Macdonald and Evans, London. There is much in his teaching which could be applied to movement in the utterance of the Word and a great deal of research waits to be done in training the messengers of the Word in this art. The T'ai Chi Ch'uan is a classic application of these principles under the rigidity of a detailed pattern. What waits to be done is the flexing of this pattern to meet the mood of the moment and to match the movement to the Word. This is a matter both for groups of people as in the Mass and for individuals as in preaching.

It is in preaching that the other form of uttering the Word through gesture comes into its own. In the Eastern tradition the spoken word is always accompanied by varied gestures: the hands, the eyes, the whole body plays its part. We see this in our Lord Himself. He too used His hands and eyes: His whole body spoke. In the art of rhetoric certain principles of gesture are included but in these days anything of that kind is suspect as unnatural and embarrassing. So it is if used unskilfully but one has only to watch a child using gesture to realise that this is an effective way of communicating thought which brings added power to the spoken word. The messenger of the Word should be trained in this art and encouraged to make his own exploration so that when he speaks his listeners may both see and hear the Word. If he does this first of all in his contemplative prayer these movements will be spontaneous and full of meaning when he speaks and they will liberate his whole personality.

So contemplation becomes something more than a way to God. It

166

is also a way from God to the world. It is a movement which goes into stillness and which moves from that stillness into action. And the action is the expression and communication of the power of God. All this is intimately related to the ministry of the gospel and in these days there is an urgent need to apply the arts of sound forms of contemplative prayer to the training of those messengers who will otherwise sound the trumpet given to the Church with an uncertain note.

Chapter 6

Acts of Contemplation

Father Baker in his book *Holy Wisdom* or 'Directions for the Prayer of Contemplation' concludes with a series of practical instructions for this prayer which he calls 'Certain Patterns or Devout Exercises'. When St. Ignatius drew up his instructions for meditation he put them all in the form of practical exercises, almost a drill book for religious. Patanjali in the Sutras is all the time concerned with practical rather than theoretical contemplation and in his tradition prayer has always been considered something to be done rather than discussed.

For this reason the following exercises in contemplation have been drawn up as an attempt to apply in practice the various contemplative principles which have been described in the previous sections of this book. They are based on the experiences of a contemplative family during more than five years of exploration. They are open to many modifications which we shall not hesitate to make for ourselves and as regards others they may be of some help in discovering a practical road to their own way of contemplative training.

If contemplative prayer is about all the God-directed actions of human life then these acts are about a variety of living experiences. Some of them may seem trivial and beneath the dignity of contemplation. For us there is nothing too small or too great to be included. This puts us in harmony with St. Paul who wrote: 'Whatsoever things are true, whatsoever things are honest, whatsoever things are just, whatsoever things are pure, whatsoever things are lovely, whatsoever things are of good report: if there be any virtue, and if there be any praise, think on these things' (Philippians 4 : 8).

The description of these acts will be brief, leaving the contemplative free to fill in the details from his growing experience. It will be limited to suggestions about the time of the contemplative act, the outward sign or symbol, the use of the body and the main exercises of the heart. These brief suggestions will only be of value when used repetitively for a long time. They are intended to build up habits.

The place of these acts is both external and internal. Externally

168

they require a holy place. This may be a room or at the most a simple prayer mat. Keeping this holy place will be most conducive to prayer. The internal place of these acts is the heart. They may be done privately or with a group of like-minded people, not exceeding under normal conditions, seven.

A Hindu who regularly practised contemplative prayer once talked about the way in which his prayer was done. We are of course in no way bound to imitate in detail his practices any more than we are bound by every part of Patanjali's teaching or the teaching of anyone else. But sometimes looking at one's own village from the other hill helps us to see more clearly and a good practice of another tradition can without any compromise be incorporated into one's own.

The object of his prayer he described as mukti or liberation from the ego and the ego-self and for this he practised a discipline of the heart. This he made clear was a real inward discipline, an activity which led to contemplative stillness, yet he insisted that it involved a good deal of planned external action as well. He gave us this outline of that activity.

It began with early rising, a cold bath, breathing exercises and a number of physical postures, especially the surya namaskar. Then in a meditation posture the prayer began at the heart centre, in the lotus of the heart.

The focus around which the contemplation took place was an image of the particular manifestation of God which was in his tradition. In his case it was an image of the divine manifestation in the form of Vishnu. This image he insisted was made from a symbol and not what would be called a graven image or idol and in all his devotions he used it not as God but as an icon through which God became present and could be worshipped in His divine Being.

This worship began with the lighting of the lamps in the heart. Its form was based on the daily external temple worship carried out by the Brahmin priest. It was of childlike simplicity but with mature and profound implications for those who could sympathise and understand. The heart image was anointed and fed and then put to rest. Each of these actions was punctuated with long pauses for recollection and silence. For instance, the food having been offered there was a long pause while it was received and eaten. At the end of this active service there followed a period of receptive waiting and then the God gave his blessing (prasād) which was shared with the members of the household and followed by a period of thanksgiving. All this our friend insisted took place in the heart.

One of the dangers this kind of contemplation avoids and trains us to avoid is quietism. Perhaps his way seems to us over-active and over-organised, but it avoids the danger of merely sitting still and doing nothing which are the symptoms of that paralysis of prayer which is quietism. Contemplative prayer demands complete action of certain kinds in which only the wisely trained can fully share. Loving communion with the living God requires the use of all the faculties in actions which often leave us exhausted. Contemplation is not primarily about relaxation but about love. That is why the symbol of this prayer is not a man relaxed in the corpse posture but a king reigning from the tree.

The actions prescribed by this Indian friend can be divided into three groups: those preliminary to the prayer, the actions leading to contemplation and the receptive climax.

There is no need to elaborate on the preliminary exercises. The important thing is that this introduction should not be left out or hurried. It is like the regular maintenance of a machine. It makes sure that it starts quickly and works efficiently. The actions leading to contemplation require greater thought and planning.

First, the place and the focus. The place is one of the centres of consciousness usually the heart. The focus is always a sign of the incarnate Lord in His being and action. St. Bernard used to remind his monks when they grumbled at having to rise early for prayer that God was already there and waiting for them before they entered the 'chapel. This is true of the divine presence in the heart. Our Indian friend recognised this by lighting lamps in the heart. Faith is described as the uncreated light in the heart and it is by stirring up our heart in faith that we intensify this light.

The symbols of contemplation are many, changing and repetitive. In the following exercises a variety of symbols are suggested which relate to the particular form of contemplation. They are given to stimulate others to make their own discoveries. Sometimes the symbol grows in the heart, like the imprinted images mentioned by St. John of the Cross. Sometimes it grows out of long and careful thought. The collection of a number of effective symbols is one of the essential conditions of sustained contemplation.

The actions of contemplation are largely controlled by the symbol and its image. If one of the sacramental signs is the image then we reproduce in the heart the actions of that particular sacrament. If the symbol belongs to one of the mysteries of our Lord or our Lady then we reproduce as much of that mystery in the heart as we need to reach contemplative silence. During this stage some form of colloquy is essential and it is well to remember that our Lord is the master of this mantra-type of communication. This means giving time to periods of listening as well as speaking during this prayer so that we may 'hearken what the Lord God would say to us'. Better to leave the action of this part of the contemplation unfinished than to end in haste and shallowness.

These actions lead to the climax of contemplation, reception and communion with God who gives His Spirit as the divine gift (prasād). We receive Him to share Him with others. This leads us from our prayer into the active balance of life. This may take the form of intercession or direct service, either of which is a communication of the Spirit. The salutation between those who know and share this mystery must always be:

> The Lord be with you.
> And with your Spirit.

In the great eucharistic prayer of the Church there are two essential moments: the epiclesis when the presence of the Holy Spirit is invoked; the anamnesis when the saving acts of Christ are again made present and effective through the eucharistic symbols. Both mysteries form the heart of every act of contemplation.

Silence is the instrument through which we reach the highest rungs of the ladder of contemplation. This was the teaching of Father Benson who summed up the results of true silence in the rule of life he gave the Society in this way: 'Silence is one of the chief joys of the religious and imparts to all his actions strength, tranquillity and perfection; for in silence the soul holds blessed communion with God, feeds upon the grace of past sacraments, contemplates the true hope of the eternal reward and rises up to the demands of the divine will in the joyous correspondence of grateful love' (c. 24).

In this summary all the highest states of union with God are included: vision, response and the union sometimes described as the Spiritual Marriage. But the silence which leads to these states is not merely a physical silence, an absence of sound and of words. It is what Father Benson calls religious silence and this makes demands on the body and the heart in terms of a total attention to the indwelling Lord. Some of the ways to this silence have been described already. It will be indicated as the goal of all the exercises which are going to be outlined in the following plan. As silence takes so many forms no attempt will be made than to indicate that the climax of the contemplative exercise is one of the degrees of silence.

All the acts of this section are based upon a twofold approach to stillness and the interior activity of the heart.

Stillness is by no means an attempt to achieve a state of 'at rest' or relaxation or reduced blood pressure. These are not states of any contemplative significance. The stillness which is aimed at is a firm position which is full of muscular feeling and is alive with the sense of balanced poise and responsive to the energy of the Spirit. It resembles Masefield's lovely description of the ship as in a state of 'swiftness at pause', like the servant of the psalms whose eyes are upon the hand of the master, ready to react to the slightest indication of his will. Stillness is a state of alert health, full of joy, in perfect balance between repose and action.

The interior activity of the heart is described in the Western tradition as one of anamnesis and in the Eastern tradition as samyama. Both these words describe states of intellectual activity which are the result of the full use of memory, imagination and love. These faculties are used, not on fantasy material in the heart but on actual material in the outside world. Sometimes memory selects from written tradition as when an incident in the Bible is used as the raw material for the imagination. The classic example of this form of anamnesis is the eucharist and the Ignatian exercises. Sometimes an outside object or symbol supplies this raw material as in so many of the meditations described in Book 3 of the Yoga Sutras and in the ceremonies and icons of the Church. On this selected material, always sifted by memory the imagination plays, making out of it an intellectual structure which is far removed from fantasy and as it is linked up with the emotions attains a life of its own. This imaginative structure makes the past present, gives to distant objects what Shakespeare calls 'a local habitation and a name'. In this way Christ manifests himself in the heart: the image brings the person it represents. And it is on this image that the discursive powers of the mind work, penetrating understanding, comparing until the contemplative becomes an integral part of the being of the image and assimilates and feeds upon the Lord. It is here that the image performs its final work. It becomes a kind of vehicle for carrying the contemplative into the Presence. As St. Peter says of the Transfiguration voice, it was the voice of the sublime Presence and revealed Him and led to Him. Like the cloud at the Transfiguration, it carried the disciples into the heart of the Lord Himself. This is what is contained in a total act of anamnesis, so clearly demonstrated in the eucharist yet by no means confined to that sacrament. Every object and every event can be used contemplatively in that way. And equally this is true of the act of samyama which leads, as Patanjali emphasises, not merely to intellectual clarity but to a participation in the power and glory of God. Persevering practice in this essential contemplative prayer technique, using the materials provided in these exercises, can lead to this goal.

Karl Barth in his exposition of Jesus as the Lord of time makes these helpful comments which throw light on both the action of the Holy Spirit and the Incarnate Lord in the act of contemplative prayer. He combines both the acts of epiclesis and anamnesis and emphasises the work of the Holy Spirit in making the Jesus of yesterday the Jesus of today. The principles he enunciates are the principles which transform the acts of contemplative prayer from mere reminiscence to living participation in the life of Christ in his kingdom. They are fundamental to the reality of all our relationships with God: 'After Easter and Pentecost, the primary conviction of the New Testament community is that the man Jesus is really but transcendentally present, in a way which could not be said of its contemporary members and other men of their age. His past history, His yesterday, cannot be understood or portrayed as a thing of the past, a thing of yesterday. The yesterday of Jesus is also today. The fact that He lives at the right hand of God means that even now He is absolutely present temporally. And to His own on their further journey into time, in and with the witness continually to be proclaimed and heard by them, He has given them His Spirit, the Holy Spirit. But where the Spirit is, there is more than a mere tradition or recollection of Jesus. Of course there is tradition and recollection as well. But the message of His past is proclaimed, heard and believed in order that it should be no longer past but present. Life is lived in contemplation of the kingdom already come, in which everything necessary has been done for the full deliverance and preservation of man, for the fulfilment of the divine covenant ... This history, this time, is not merely past but present, overlapping objectively as it were the present time of the apostles and their communities, pushing beyond its own frontiers to those of this other time and beyond. These men do not make or feel or know themselves the contemporaries of Jesus. It is not they who become or are this. It is Jesus who becomes and is their Contemporary. As a result of this, His past life, death and resurrection ... have the significance and force of an event ... which is decisive for their present existence' (Karl Barth, *Church Dogmatics*, Vol. III, p. 467, T & T Clark, 1968).

1

PRELIMINARY EXERCISES

The body plays an integral part in every act of contemplation. It shares in the divine life because the Word has taken it into Himself and in His own Person brings about the supreme mystery of interchange between the human and divine natures. This is a union of eternal significance in which both natures preserve their being without confusion and interpenetrate each other. The renewal and development of our human nature, whatever the ways we use and

173

however limited, enable it to participate more completely in the divine life of God. The acts described in this section are patterns of the way in which our humanity can be thus trained. It is important to insist that this is not done by our own unaided efforts, which would be a pelagian error, but by our response to the grace given by the indwelling Spirit. They should be adapted to age, health and opportunity.

The preliminary acts are therefore primarily physical but they divide into three classes: those which are exclusively physical; those which combine symbolic meaning with movement; and then corporate physical acts which are a combination of both.

1. PHYSICAL ACTS. The purely physical acts which are about to be described have been summarised by Yehudi Menuhin as designed to prepare the body as a dedicated offering, not merely a burnt sacrifice but an instrument 'focused in attention and will, offering in simplicity and innocence'. While they are being performed the mind is kept empty by being centred on the eternity of God (ananta) and the climax of each posture is a stillness of silence. The acts here described are a small selection from many but they have been tested by some for many years and found adequate for the purpose we have in mind. To them may well be added other forms of physical movement such as gardening or a non-competitive sport. It is important to choose what is suitable to the age and physical capacities of each person. The techniques of the movements should be mastered with at least as much perseverance as is needed for a musical instrument. Breathing and movement should be harmonised.

1. Standing in the vertical (tādāsana)
Movements into stillness:

Stand with the feet parallel.
Straighten the backbone from the base of the spine to the neck.
Balance the head on the spine with the eyes directed to the tip of the nose.
Press back the shoulders into an imaginary horizontal axis.
Relax the centres in the head, eyes, throat, heart, solar plexus, genitals and base of the spine.
Breathe through the nose, using the abdominal muscles to control the breathing rhythm.

Time: 5 minutes.

174

2. The death posture (*shavāsana*)
Movements into stillness:

Lie flat on the back,

Hands away from the sides, palms facing upwards.

Stretch the spine from the base.

Keep the eyes closed and unfocused.

Relax in all the centres as for the previous posture.

Breathe through the nose, abdominally.

Keep the mind still, turned towards God.

Time: 5 minutes.

3. Shoulder Stand (*sarvangāsana*)
Movements into stillness:

Lie flat on the back.

Breathe in and raise the legs, held straight, at right angles.

Place the hands against the back as a supporting strut.

Breathe out and bring the centre of balance to the shoulders.

Breathe in and raise the legs to a vertical position.

Bring the chest forward to touch the chin.

Remain in this position for some twenty abdominal breaths.

Return gently to the original position.

Time: 20 seconds to begin, lengthening to about 2 minutes.

175

4. The Plough (halāsana)
Movements into stillness:

Move into the first part of the shoulder stand

With the legs raised to the vertical.

Bring the arms over the head and rest them on the floor.

Breathe out and lower the legs, held straight, to the floor,

Behind the head, the toes lightly touching the ground.

Remain in this position, breathing abdominally, for some

Twenty breaths. Return to first position and relax.

Time: 20 seconds to begin, lengthening to about 2 minutes.

5. The Backstretch (paschimottānāsana)
Movements into stillness:

Sit with the legs stretched out in front, back straight.

Breathe out and take hold of the toes.

Extend the spine from the base, keeping the back concave.

Breathe out, bend forwards and widen the elbows.

Pull the trunk forward and touch the forehead to the knees.

Rest the elbows on the floor.

Remain, breathing from the abdomen, in this position

For some twenty breaths. Return to first position and relax.

Time: 20 seconds to begin, lengthening to about 2 minutes.

6. *The Cobra* (*bhujangāsana*)
Movements into stillness:

Lie on the floor, face downwards.
Breathe in and raise the trunk.
Bring the hands forward and with
    their help complete the
Movement.
Keeping the pelvis on the floor
    breathe from the abdomen
For some twenty breaths.
Return to the first posture and
    relax.

Time: 20 seconds to begin, lengthening to 3 minutes.

7. *The Headstand* (*shirshāsana*)
Movements into stillness:

Kneel and rest the forearms on the
    ground,
The elbows not wider than the
    shoulders.
Interlock the fingers.
Cup the back of the head into the
    hands.
Raise the knees from the ground
And walk towards the head.
Breathe in and lift the legs off the
    ground,
Bending them at the knees.
Using the muscles of the pelvis
Straighten the legs along the ver-
    tical axis
Running from the head to the base
    of the spine.
Correct the balance by moving the
    pelvis and the legs.
Thrust the legs upwards and keep
    the body still.
Breathe from the abdomen for
    some twenty breaths.
Return slowly and gently to the
    first position
And relax, resting on the heels
    with the back straight.

Time: 20 seconds to begin, lengthening to about 3 minutes.

8. *The Folded Leaf* (*virāsana*)
Movements into stillness:

Sit on the heels with the back straight.

Breathe out and bend the back from the pelvis,

Then from the shoulders and the neck

Until the forehead touches the ground

And the buttocks remain on the heels.

Relax the arms, palms upwards, along the sides.

Remain in this position, breathing abdominally,

For some twenty breaths.

Return to the first position and relax.

Time: 20 seconds to begin, lengthening to about 5 minutes.

9. *The Tree* (*vrkshāsana*)
Movements into stillness:

Stand in the vertical posture.

Move the weight on to the right foot.

Breathe in, placing the left foot against the right knee.

Breathe out.

Breathe in, raising the arms above the head.

Open the hands and then lower the arms.

Breathe out as they come down.

Join the hands over the solar plexus centre.

Relax in this position for some ten breaths.

Repeat the posture, using the other leg.

10. *Sleep* (*nidrā*)
Sleep is a complicated series of movements leading to the states of deep and shallow sleep. Not all of these movements are under our

178

own control but we can prepare for some of them and co-operate with others, especially the mental and emotional responses demanded in dreams. Artificial stimulation for sleep, such as barbiturates must at all costs be avoided.

Movements into stillness:

Undressing and washing should be done slowly.

A period of light reading.

The corpse posture for some five minutes of abdominal breathing.

Concentrate on one image and then relax the mind,

Directing the attention towards God.

Practice relaxing the mind by putting the eyes out of focus.

Slide into sleep.

Concentration themes:

Defend us from all perils and dangers
Of this night (Collect B.C.P.).
So He gives His beloved
Sleep (Psalm 127).
Sleep that knits up the ravell'd sleeve of care,
The death of each day's life,
Sore labour's bath,
Balm of hurt minds,
Great nature's second course,
Chief nourisher in life's feast (Shakespeare, *Macbeth*, Act 2).

11. Breathing

This is not an interference with the natural breathing but a removal of obstacles to this breathing and then a contemplative watching of the rhythm as an outward sign of the life and presence of the Holy Spirit.

Removal of obstacles:

Adopt one of the meditation postures.

Sit in a firm and pleasant position.

Put the eyes out of focus.

Keep the attention on a symbol of the Spirit

Centred near the solar plexus.

Clear the nasal passages,

179

Closing one and breathing gently through the other.

Relax all the centres of consciousness.

Contemplation of the breathing rhythm:

A symbol is helpful to keep the mind attentive.

Sometimes counting each breath is useful.

The breathing rhythm must in no way be interfered with.

The wind blows where it will:

So with the Spirit as he breathes.

This breathing will usually become slower and shallower.

Time: This exercise may go on for a long time. To begin with, not less than 10 minutes. This may be lengthened to form the main part of the act of contemplation.

12. Other forms of physical movement.

Under this heading comes:

Athletic exercises such as running and team games.

The competitive element must be subordinated to the attainment of contemplative stillness and at the end of any form of this exercise there should be a period of corporate stillness.

Music.

Manual work.

The pattern for each of these movements is the same as for the postures. It requires the mastery of the physical technique and then the performance in harmony with the breathing and the mind emptied of discursive thought.

2. SYMBOLIC ACTS. Because creation is a sacramental mystery every outward sign and movement has an inward and spiritual meaning. So with the acts of the body. They all express something of the indwelling spirit. The actions about to be described have been deliberately chosen to express certain hidden truths about man and his relationship to the world and to Christ and to his neighbour. They reach their most complete form in the sequence of movements connected with the Eucharist and the Holy Week ceremonies. The physical acts are distinguished by their symbolic meanings. When used with the co-operation of the mind and the will these acts develop the mystery they represent in both the individual and the group with which they are shared. For this reason certain suggested meditation responses are given to direct these faculties in taking their part in the movements.

1. Self-Denial (pādahastāsana)
Movements into stillness:

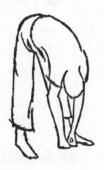

Stand in the vertical posture
With the hands joined over the heart centre.
Raise the arms over the head and breathe in.
Retract the abdomen and bend at the pelvis,
Making the back concave.
Take hold of the feet and bend the back at the shoulders.
Lower the head to the knees and draw the trunk inwards.
Relax in this posture for some twenty breaths.
Return gradually to the first position and relax.

Meditation responses:
Leave self behind;
Take up your cross;
Come with me (Mark 8 : 34).
The life I now live is not my life,
But the life which Christ lives in me (Galatians 2 : 20).
We are not worthy
So much as to gather up the crumbs
Under your table (Series 3).
Loving silence for 5 minutes.

181

2. Standing in the Cross (tādāsana)
Movements into stillness:

Perform the vertical posture already described.

Image the vertical axis of the cross Passing from the feet, through the spine to the head.

Image the horizontal axis passing through the shoulders.

Relax the centres and breathe abdominally.

Remain in this posture for five breaths and relax.

Meditation responses:

Your body is a shrine of the indwelling Holy Spirit (1 Corinthians 6).

You are Christ's body (1 Corinthians 12).

If there is a physical body, there is also a spiritual body (1 Corinthians 15).

What a piece of work is a man.

How noble in reason.

How infinite in faculty.

In form, in moving, how express and admirable.

In motion how like an angel.

In apprehension how like a god.

The beauty of the world.

The paragon of animals (Shakespeare, *Hamlet*, Act 2).

Loving silence for 5 minutes.

3. Turning to Christ (*surya namaskar*)
Movements into stillness:

These twelve movements need an instructor.

They lead down to the depths of the self

And to the heights of the Lord.

He who descended in great humility

182

Was also raised in glory.
The Spirit is the instrument
Of this great journey.
The Lord its goal.
Meditation responses:
I turn to Christ (Baptism).
He made Himself nothing,
Assuming the nature of a slave.
He humbled Himself.
Therefore God raised Him to the heights.
Jesus Christ is Lord (Philippians 2 : 6).
Holy, holy, holy Lord,
God of power and might,
Heaven and earth are full of your glory.
Hosanna in the highest (Series 3).
Loving silence for 5 minutes.

4. Walking in Christ
Movements into stillness:

Stand in the vertical posture.
Shift the weight to the right foot.
Breathe in and raise the left leg.
Hold the breath and breathe out as
the left leg reaches the ground.
Keep the eyes fixed on a point
some three feet ahead.
Repeat this movement using the
other leg.
This meditative walk should be
continued for some 5 minutes.

Responses:
God be in my head, and in my understanding;
God be in my eyes and in my looking;
God be in my mouth and in my speaking;
God be in my heart and in my thinking;
God be in my emotions and in my feelings;
God be in my instincts and in my loving;
God be at my end and at my departing (Sarum prayer).
Loving silence.

5. *Cosmic Christ*
Movements into stillness:

Stand in the vertical posture.
Breathe in and raise the hands
 from the sides.
Hold them outstretched.
Breathe out and bring them to-
 gether
At the heart centre.

Meditation responses:
> He is the image of the invisible God;
> His is the primacy over all created things (Colossians 1 : 15).
> Through Him you have created all things
> From the beginning
> And formed us in your own image (Series 3).

Loving silence for 5 minutes.

6. *The Head of the Body*
Movements into stillness:

Stand in the cross.
Turn right towards the neighbour.
Move towards him with out-
 stretched arms.
Give the kiss of peace.
Receive the kiss of peace and
 return to first posture.

Meditation responses:
> When the disciples were together
> Behind locked doors,
> For fear of the Jews,
> Jesus came and stood among them (John 20 : 19).
> O God, who hast knit together thine elect
> In one communion and fellowship
> In the mystical body of Thy Son (Collect).
> Through Him you have made us
> A people for your own possession (Series 3).

Loving silence for 5 minutes.

3. CORPORATE ACTS OF CONTEMPLATION. There are many
ways of sharing acts of contemplation. Christian tradition uses the
meal as one of these forms and calls it an agapé, and also the
eucharist. These are both essential ways of training for contemplative prayer and should be shared regularly. Based on these patterns
are other shared movements. Recreation is one and then the contemplation of movement practised each day at the Anchorhold and the
T'ai Chi Ch'uan.

It is not possible to describe these movements in detail because
each depends on the number taking part and the conditions under
which they are done. However some general outline may be helpful
and encourage others to design their own. We have in recent years
learnt the folly of trying to make people worship according to
rubrics. We must equally avoid the folly of trying to make them
contemplate according to rules. It is enough to give the principles
and then leave each group to experiment and apply them as seems
best. The Series 3 form of the eucharist has done this for the Church.
Much on these lines still waits to be done for the other forms of
Christian prayer.

1. Meals (agapé)
 The sign: Care should be taken to arrange the room and table.
     To suggest the community and the presence of the Lord.
     There should be a central symbol of the Lord.
 Time: at least 30 minutes.
 Movements into stillness:
   Every movement is a part
   Of a liturgy of service;
   The preparation and serving,
   The clearing away and washing up
   Are all means of grace.
   The food should be plain and wholesome,
   Meeting the needs of all the senses.
   Silence against a background of carefully chosen music
   Is helpful.
 Meditation responses:
   Draw near with faith.
   Feed on Him in your hearts
   By faith with thanksgiving (Series 3).
 Conversation.

2. The Eucharistic Sequence

This is the most complete form of symbolic movement in the Western tradition and recent revisions have encouraged the development of suitable postures to accompany the new forms. This can only be done by bold experiment between small groups of people and what follows is an outline of some of the positions reached by such a group. The results must always be provisional and flexible. Series 3 is the form of the eucharist used for this exposition and the references are to the sections as they are numbered in this form.

The Word and the Prayers

1–6 The Preparation

1–4	Stand in the vertical with hands joined.
5	Meditation walk around the central focus.
6	Stand in the vertical.

7–13 Ministry of the Word

7–10   Sit in a meditation posture for the O.T. and Epistle readings.

Sing an alleluia.

11   Stand in the vertical.

After the reading of the gospel the reader takes the book round to be reverenced and then places it at the centre.

12–13   Sit in a meditation posture.

14–20 The Prayers
15–17   Sit in a meditation posture.
20   Stand in the vertical.

The Communion

21–2 The Peace
21   Stand in the cross
22   The cosmic embrace.

23–5 The Taking of the bread and wine
23   A selection of Yoga postures or part of the T'ai Chi Ch'uan.
24   Meditation walk.

26–9 The Thanksgiving
27   Cosmic embrace.
29   Extend right hand towards the elements.
           Join hands at the heart centre for the acclamation.
           Modified tree posture for the doxology.

30 The Breaking of the Bread

31–6 The Giving of the Bread and the Cup
32   Meditation walk to the altar.
33   Hands in communion posture.

37 After Communion
43   A meditative posture for the contemplative silence.

3. Recreation
   The sign: The room should be arranged to symbolise.
           The body of Christ.
           The guests should sit in a circle around a focus.
           A stimulator or leader is essential.
   Time: at least 30 minutes.
   Movements into stillness:
           Refreshments, such as coffee, establish relationship.
           And should be served with special care.
           We have much to learn from the Japanese tea ceremony.
           The leader starts the conversation.
           By discreetly dropping the subject into the group.
           Like a fisherman.
           Dropping his float into still water.
   Meditation responses:
           Glory to God in the highest
           And peace to His people on earth (Series 3).
           How good and joyful a thing it is
           For brethren to dwell together in unity (Psalm 133).
           True friendship is a plant
           Of slow growth,

And must undergo and withstand
The shocks of adversity (George Washington).
Jesus, redeemer of the world;
Give us your peace (Series 3)
Loving silence.

4. CONTEMPLATION OF MOVEMENT
Time: 45 minutes.
Symbol: variable, depending on the theme of the prayer.

Sequence 1. Self-Denial
(i) Stand in the Cross,
   Hands held together at the naval centre
   Eyes looking towards the nose.
   Open each of the centres using the prayer:
   God be in my head and in my understanding:
   God be in my eyes and in my looking:
   God be in my mouth and in my speaking:
   God be in my heart and in my thinking:
   God be in my emotions and in my feelings:
   God be in my instincts and in my willing:
   God be at my end and at my departing.
(ii) Perform the obeisance posture (Pādahastāsana).
(iii) Move round the centre, using the meditation walk.
   Return to the starting point.
   Stand once more relaxed in the cross.

Sequence 2. Affirmation
(i) Perform the surya namaskar three times
   With complementary breathing and the ascription:
   Glory be to the Father,
   And to the Son,
   And to the Holy Spirit.
(ii) The cosmic embrace;
   All things were made through Him.
(iii) Pass the kiss of peace to all sharing in the contemplation.
   Peace be with you.

Sequence 3. Stillness
The word posture which is ordinarily used for positions of stillness is
a translation of the sanskrit word āsana which means sitting. Each
posture is an exercise to enable the body to be held in stillness for a
long time. It should be reached by harmonising movement and
breathing. There should be a period of stillness when the position is
reached and a period of equal length in a relaxed posture afterwards.

The mind should be concentrated on the eternal attributes of God during these movements.

The following is a suggested course of postures which have been proved effective both for physical health and the development of stillness leading to contemplation.

The corpse posture (shavāsana)
Shoulder-stand (sarvangāsana)
Plough (halāsana)
Backstretch (paschimottānāsana)
Cobra (bhujangāsana)
Head-stand (shirshāsana)
Folded leaf (virāsana)

These postures should not be attempted too soon after a meal. They should not be isolated into a form of physical training since they are intended to lead to stillness and stillness requires some form of contemplative activity if all the faculties are to be properly used.

Sequence 4. Contemplation of the Spirit
The word which corresponds to Spirit in sanskrit is prānā and the rules for co-operation with the Spirit are called prānāyāma. The most intimate manifestation of this energy is breathing and so co-operation with the Spirit takes the form of breathing control. The Western tradition is that the Spirit initiates and co-operates in the spiritual life and so this part of the act of contemplation is concerned with the removal of hindrances to the free activity of the Spirit and the adequate co-operation with His working.

There are three main exercises:

(i) Mastery of one of the sitting postures.
(ii) Clearing the nasal passages.
(iii) Substitution of the natural breathing rhythm for the rythm of the Spirit.

A symbol of the Spirit such as water, wind, incense, wine, oil, flame held in the place of breathing helps concentration on the Spirit and co-operation with His infusion of the virtues and gifts intensifies awareness of His work and presence. Details of this co-operation will be found in other examples of contemplative acts.

Sequence 5. Contemplative Detachment
This is a process of withdrawing the senses from outside stimulation and centring them in the heart.

(i) Close the eyes and withdraw the other senses from outside contact.

(ii) Enter into the heart and there centre the inner senses on a point in the heart. This is done by standing in the vertical position and crossing the hands over the heart.

Sequence 6. Contemplation of the Word
A symbol of the Word is chosen for this purpose and placed in the centre. Then the following three acts of what Patanjali calls samyama or mind concentration are practised.

(i) All the senses are concentrated on the visible object. The hand is held out towards it to increase the concentration.

(ii) The contemplative moves towards the symbol and using the communion gesture with the hands closes the eyes and allows an internal image of the symbol to form in the heart.

(iii) Holding this image which is made alive by breathing the Spirit into it, the contemplative moves round the symbol using a mantra or short phrase to keep the mind flowing towards the image.

The tree posture is used at the end of each circuit for the purpose of relaxation.

(iv) The sitting posture is then taken and the image allowed to fade, either by a process of fraction or assimilation. The heart then opens to the presence of the Lord and identifies with Him. This still, contemplative posture should be held as long as possible without strain.

This contemplation of movement is capable of an infinite number of variations and should be adapted to meet the needs of the individual as well as the contemplative group. It also provides a pattern for other forms of contemplation.

5. THE CONTEMPLATIVE DANCE—T'AI CHI CH'UAN. In a discussion between a Taoist and a Buddhist the Taoist said: 'Meditation in activity is a million times superior to meditation in repose. The stillness in stillness is not real stillness. Only when there is stillness in movement does the universal rhythm manifest itself.' This is the principle behind the contemplative dance. Through movement stillness is gained and in the stillness of movement the presence of God is realised. This is the teaching of T. S. Eliot. The dance and the stillness are one.

The T'ai Chi Ch'uan is one of many forms of dance which has been designed to lead to this stillness through movement. It was practised by early Taoist monks and is sometimes attributed to Chang San-Feng who lived roughly between A.D. 1260 and A.D. 1360. He lived in a monastery in central China and spent his life creating these movements. He died at the age of 74 and after his

190

death the dance continued to be practised by monks and was handed down by them and shared with certain distinguished families. There are many ways of doing it today and this freedom is part of the essence of the movements. There are 108 of them which once mastered lead the body, mind and spirit into a harmony of contemplative awareness.

The mastery of these movements makes considerable demands and it is said that the dance must be practised for at least ten years before its real effects are experienced. But all the time it has its beneficial results: slowly the body is transformed, the movements become smoother and more flowing, the breathing becomes freer and deeper and the thoughts clarify. This is not the place to describe the movements which in any case cannot be grasped without individual tuition, but some of them may be easily learnt and even a reduced form of the dance can bring great benefits.

In using this dance as a contemplative act the following points should be observed:

1. A contemplative symbol should be set up. This may well take the form of an icon fixed on the wall of the room where the dance is performed. The icon should be venerated both at the beginning and the end of the dance.
2. The heart should be kept free for images of the dance during the performance. This is done by following the movements with the eyes and harmonising them with the movement of the Spirit.
3. At the end of the dance there should be a considerable period for recollection and inner stillness. During this time the same acts as have been described for using the image and meditating upon it should be practised.

Some of us see a similarity between the T'ai Chi Ch'uan and the Indian form of the 'Lord of the Dance' in the figure of Shiva Nataraj.

This wonderful sculpture has been described in this way: 'Shiva's dance is not an empty myth, but an image of the Energy which science must postulate behind all phenomena ... its significance is threefold: first, it is the image of his rhythmic play as the source of all movement within the cosmos which is represented by the arch: secondly, the purpose of his dance is to release the countless souls of men from the snare of illusion: thirdly, the place of the Dance, Chidambaram, the centre of the universe, is within the heart' (Jon and Rumer Godden, *Shiva's Pigeons*, p. 220, Chatto and Windus, 1972).

Heinrich Zimmer analyses the idea in much the same way, writing of Shiva as 'the Cosmic Dancer' and as the expression of the eternal energy of creation. Such an idea has penetrated to Christianity where our Lord is identified with the Lord of the Dance.

The Indian and Chinese approach to breathing is very much the same. For the Indian, breathing is a reception of prānā, the energy of the universe and in all its forms the object is to receive and use this energy as completely as possible. For the Chinese, breathing is the reception of Chi, the life breath of the earth, and although the Yoga physical postures are not generally used by Chinese ascetics they have developed techniques of breathing similar to those found in the breathing exercises of Hatha Yoga.

Arthur Wayley in his book *The Way and Its Power* writes of the Chinese theory of breathing as follows: 'The breathing of the Sage is not like that of ordinary men: he breathes with every part of him right down to the heels. He keeps the Great Treasure (i.e. the initial life-breath) intact and uses only the new breath. He sees to it that his "clarified breath" is daily renewed, his evil breath entirely eliminated. The breathing of the Sage ... must be like that of an infant. Later Taoist writers go a step further, saying that it must be like that of a child in the womb' (Arthur Wayley, *The Way and Its Power*, p. 118, Allen & Unwin, 1968).

Yin and Yang literally mean the dark side and the sunny side of a hill. They correspond to the categories of male and female, weak and strong, dark and light. Yin is the vital energy (Chi, the life-breath of earth) and Yang is the life-breath of heaven. The object in spiritual asceticism in the teaching of the Yin-Yang philosophers was not the triumph of one or other of these forces but the attainment of a perfect balance between them.

This teaching can be applied both to breathing and movement. The in-breath is a Yin energy: the out-breath, a Yang. The withdrawing movement is Yin: the aggressive, Yang. The upward movement of the leg in walking is Yin: the downward movement, Yang.

The purpose of the dance is to harmonise movement and breathing and so to bring the whole being into a state of resolved and balanced tension of Yin and Yang energies.

Behind the movement of the dance is a controlling allegory. This is used, not so much as material for discursive thought during the dance as concentration material for holding the mind still and in balance as the movements are performed. Some of the main themes of this allegory, though by no means all, are given in the following outline.

Part One

Grasp bird's tail.
Bird's beak.
Hand strums lute.
White stork spreads its wings.
Twisted step, parry and punch.
Carry tiger in your arms and return to the Mountain.

Part Two

Step back and repulse the monkey.
Magic bird standing on one leg.
Looking for needle at the bottom of the sea.
Shooting the Arrow.
No beginning, no end.
The kicking section.
Carry tiger to the Mountain.

Part Three

Parting of wild horse's mane.
Four corners of the earth.
Snake creeps down to water.
Golden cock stands on one leg.
Step up to form the seven stars.
Retreat step and ride tiger.
Rising out of the mire.
Bend bow and shoot tiger.
Carry tiger to the Mountain.

2

ACTS OF CONTEMPLATION IN THE HEART

There is an innumerable number of possible contemplative acts in the heart. They vary from tradition to tradition and are an interiorisation of many of the forms of prayer used by the members of these traditions. The Christian tradition is particularly rich in such forms. They are to be found in the Divine Office and in the liturgical mysteries, in the eucharist and in the sacraments, besides those associated with Christian symbols and art and architecture. Those mentioned in this selection are a small number which have been used for many years and proved their value in training the heart in contemplation both of the Spirit and the Word. Each individual will eventually select his own.

The heart considered as the place of contemplation is a nexus of mind, emotions and will. The Sanskrit word which corresponds to this centre is chitta. It is much more than a mental faculty concerned with discursive thought. It is the centre of the new man, of the total spiritual powers of human nature, the point where God indwells and communicates with man. The heart raised to mature activity is the contemplative apex of man, the instrument of supreme insight into the mystery of God.

One of the clearest models of the ways to contemplation in the heart is given in Blake's *Book of Job.* There he provides the mind with imaginative material in the form of the engraving. This is enriched with the verbal materials of his Bible quotations. Under the control of these images and words the heart is led to share in the contemplative insight which Blake intended to communicate. These acts of contemplation in the heart will follow a similar pattern. There will be a controlling sign or image. There will be some verbal material to focus and stimulate the mind. In the period of imageless silence some form of insight should normally follow. But the aim is not this insight so much as the stillness of heart which makes possible response to the movement of the Spirit and the utterance of the Word which go on continually within it.

No references are made in these exercises to any physical acts but they assume the mastery of a suitable contemplative posture. There are many from which to choose. The three yoga postures are: the siddhāsana, the sukhāsana and the padmāsana. These are difficult to achieve by beginners but perseverance and practice often bring mastery in a short time. Other less demanding postures are achieved by using a prayer stool or a straight-backed chair. The vital physical condition at this stage of contemplation is a complete stillness. When the body is restless the heart becomes clouded and unsteady and contemplation is impossible.

Three acts control this kind of contemplation. They are memory, imagination and love. The memory is the faculty by which the mind selects from the objective material what it needs for making the internal image. Sometimes this objective material is a physical object in the form of a symbol but often it is a past event recorded in the Bible or lifted out of past experiences. When the memory operates on the material in this way it makes the first act of a memorial or anamnesis; it supplies the material needed by the imagination to lift the past event into the present and to interiorise the object in the heart. This is quite different from fantasy. It is a creative act and the resulting image is a real and living vehicle for communicating the Lord and His grace in the heart. Blake fully understood this 'divine power of the imagination'. In these days of so many fantasy images it is not easy to train the imagination for this contemplative purpose. And then the image is not lifeless but quickened by the Spirit of

Love. It is an instrument which communicates the love of God and stimulates the heart to reciprocate that love.

1. ACTS OF CONTEMPLATION OF THE SPIRIT IN THE HEART. There are three instruments for contemplating the Spirit in the heart: the symbols of the Spirit as they are given in the Christian tradition; the rhythm of breathing in the Body of Christ; and the mysteries of our Lady who is described as 'the shrine of the Holy Spirit'. In her we see the Spirit working and her response is the model of our own. These three instruments are the basis of the acts which follow.

1. Cleansing by the Spirit
    Time: 30 minutes
    Sign: Water and baptism.
    Movements into stillness:

Reproduce in the heart
With memory and imagination
The sacraments of initiation.
Visualise the water of life flowing
    through the heart,
Making all things new.
Contemplate the den of robbers
Transformed into the house of
    prayer.

Meditation response:
Almighty God,
To whom all hearts are open,
All desires known,
And from whom no secrets are
    hid:
Cleanse the thoughts of our
    hearts,
By the inspiration of your Holy
    Spirit (Series 3).

Loving silence.

2. Reception of the Spirit
Time: 30 minutes
Sign: Sound. The Annunciation
Movements into stillness:

Loving silence.

Reproduce in the heart St. Luke
1 : 26–38.
With memory and imagination.
The angel went in and said to her
Greetings, most favoured one.
She was deeply troubled.
The Holy Spirit will come upon
you,
And the power of the Most High
will overshadow you.
I am the Lord's servant;
As you have spoken,
So be it.

Meditation response:
Pour your grace into our hearts
That as we have known the incar-
nation of your Son
By the message of an angel,
So by his cross and passion
We may be brought unto the glory
Of his resurrection.

3. Rejoicing in the Spirit
Time: 30 minutes.
Sign: Wind. The Visitation.
Movements into stillness:

Reproduce in the heart St. Luke
1 : 39–56.
With memory and imagination.
Mary went to a town in the
uplands of Judah.
She greeted Elizabeth.
When Elizabeth heard Mary's
greeting
The babe stirred in her womb.
God's blessing is on you above all
women,
And his blessing is on the fruit of
your womb.

196

Meditation response:
Tell out, my soul, the greatness of
the Lord,
Rejoice, rejoice, my spirit, in God
my Saviour.
So wonderfully has He dealt with
me,
The Lord, the Mighty One. (Magnificat.)

Loving silence. Exercise the other emotions: grief, fear, hope.

4. Sacrifice through the Spirit
Time: 30 minutes.
Sign: Incense. Presentation.
Movements into stillness:

Reproduce in the heart St. Luke
2 : 22–40.
With memory and imagination.
They brought him up to Jerusalem
To present Him to the Lord.
He took him in his arms
And praised God.

Meditation response:
This day, Master, thou givest thy
servant
His discharge in peace;
Now thy promise is fulfilled.
For I have seen with my own eyes
The deliverance which thou hast
made ready,
A light that will be a revelation to
the heathen,
And glory to thy people Israel.

Loving silence.   (Nunc Dimitis.)

5. *Suffering in the Spirit*
Time: 30 minutes.
Symbol: Wine. Mary at the Cross.
Movements into stillness:

Loving silence.

Reproduce in the heart St. John
  19 : 25–7.
With memory and imagination.
But meanwhile near the Cross
  where Jesus hung
Stood his mother.
Jesus saw his mother,
With the disciple whom he loved
Standing beside her.

Meditation response:
Woman, there is your son.
Son, there is your mother.
The disciple took her into his own
  home.

6. *Rebirth in the Spiritual body*
Time: 30 minutes.
Symbol: Oil. Resurrection.
Movements into stillness:

Reproduce in the heart St. John
  20 : 11–18.
With memory and imagination.
She peered into the tomb.
She saw two angels in white sitting
  there.
She turned round and saw Jesus
  standing there.
Jesus said, Mary.
She turned to him and said,
Rabbuni.

Meditation response:
We thank you
For the glorious pledge of the
  hope of our calling
Which you have given us in your
  saints;
that, following their example

198

and strengthened by their fellowship,
we may run with perserverance
the race that is set before us,
and with them receive
the unfading crown of glory
(Series 3).

Loving silence.

7. *Glory from the Spirit*
Time: 30 minutes.
Sign: Crown. Pentecost.
Movements into stillness:

Reproduce in the heart Acts
2 : 1–4.
With memory and imagination.
They were all together
In one place.
Suddenly there came from the sky
a noise
Like that of a strong driving wind
Which filled the whole house
where they were sitting.
There appeared to them tongues
like flames of fire
Dispersed among them
And resting on each one.

Meditation response:
By that same Spirit
We are led into all truth
And are given power to proclaim
your gospel to the nations
and to serve you as a royal priesthood (Series 3).

Loving silence.

8. *Affective prayer*
Time: 30 minutes.
Sign: candle.
Movements into stillness:

Concentrate on the sexual centre
And relax.
Direct the energy of this centre
Into the heart.
Use it to light a flame in the heart.
In the early stage use the medita-
   tion walk
To achieve control and remove
   tension.

Meditation response:
Christ is the head of everyman.
I take thee to my wedded husband
to have and to hold
from this day forward
for better for worse,
for richer for poorer,
in sickness and in health,
to love, cherish and to obey,
till death us do part,
   according to God's holy ordinance.

Loving silence.

9. *Vocal prayer*
Sign: prayer mat.
Movements into stillness:

The attention should be focused in
the heart and throat centre.
The words should be addressed to
The Lord in the heart in the power
   of the Spirit.
Recitation on a note increases
   concentration.

Meditation response:
The words and ceremonies of the
   Office.

Loving silence of at least 10 minutes at the conclusion of the prayer.

10. Mass in the heart

Signs: the symbols and ceremonies of the Mass.
Movements into stillness:

The place of the eucharist is the heart
Here all the actions are reproduced with
Memory and imagination.
The actions are addressed to the Lord in the heart.
There He is met and assimilated.

Meditation response:
The words and ceremonies of the Mass.

Loving silence of at least 10 minutes at the conclusion of the prayer.

11. Intercession in the heart

Signs: images of the subjects of the prayer.
Movements into stillness:

The subjects of the prayer are reproduced in the heart
Through memory and imagination.
They are breathed upon by the Spirit:
They are assimilated in loving sympathy.

Meditation response:
The Lord's prayer.

Loving silence of at least 10 minutes to receive the grace prayed for.

12. Work in the heart

The place for rehearsal of work to be done and recollection of work completed is the heart. Our Lord approached and concluded all his work in this way. This prayer is an attempt to follow his example.

Sign: work to be done.
Movements into stillness:

> The work is reproduced in the heart
> By memory and imagination.
> It is animated by the Spirit.
> The actions relating to the work are done in the heart.

> Meditation response:
> The Lord God planted a garden
> And there he put the man
> Whom he had formed
> To dress it and keep it (Genesis).
> But for the Virtuous things you do,
> The Righteous Work the Public Care,
> It shall not be forgiven you (Chesterton).
> Grant us so to labour
> That the works of your redeeming love
> May be revealed in our lives
> In the beauty of holiness.

Loving silence for at least 10 minutes to give thanks for the work done.

2. ACTS OF CONTEMPLATION OF THE WORD IN THE HEART. The Word in the heart begins as an image which becomes a sound and then leads into silence. All the acts of contemplation on the Word therefore follow the sequence of sign, sound and silence. Of course the sound often takes the form of words but in order to reach silence these words should be simplified, eventually to a single sound leading to silence. The present-day emphasis on speaking with tongues may be an instinctive recoil from an over-emphasis on a verbal form of the faith, and an attempt to move to a less verbal and more simple communication with the Lord. What needs to be watched is the danger of making the sound as complicated as the rejected words and to search for a replacement language in the form of speaking with tongues. This would be to replace the semantic error with semantics in an even more complicated and obstructive form. The Eastern satisfaction with the sound OM is a wiser insight than this.

In giving some acts of contemplation of the Word the traditional mysteries of the Incarnate Lord have been followed but there is no reason why others should not be used from the rich material available both in the Bible and in the whole of creation. These acts are selective and perhaps sound enough to form a pattern for the many others that can be used. It is necessary to emphasise that the selected acts are not ends in themselves but exercises to lead to the contemplation of the Word. When He has been heard the exercises can be put aside and the music played.

1. The Incarnation of the Word
  Time: 30 minutes.
  Sign: Open hands. The Nativity.
  Movements into stillness:

Reproduce in the heart St. Luke 2 : 1–20.
With memory and imagination.
She gave birth to a son, her first-born.
She laid him in a manger.
We must go straight to Bethlehem
And see this thing that has happened,
Which the Lord has made known to us.
The shepherds returned
Glorifying and praising God.

Meditation response:
By the power of the Holy Spirit
He took our nature upon him
And was born of the Virgin Mary his mother,
That being himself without sin
He might make us clean from all sin (Series 3).

  Loving silence.

2. *The Manifestation of the Word*
Time: 30 minutes.
Sign: The star. Epiphany.
Movements into stillness:

Reproduce in the heart St. Matthew 2 : 1–12.
With memory and imagination.
Where is the child
Who is to be born king of the Jews?
The star which they had seen at its rising
Went ahead of them
Until it stopped over the place where the child lay.
Entering the house,
They saw the child with Mary his mother.

Meditation response:
Because in coming to dwell among us as man,
He revealed the radiance of his glory,
And brought us out of darkness
Into his own marvellous light (Series 3).

Loving silence.

3. Temptations and ministry

Time 30 minutes.
Sign: Cross. Temptations in the wilderness.
Movements into silence:

Reproduce in the heart St. Mark
    1 : 12–13.
With memory and imagination.
The Spirit sent him away into the
    wilderness.
And there he remained for forty
    days
Tempted by Satan.
He was among the wild beasts;
And the angels waited on him.

Meditation response:
Through him you have given us
The Spirit of discipline
That we may triumph over evil
And grow in grace (Series 3).

Loving silence.

4. The Transfiguration

Time: 30 minutes.
Sign: Loaf. Transfiguration.
Movements into stillness:

Reproduce in the heart St. Mark
    9 : 2–8.
With memory and imagination.
Jesus took Peter, James and John
    with him
And led them up a high mountain
Where they were alone.
And in their presence he was
    transfigured.
This is my Son, my Beloved;
Listen to him.

Meditation response:
Grant that in faith beholding the
    light of his countenance

We may be strengthened to bear
his cross,
And be changed into his likeness
From glory to glory (1928 BCP).

Loving silence.

5. *Crucifixion*
Time: 30 minutes.
Sign: Chalice. The Crucifixion.
Movements into stillness:

Reproduce in the heart St. John
19 : 23–37.
With memory and imagination.
The soldiers having crucified
Jesus,
Took possession of his clothes,
And divided them into four parts.
Jesus said:
I thirst.
Having received the wine he said:
It is accomplished.
He bowed his head
And gave up his Spirit.

Meditation response:
For our salvation
He was obedient even to death on
the Cross.
The tree of defeat became the tree
of glory:
And where life was lost
There life has been restored
(Series 3).

Loving silence.

206

6. *Resurrection*

Time: 30 minutes.
Sign: Candle. Resurrection.
Movements into stillness:

Reproduce in the heart St. John 20 : 1–9.
With memory and imagination.
They were running side by side,
But the other disciple outran Peter
And reached the tomb first.
He peered in,
He went in.
He saw and believed.

Meditation responses:
By his death he has destroyed death
And by his rising again
He has restored to us eternal life (Series 3).

Loving silence.

7. *Ascension*

Time: 30 minutes.
Sign: Crown. Ascension.
Movements into stillness:

Reproduce in the heart Acts 1 : 9–11.
With memory and imagination.
As they watched he was lifted up,
And a cloud removed him from their sight.
This same Jesus
Who has been taken away from you up to heaven
Will come in the same way as you have seen him go up.

207

Meditation response:
In his risen body
He appeared to his disciples
And in their sight was taken up
into heaven,
To reign with you in glory (Series
3).

Loving silence.

Paraphrased Extracts from the Yoga Sutras

Geraldine Coster was speaking for most of us when she wrote: 'Very few western readers are acquainted with the Yoga Sutras and those who do read them find them for the most part incomprehensible. There exist several English translations but where these have been made by Hindus the phraseology used is very misleading to the European reader, and where they have been made by English students the endeavour to render them intelligible has often led to a very wide departure from the original' (Geraldine Coster, *Yoga and Western Psychology*, p. 99, Motilal Banarsidass, 1968).

Translation is one problem: selection is the other. Much of the Yoga Sutras deals with matters which are not of interest to our Western traditions and to include this material would unnecessarily complicate the task of both reader and writer. Jack Winslow was well aware of this when he limited himself to the eight limbs of the Yoga Sutras. This was too severe a limitation for our purpose and so we have been more generous in our selection. But we have observed the twofold principle of paraphrase as regards translation and selection as regards the extracts given in this appendix. In both methods we have used the Yoga Sutras as illustrative material from a classic Eastern tradition which is always subordinated to the main purpose of exploring the art of contemplation. As far as possible the aim has been to give as wide an introduction to the Yoga Sutras as is compatible with the larger theme. It is to be hoped that many others more competent in sanskrit will undertake other translations and paraphrases and will include, perhaps in smaller print, those other parts of the Sutras which have not been included here.

In order to have a controlling structure for the selections from the Sutras they have been grouped under the following headings which as far as possible follow the general outline of the exploration which has been described in this book. Not always has it been possible to achieve an exact correspondence but it has seemed near enough for our purpose and we hope will encourage readers to develop for themselves the fascinating task of discovering in Patanjali so many of the fundamental features of their own contemplative tradition.

The headings under which our selections have been arranged are:

1. Contemplation
2. Materials of contemplation:
   1. Images
   2. The Lord

1

CONTEMPLATION

1 : 1   The Yoga Sutras
Are a present-day exposition
Of the way to contemplative union with God (yoga).

1 : 2   Contemplative union with God
Is brought about
By mastering the images in the heart.

1 : 3   When this mastery is achieved
The contemplative abides
In his true self.

1 : 4   Without this mastery
The contemplative is distracted
By the images in his heart.

1 : 17   Contemplation with an image (samprajnātā samādhi)
Passes through these stages:
discursive thought (savitarka samādhi);
reflection (savichārā samādhi);
joy (sānanda samādhi);
simple awareness (sasmitā samādhi).

1 : 18   Contemplation without an image (asamprajnātā samādhi)
Other than those imprinted on the mind
Is that activity of the heart
Which follows the cessation of images.

1 : 19   Imageless contemplation arises from
A complete absorption
In the mystery of primary creation.

1 : 20   Imageless contemplation is the result of
Faith (shraddhā), unwavering energy (viryā)
Memory (smrti) and perfect understanding (prājnāpurvaka).

210

1 : 21 Imageless contemplation comes to those
Who strive energetically (samveganām).

1 : 22 Progress varies in proportion as the application is
Half-hearted (mrdu), lukewarm (madhya) or intense (adhimā-
tratvāt).

1 : 23 Imageless contemplation arises from
Devotion to the Lord (Ishvara pranidhāna).

111 : 4 When concentration, meditation and contemplation
Are practised in one sequence on an object
They form an act of total contemplation (samyama).

111 : 5 The mastery of samyama
Leads to the light
Of perfect insight (prajnā).

2

MATERIALS OF CONTEMPLATION

Patanjali, following the Sankhya philosophy, includes primary nature
(prakrti) and the emotional energies (gunas) among the contemplative
materials and with them such influences as heredity (karma) and the bodily
functions but these are all described in an idiom which is far removed from
modern scientific jargon and hard to translate into present-day language.
For our purpose the materials of contemplation most important are images
and the Lord.

1. IMAGES. We have translated the word vrttis as images. Actually this
word means a wave or mental vibration. It is used of a movement in the
mind. It need not be merely visual. It can be formed by any or all the senses
and react upon them. But so can an image. In the west we most ordinarily
think of mental movements as images rather than waves or vibrations and so
this word has been used.

1 : 5–11 Sources of images
1 : 5 The images of the heart arise from five sources.
Some are hindrances; some are helps
To contemplation.

1 : 6 The five sources of images are:
Right knowledge (pramāna); wrong knowledge (viparyaya);
Fantasy (vikalpa); sleep (nidrā); and memory (smrti).

211

1 : 7   Images arising from right knowledge are based on:
         Sense perception (pratyaksha); right reasoning (anumāna);
         Sound tradition (āgamā).

1 : 8   Images arising from wrong knowledge
         Are based on a false perception
         Of a real object.

1 : 9   Images arising from fantasy
         Are based on words alone
         And have no objective reality.

1 : 10   Images arising from sleep
         Are based on imagination alone.

1 : 11   Images arising from memory
         Are based on past experience.

1 : 12–16 Mastery of images
   1 : 12   The mastery of the images in the heart
            Comes from practice (abhyāsa) and
            Non-attachment (vairāgyā).

   1 : 13   Persistent practice is a persevering effort
            Towards the mastery of the image in the heart.

   1 : 14   This persistent practice develops into a deeply-rooted habit
            When repeated for a long time,
            Without interruption
            And with perfect devotion.

   1 : 15   Non-attachment is perfect mastery of desires
            By one who has ceased to crave
            For objects, visible or invisible.

   1 : 16   The highest non-attachment comes
            From awareness of the true self (Purusha)
            And the cessation of every desire.

2. THE LORD (ISHVARA) 1 : 24–9
   1 : 24   Ishvara is the Supreme Self (Purusha)
            Who is without hindrances (klesha)
            Karma and inherited defects (vipakashayair).

   1 : 25   In him is the highest form of knowledge
            Which in others
            Is only in germ.

212

1 : 26   Unlimited by time
         He was the teacher of the teachers
         Of ancient times.

1 : 27   His manifesting symbol (vachaka)
         Is the word of glory (pranava) OM.

1 : 28   This should be constantly repeated (japa)
         With meditation on its meaning.

1 : 29   Through this repetition of the word
         With meditation
         Distractions disappear and consciousness turns inwards.

3

OBSTACLES TO CONTEMPLATION

This section introduces the most valuable part of the Sutras for our Western tradition. It analyses the obstacles to contemplation under the headings of distractions and hindrances and then proceeds to give a method of training to reduce them and develop the heart in ways of contemplation. It shows remarkable psychological insight and supplies sound material for applying much of the method to our own Western needs.

1. DISTRACTIONS (VIKSHEPAS)
1 : 30   There are nine mental distractions
         Which obstruct contemplation:
         disease (vyādhi) which disturbs the body;
         languor (styāna) which weakens the mind;
         doubt (samshaya);
         carelessness (pramāda);
         laziness (ālasya);
         worldly-mindedness (avirati);
         illusion (bhrānti darshana);
         non-completion of a stage (alabdha bhumikatva);
         instability (anavasthitattva).

1 : 31   The symptoms of these distractions are:
         sadness (dukha);
         anxiety (daurmansya);
         unsteadiness of body (angamejayatva);
         irregular breathing (shāvasaprashvāsa).

1 : 32–9 Ways of mastering mental distractions
1 : 32   Mental distractions are overcome
         By concentration on a single truth (eka-tattvābhyāsah).

213

1 : 33   The heart is cleansed
By cultivating attitudes of:
friendliness (maitri);
compassion (karunā);
gladness (mudita);
indifference (upeksha) towards happiness, misery, virtue, vice.

1 : 34   By the expiration and retention of the breath.

1 : 35–9   Steadiness comes from:
applying the powers of reason to sense perception;
concentrating on the inner light;
meditation on a fully integrated person;
a dream or deep sleep experience;
a subject of one's own choice.

2. *HINDRANCES* (*KLESHAS*). Patanjali's teaching about the hindrances to contemplation is one of the basic parts of his work. These hindrances are not merely defects to a balanced life or offences against God. They obstruct contemplation and when removed the contemplative is able to live his intended life. In some ways they resemble the Christian teaching about sin but they view sin much more in the light of a cloud between the soul and God than in terms of a breach of the divine law.

2 : 3–9 The hindrances described

2 : 3   The hindrances are:
ignorance (avidyā);
egoism (asmitā);
desire (rāga);
aversion (dvesha);
over-attachment to life (abhinivesha).

2 : 4   Ignorance is the field
In which the other hindrances grow.
These hindrances exist in the following forms:
dormant, reduced, alternating and developed.

2 : 5   Ignorance leads a man to assume
That the transient is eternal,
The impure, pure.
The painful and non-Atman to be
Eternal, pure, good
And the true Self.

2 : 6   Egoism is the confusion of identity between
The object of contemplation (Purusha)
And the instrument of contemplation (the ego).

2 : 7   Desire is being absorbed
In pleasure.

2 : 8   Aversion is being absorbed
In pain.

2 : 9   Over-attachment to life
         Dominates even the wise.

2 : 10–11 Principles for overcoming the hindrances to contemplation
2 : 10   The hindrances
         In their undeveloped form
         Should be overcome
         By tracing them back to their sources.

2 : 11   The hindrances
         In their developed form
         Should be overcome
         Through meditation.

4

PRIMARY CONTEMPLATIVE TRAINING

2 : 1   Physical discipline (tapas)
         Self-study (svādhȳaya)
         Devotion to the Lord (Ishvara pranidhāna)
         Are the forms of active contemplation (kriya yoga).

2 : 2   This discipline leads to contemplation
         And reduces the hindrances.

5

ADVANCED CONTEMPLATIVE TRAINING

2 : 28–9 The Eight-limbed Yoga (Ashtanga Yoga)
2 : 28   Through the practice of the eight-limbed yoga
         Comes the destruction of impurities
         And the growth of spiritual illumination,
         Developing into awareness of the divine presence.

2 : 29   There are eight limbs of yoga:
         Restraints (yama); observances (niyama)
         Posture (āsana); regulation of prānā (prānāyāma);
         Introversion (pratyāhāra);
         Concentration (dhāranā); meditation (dhyāna); contemplation
            (samādhi).

2 : 30–1 The Five Restraints

2 : 30   The restraints are:
Non-killing (ahimsā); truthfulness (satya); non-stealing (asteya);
Continence (brahmachārya); non-covetousness (aparigrahā).

2 : 31   These restraints are not limited to
A particular class or country,
To the past, present or future:
They are universal.
They are the natural law (mahat vritam).

2 : 32 The Five Observances

2 : 32   The observances are:
Purity (shaucha); contentment (samtosha);
Physical discipline (tapas); self-study (svādhyāya);
And devotion to God (Ishvara pranidhāna).

2 : 33–45 Principles and results of practising the restraints and observances

2 : 33   In order to overcome distracting forces
Their opposites should be practised.

2 : 34   Opposite actions should be cultivated
Because all destructive instinctive forces,
Whether performed or caused to be done or approved,
Whether motivated by greed, anger or delusion,
Whether in mild, moderate or intense form,
Cause infinite suffering and ignorance.

2 : 35   When man is firmly established in non-violence
His presence destroys hostility.

2 : 36   When a man is established firmly in truth
The result of his actions is truth.

2 : 37   When a man is firmly established in non-stealing
All jewels belong to him.

2 : 38   When a man is firmly established in continence
He gains energy.

2 : 39   When a man is firmly established in non-covetousness
He achieves a knowledge of the mystery of existence.

2 : 40   When a man is firmly established in purity
He guards his body from contamination with others.

2 : 41   When a man is firmly established in mental purity (sattva-
shuddha)
He attains serenity of mind,
Cheerfulness and one pointedness (ekāgrya)

Control of the sense organs (indriya)
And fitness for union with the Atman.

2 : 42   When a man is firmly established in contentment
He attains supreme joy.

2 : 43   When a man is firmly established
By the destruction of impurity
Through mortification
He attains special powers (siddhis)
In the body and sense organs.

2 : 44   When a man is firmly established
In self-study
He attains union with the deity
In the form he has chosen.

2 : 45   When a man is firmly established
In devotion to the Lord
He attains perfect contemplation (samādhi).

2 : 46–8 Postures
2 : 46   Postures should be
Firm (sthira) and pleasant (sukham).

2 : 47   Postures are achieved by
Relaxation of tension
And meditation on the eternity of God (ananta).

2 : 48   When posture is mastered
Extremes (such as heat and cold) do not disturb.

2 : 49–53 Regulation of prāna
2 : 49   When posture has been mastered
Prānāyāma follows.
This is the cessation of
Inspiration (shvāsa) and expiration (prashvāsa).

2 : 50   Prānāyāma is
External, internal or suppressed modification (vrittir).
It is regulated by
Place, time and number,
And grows in length and subtlety.

2 : 51   The fourth form of prānāyāma
Is a transcending of the ordinary out-in breathing.

2 : 52   Through mastery of prānāyāma
The veil over the inner light (prakāsha-āvaranam)
Is removed.

2 : 53 Then the brain (manasah) becomes capable
        Of concentration (dhāranā).

2 : 54 Sense-withdrawal
  2 : 54 Sense—withdrawal is an exercise by which
          The sense organs (indriyas)
          Are withdrawn from outside objects
          And centred in the heart.

3 : 1 Concentration
  3 : 1   Concentration is a focusing of the heart
          On one centre (desha-bandha).

3 : 2 Meditation
  3 : 2   Meditation is an uninterrupted flow of the mind
          Towards the object of concentration.

3 : 3 Contemplation
  3 : 3   Contemplation is a union
          Between the ego and the object of contemplation.

6

FREEDOM (KAIVALYA)

Patanjali makes no attempt to describe this freedom. He points out some of
the ways by which it can be experienced. In this reticence he is in harmony
with the greatest teachers of all the main spiritual traditions who are content
to affirm: His service is perfect freedom. The following are some of the
sutras which describe the ways to this freedom.

  3 : 56 Freedom (kaivalya) comes from
          A balanced purity between the heart
          And the Lord.

  4 : 5   The activities of the many created hearts
          Are directed by the Supreme Heart.

  4 : 29 When there is no selfish desire,
          Or personal attachment,
          Or ulterior motive,
          When discriminating knowledge is continuous,
          Then comes the rain-cloud contemplation (dharma-megha-
          samādhi).

  4 : 30 From this comes
          Freedom from hindrances and actions.

4 : 31　When dharma-megha-samādhi comes
　　　　The heart is uncovered,
　　　　Freed from impurities
　　　　And united with the universal mind
　　　　The manifested universe in comparison with this experience is
　　　　　small.

4 : 32　At this point
　　　　The succession of changes in the emotions (gunas) ends
　　　　Because they have completed their purpose for the individual.

4 : 34　Freedom comes
　　　　When the emotions have ceased from action
　　　　For the sake of the individual self
　　　　And have returned to their original stillness:
　　　　Or when the Supreme Mind is established
　　　　In its true form.

7

SOME EXERCISES IN CONTEMPLATION (SAMYAMA)

A selection has been made from this variety of exercises to include some
most suitable to our own tradition. Of course they can be multiplied
indefinitely. Patanjali plays down the results of such exercises and insists
that they must not be done merely for the sake of such experiences nor must
the contemplative rest in any of them. The following two Sutras emphasise
this point.

3 : 51　By non-attachment to spiritual powers
　　　　The seed of bondage is destroyed
　　　　And freedom (kaivalya) follows.

3 : 52　There must be a complete detachment
　　　　From matter, pride and the attainment of high position
　　　　In order to avoid a fall from grace.

3 : 16–52 Contemplative exercises
　3 : 18　Concentration on memory recollections (samskara)
　　　　　Brings a deep knowledge of past experiences.

　3 : 19　A mental image
　　　　　Brings insight into the heart.

　3 : 24　Meditation on friendliness and compassion
　　　　　Leads to mental, moral and spiritual strength.

3 : 25   Meditating about strong things
          Brings strength.

3 : 26   Meditation on the uncreated light (aloka)
          Brings understanding of
          Spiritual, hidden and distant things.

3 : 30–5 Concentration on
          The solar plexus, throat, eye, head and heart centres
          Leads to special insights.

3 : 36   Concentration on the true Self
          Brings knowledge of that Self.

3 : 44   By meditation on the spiritual state
          The images of the heart become real
          And the ignorance which conceals Reality
          Is destroyed.

3 : 49   By meditation on the pure heart and the Self (purusha)
          Comes omnipotence and omniscience.

Acknowledgements

The author and publishers acknowledge the permission of the following to use copyright material:

   T & T Clark Ltd. for *Church Dogmatics*, Volume 3, by Karl Barth.
   Lutterworth Press, for certain illustrative material which appeared in the same author's book *Oriental Meditation*.